MONARCH NOTES AND STUDY GUIDES

THE OLD TESTAMENT

by

Robert Ackerman
Department of English
State University of New York, Stony Brook

Ruth H. Blackburn, Ph.D.
Assistant Professor of English
State University of New York
Stony Brook

Unicio J. Violi, Ph.D.
Assistant Professor of English
Fairleigh Dickinson University

Distributed by

MONARCH PRESS, INC.

387 Park Avenue South
New York, N. Y. 10016

CONTENTS

PREFACE

The primary aim of this book is to provide the student with a guide to the understanding of the Old Testament (O.T.) for, notwithstanding the classical purists who sneer at any kind of "guide" with its clutter of introductory notes and critical apparatus as companion to a great, traditional classic of literature, there can be little but superficial understanding of the monumental complexities inherent in the Old Testament without one. The Old Testament is of ancient, oriental vintage, written in another age, whose mores, morals, customs, concepts, traditional ways of thought and expression have undergone significant changes. Those who plead with us to "Read the Bible!" as if it were some popular tale of mystery and adventure, without regard to an understanding of the milieu in which it was composed are serious misleaders indeed. Such a reading invites a sense of bafflement and frustration on the part of the reader, and he is likely to think the book a horrendous mixture of queer folktale and legend embedded in a mass of unintelligible gibberish. To guide the reader then into a sympathetic understanding and comprehension of this greatest of books is the primary purpose of this guide. Armed with the minimal critical commentary and introduction provided in this book (an exhaustive commentary would take up forty books the size of the *Encyclopedia Britannica!*), the reader will find his way through the Old Testament made easier, more intelligible, and (we hope) much more interesting.

It is obvious that such a guide as this can be no substitute for the reading of the Old Testament itself, and it is not intended as such. The instructor, the student, and all interested laymen, however, will find the information contained herein a minimal body of knowledge necessary for an increased pleasure in their reading of the Bible:

1. He will find a clear and intelligible review (paraphrase) of the entire Old Testament, including the Apocrypha.

2. He will find the commentary clear and ordered, without any special bias for any single critical school. The latest findings of the best scholars, without regard to their theological attachments, have been incorporated into this work (see Bibliography for works consulted). When the various schools are in dispute on certain matters of interpretation and viewpoint, an attempt is made to record the differences.

3 He will find the introductory essays of indispensable value; we recommend that they be read *first,* since they contain information of vital importance to an understanding of the rest of this book.

4. He will find the King James Version (KJV) used throughout this guide because:

a. It is the greatest and most well-known translation in English.

b. It is used in most of the college classes in such courses as "The Bible As Literature" etc.

c. Its language has become familiar to all English-speaking peoples because of its pervasive influence.

5. He will find all books cited in the text listed again in what we think is an extensive and useful Bibliography.

6. He will find an introductory essay preceding each book of the Bible; this essay will lay out the main outlines and give necessary information for a proper understanding of the book to follow.

7. He will fiind all new and unusual terms and concepts defined as he reads along, and, in addition, he will find that we have written in what we think is a clear and uncluttered prose.

In summary, then, we feel we have composed a student review-guide which stands unrivalled in its field for clarity, accuracy, and completeness. Judge for yourself.

The Authors:
ROBERT ACKERMAN
RUTH H. BLACKBURN
UNICIO J. VIOLI

INTRODUCTION

ARCHEOLOGY AND THE BIBLE

Before providing the reader with an historical background to the Old Testament, it might be wise to indicate briefly how the exciting archeological discoveries of the nineteenth and twentieth centuries have tended to support the main outlines of the history of the early Hebrews as laid out in the Bible.

1. *The Rosetta Stone*
In 1799 one of Napoleon's French officers found a block of basalt stone 45″ X 28″ in size, which now lies in the British Museum. A French scholar, Francois Champollion, succeeded in translating the hieroglyphics, and thereby opening up the secrets of Egyptian civilization, one of the greatest ancient civilizations, and one which contributed in no small way to our understanding of the Bible.

2. *The Rocks of Behistun*
In 1857 Henry C. Rawlinson succeeded in deciphering the Persian and Babylonian cuneiform wedge-shaped characters carved on the face of the rocks of Behistun, thereby unlocking the secrets of another great ancient civilization which had had profound effects upon the Hebrews.

3. *The Cuneiform Tablets at Nineveh*
In 1872 George Smith deciphered a cuneiform tablet containing a Babylonian account of a flood, which closely resembles the story of the Flood in Genesis 7 and 8. The tablet dates from the seventh century B.C.

4. *The Creation Tablets*
In the same area were found two stories of the creation of the world dating from the second milennium B.C., which may have influenced the account given in the very beginning of Genesis.

5. *The Code of Hammurabi*
In 1901 De Morgan, in charge of a French expedition, came upon stone tablets inscribed by King Hammurabi at least six hundred years before the time of Moses. They consist of codified laws which considerably influenced the so-called Mosaic laws of the Pentateuch (first five biblical books). In 1952 Professor Noah Kramer discovered a legal code prescribed by Ur-Nammu, a Sumerian king who ruled *before* the time of Hammurabi himself. Notable is the fact that the code of Ur-Nammu was less harsh and barbaric than that of Hammurabi.

6. *The Poem of the Righteous Sufferer* (about 2000 B.C.)
This is a Babylonian poem which bears close resemblances to the Book of Job, about a righteous man who suffers and questions the fairness of the gods.

7. *The Royal Tomb of King Meskalam-dug* (3300 B.C.)
C. Leonard Woolley, directing an expedition at ancient Ur of Sumeria (near the north end of the Persian Gulf), discovered evidences of human sacrifice in this tomb. This proves that such sacrifices existed in the fourth milennium and became widespread in Canaan, the land later taken over by the ancient Hebrews.

8. *The Ziggurat*
Among the Ur discoveries of Professor Woolley were ziggurats, mounds (200′ X 150′ at the base) reaching high into the air. Stairs led to the Holy of Holies on the top of the

structures. Resemblances to the biblical tower of Babel are obvious. Again we see the influence of Sumerian and Babylonian religious customs upon the Canaanites and Hebrews. The "high places" of the Canaanite agricultural god Baal can only be understood in the light shed by our knowledge of Sumerian and Babylonian civilizations. Incidentally, a number of "high places" shrines of the Canaanites and Hebrews have recently been uncovered in Palestine.

9. The Mesopotamian Flood
Woolley and Langdon discovered unmistakable evidence of a flood that must have destroyed most of Mesopotamian civilization about 3200 B.C. The legend of the flood has now a basis in actual history!

10. The Nuzu tablets (second milennium B.C.) shed light upon our understanding of Hebrew inheritance customs; the Letters of Tell el-Amarna discovered in Egypt give us information about Palestine before

Joshua's time; and there is the identification of the ancient "Habiru" (Hebrews?) around 1360 B.C.; the Papyri of Elephantine (Egypt, fifth century B.C.) indicate Jewish settlements there in the fifth century B.C. Other discoveries such as the Tomb of Tutenkhamon (pre-Hebraic monotheism), the Temples of Dagon and Ashtoreth (Canaanite temples), the Royal Library of Boghaz-Keui (in Turkey), and the well popularized Dead Sea Scrolls are but a few of the many important archeological findings still to be mentioned. In recent years new discoveries are being made with almost bewildering rapidity, and most have served so far to substantiate basically the historical accounts given in the Hebrew Bible. The interested student is referred to George A. Barton's Archeology and the Bible (7th ed.), 1937; Frederick Kenyon's The Bible and Archaeology, 1940; and G. Ernest Wright's Biblical Archaeology, 1954. See Bibliography for further references.

HISTORICAL BACKGROUNDS OF THE OLD TESTAMENT

About 3000-2000 B.C. there arose the first great civilizations of Asia Minor and Egypt, the Early Bronze Age. Irrigation made vast farming projects possible; agriculture formed the base of the civilizations of both Egypt and Mesopotamia, and its culture, art, and religions are expressions of this basically intensely agricultural civilization.

About 2000-1500 B.C. there arose an era termed the Middle Bronze Age, the age of patriarchs (the ancient ancestors of the Hebrews living as wandering, semi-nomadic shepherds); it is this period that figures in Genesis stories and legends surrounding the Hebrew patriarchs Abraham, Isaac, and Jacob. It was during this era that Hammurabi ruled (see above). Egypt was then ruled by the Hyksos invaders, and it might have been during this period that the Hebrews began entering Egypt.

About 1500-1200 (the Late Bronze Age) the Egyptians drove out the Hyksos invaders; and this is also the time of the enslavement and escape to freedom of the Hebrew slaves under Moses from Egyptian bondage. Palestine was then occupied by the Semitic Canaanites, who in turn had been strongly influenced by the great cultures of the Mesopotamian region.

About 1300 the Hebrews fled from slavery in Egypt, and after a long period of wanderings in the Arabian desert, they invaded the Canaanite lands of Palestine, which they looked upon as the land promised them by Yahweh in a sacred contract or covenant. (*Yahweh* is the proper name of the Hebrew God as given in the Old Testament. Jehovah, the Lord, are various alternative names or euphemisms used to avoid uttering the sacred proper name Yahweh (Hebrew: YHWH). The miraculous Red Sea escape and the so-called "forty years" of wanderings in the desert have not been substantiated by history. What we do know is that from 1250-1200 B.C. the Hebrews gradually settled in Canaan and after much fighting, hardship and struggle succeeded in wresting the land from the Canaanites, absorbing much of their culture and religion, and even mingling with them in inter-marriage. The struggle and wars are pictured, however, in the Old Testament as a series of rapid conquests by Joshua. The main center of Hebrew settlement was central Palestine; the fertile plains along the coast and in the north were still occupied by the Canaanites. The lower coastal plain was occupied by the Philistines, a mighty sea-faring people with a splendidly advanced culture. The culture of the Canaanites was not far behind. The Hebrews were mighty in battle but crude in their culture; yet their belief that Yahweh led them, guided them, and placed all His hopes in them as the Chosen People gave the Hebrews great strength and courage. They were loosely bound together in a federation of tribes with "judges" (military leaders) occasionally rising to positions of responsible leadership. The Hebrews adopted Canaanite methods of farming, but some still retained their semi-nomadic, provincial ways. Great states peopled and worked by numerous slaves as in the Canaanite areas was not the way for the Hebrews. Small farms and a kind of rough equality was the rule, since there was a fear among the individual tribes that centralized power would bring tyranny. The period from 1250-1020 is usually termed the Period of the Conquest and Judges (see the Book of Judges below).

About 1020-926 B.C. (Period of the United Kingdom) the Hebrews formed their first monarchy because enemy pressures required a more close-knit organization. Their first king was Saul, who fought against the Ammonites and Philistines; and he succeeded in unifying the tribes in a more solid unit.

About 1004 B.C. David became king of Judah (southern Palestine) after Saul's death; he defeated Ish-baal (Saul's son), who was the leader of the northern tribes; David captured Jerusalem from the Canaanites and made it his capital city, since it was midway between the northern and southern tribal areas. David broke the power of the Philistines, and because of the weakness of the great Egyptian and Babylonian empires, he succeeded in building an empire of his own. The rebellion of his own son Absalom was then defeated, and after that David chose Solomon, another son, to succeed him as king.

About 965 B.C. Solomon succeeded to David's throne and inherited a unified empire, rich and prosperous. Solomon's magnificence was oriental in its splendor. He built the great Temple in Jerusalem, traded widely, and managed to maintain a rule of peace and opulence. Solomon's wealth and extravagant spending resulted in popular discontent and rebellion.

About 926 B.C. the northern tribes revolted against Solomon's son Rehoboam and established the kingdom of Israel under Jeroboam. Israel was far richer than Judah both in territory and population; its land was

more fertile; and in addition it was located on the famous trade routes of the Fertile Crescent. Unfortunately, Israel had no continuous dynasties of kings, and as a result there were nineteen kings from nine dynasties in the next two centuries. In addition they had no central place of worship. And finally they were exposed to invasion by the powerful, newly rising empire of the Assyrians.

About 882 B.C. Omri became king of Israel and scored many military victories in the trans-Jordan areas. He married his son Ahab to Jezebel, a Phoenician princess.

About 871 B.C. Ahab became king of Israel (the northern kingdom). His wife Jezebel imported hundreds of Baal priests of Canaanite extraction, who proved of widespread effectiveness. Against her the mighty prophet Elijah thundered and railed; the famous defeat of the "prophets of Baal" in contest with Yahweh and Elijah on Mount Carmel (I Kings, Chapter 18, verses 17-40; hereafter, biblical references will be given as I Kings 18:17-40, for example) is largely legend, but it does reveal the rise of a new religious conservatism.

About 845 B.C. Jehu led a revolution and wiped out Ahab, Jezebel, and all their relatives as well as the professional Baal priests. Ostensibly all forms of worship were now centered in Yahweh, but Canaanite practices constantly cropped up. Elisha the prophet endorsed Jehu's activities.

About 787 B.C. Jeroboam II became king, and it is under him that Amos arises, the first writing prophet.

In 722 B.C. Samaria, the capital city of Israel, is captured by the Assyrians.

Judah (the southern kingdom), although poorer and less fertile than Israel, still had only one dynasty throughout her entire history (David's); it had Jerusalem and the Temple of Solomon with a firmly established priesthood that gained in power and influence.

In 742 B.C. Ahaz became king of Judah and joined in league with Assyria, becoming its vassal. Hezekiah, the son and successor of Ahaz, paid tribute to Assyria but later attempted revolt. Sennacherib, the Assyrian king who had succeeded Sargon II, crushed the revolt and laid siege to Jerusalem, only to spare it and leave Hezekiah as ruler. In 696 B.C. Manasseh (Hezekiah's son) became king; then in 639 his grandson Josiah ruled. A threat of a Scythian invasion arose, and not long after a book of law was found in the Temple. This book became the basis of Josiah's so-called "reform" in religious practices and law. Local altars of sacrifice were abolished, and all worship was centralized in Jerusalem (see Introduction to the Book of Deuteronomy).

In 598 B.C. the Babylonian king Nebuchadnezzar (alternate spelling: Nebuchadrezzar) captured Jerusalem and thousands of Jews were exiled, many to Babylon itself. In 586 B.C. Nebuchadnezzar crushed a revolt under Zedekiah and this time totally destroyed Jerusalem, and again deported thousands to Babylon.

In Babylon many Jews readily absorbed Babylonian ways, customs, and religious practices, but on the other hand many remained faithful to their monotheistic god Yahweh. The prophets of the Exile were Ezekiel and Deutero-Isaiah. The Persians arose now as a mighty empire and conquered Babylon (539 B.C.). Cyrus the Persian allowed the Hebrews to return to Palestine if they so wished. A minority actually did return in spite of the more attractive conditions of life in Babylon. The real leadership of Judah passed to the priests, and under their encouragement and

pressure the Temple was rebuilt— no little debt for this success is owed to the prophets Haggai and Zechariah. The Temple was dedicated in 516 B.C.

About 445 B.C. Nehemiah returned to Jerusalem and succeded in urging his fellow-citizens to build a protective wall around Jerusalem, thus laying down a firmer structure of civil government. Nehemiah wrote the story of his own life (which see, below). A scribe (scholar) named Ezra also returned from Babylon, and through his efforts the Jews of Jerusalem adopted the completed Law as their communal standard in religious and civil life. From now on the Law was fixed for all Jews, except for those unwilling to adopt the standard, such as many of the Diaspora (Jews not settled in Palestine) and the Jews around Samaria in Palestine (i.e., Samaritans).

Post-Exilic Period 445-63 B.C.
From 333-198 B.C.: Alexander the Great (356-323) defeated the Persians, spread Greek culture wherever he conquered, and even after his death in 323 B.C. Hellenism continued to spread.

Alexander's empire was divided among the Ptolemies of Egypt and the Seleucids of Syria, Palestine going to the Ptolemies. The high priest, along with some leading citizens, ruled Judea; and the Temple was the center of worship for *all* Jews, both in and out of Palestine. By the end of the third century the official books (canon) of the Bible included the Law and the Prophets (see below). Greek became the international language during this period, even for Jews of the Diaspora. A translation of the Bible was prepared for the non-Hebrew-reading Jews. Their tongue was Greek (Koiné Greek), and the Greek translation of the Hebrew Bible is called the Septuagint.

CHIEF POWERS, 2000 — 1000 B.C.

	EGYPT	HEBREWS	MESOPOTAMIA
2000	XII Dynasty		Hurrians Amorites
1900			
1800	Hyksos Invasion	Abraham c. 1750?	Hammurabi c. 1728?-1686?
1700			
1600	XV — XVII Dynasties (Hyksos)	Joseph and Family to Egypt	Babylonian Decline Hittite Empire
1500	XVIII Dynasty Hyksos Expelled Thutmose III c. 1490-1435 Amenhotep III c. 1406-1370		
1400	Akhnaton c. 1370-1353		New Hittite Empire Rise of Assyria
1300	XIX Dynasty Seti c. 1308-1290 Rameses II c. 1190-1224 Merneptah c. 1224-1216	The Exodus c. 1290	
1200	XX Dynasty	The Judges	
1100		Fall of Shiloh c. 1050 Samuel Saul 1020-1000	
1000	Decline of Egypt XXI Dynasty XXII Dynasty	David 1000	Tiglath-Pileser I c. 1114-1706

CHIEF POWERS, 2000 — 1000 B.C.—Continued

			ASSYRIA
	SAMUEL		
	Saul, 1020-1000		Tiglath-Pileser I revives Assyrian Empire
1000	David 1000-961		
	NATHAN		
950	Solomon 961-922		Decline of Assyria

THE DIVIDED KINGDOM

	ISRAEL	JUDAH	ASSYRIA
	Jeroboam I 922-901	Rehoboam 922-915	Revival of Assyria
		Abijam 915-913	
		Asa c. 913-83	
900	Nadab 901-900		Adad-ninari II 912-890
	Baasha 900-877		Ashur-nasir-pal II 883-859
	Elah 877-876		
	Zimri 876		
	Omri 876-869		
	Ahab 869-850	Jehoshaphat 873-849	Shalmaneser III 859-824
	ELIJAH		
850	Ahaziah 850-849		Battle of Qarqar 853
	Jehoram 849-842	Jehoram 849-842	
	ELISHA	Ahaziah 842	
	Jehu 842-815	Athaliah 842-837	
		Joash 837-800	Shamshi-Adah V 824-811
	Jehoahaz 815-801		
800	Jehoash 801-786	Amaziah 800-783	Adad-nirari III 811-783

THE GREAT PROPHETS and THE KINGS OF ISRAEL AND JUDAH

	ISRAEL	PROPHETS	JUDAH	ASSYRIA
800	Jeroboam II 786-746		Uzziah 783-742	(Period of Assyrian weakness)
750	Zechariah 746-745	AMOS	(Jotham co-regent) Jotham 742-735	Tiglath-Pileser III 745-727
	Shallum 745			
	Menahem 745-738	HOSEA		
	Pekahiah 738-737			
	Pekah 737-732	ISAIAH	Ahaz 735-715	Shalmaneser V 727-722
	Hoshea 732-724	MICAH		Sargon II 722-705
	Fall of Samaria 722/721			
700			Hezekiah 715-687	Sennacherib 705-681
			Sennacherib invades 701	
			Manasseh 687-642	
				Esarhaddon 681-669
650				Asshurabanapal 669-633?
			Amon 642-640	Asshur-etil-ilani 634-629?
			Josiah 640-609	
			Deuteronomic Reform 622	Sin-shan-ish-Kun 626-612
		JEREMIAH		
		ZEPHANIAH		
		NAHUM	Jehoahaz 609	Fall of Nineveh 612
600			Jehoiakim 609-598	BABYLONIAN EMPIRE
		HABAKKUK	Jehoiachin 598/597	Nebuchadrezzar 605/4-562
		EZEKIEL	Zedekiah 597-587	Battle of Carchemish 605
			Fall of Jerusalem 587	

EVENTS AND PROPHETS FROM AFTER THE EXILE TO 400 B.C.

	THE HEBREW PROPHETS	BABYLON	MEDIA	PERSIA
			Cyaxares 625-585	
600	1st deportation 597	Nebuchadrezzar 605/4-562	Astyages 595-550	
	2nd deportation 587			
	3rd deportation 582			
		Nebuchadrezzar invades		
		Egypt 568		
		Amel-marduk 5625-60		
		Neriglissar 560-556		
		Nabonidus 556-539		Cyrus overthrows Astyages 550
550	II ISAIAH			PERSIAN EMPIRE
		Cyrus takes Babylon 539		Cyrus 550-530
		Edict of Cyrus 538		Cambyses 530-522
				Darius I 522-486
	Zerubbabel			
	Rebuilding of Temple 520-515			
	HAGGAI, ZECHARIAH			
				Marathon 490
500	OBADIAH			Xerxes 496-465
				Thermopylae,
				Salamis 480
				Artaxerxes I 465-424
	MALACHI			
450	Ezra's mission 458?			Peace of Gallias 449
	Nehemiah gov. 445-			Xerxes II 423
	Ezra's mission 458?			Darius II 423-404
				Artaxerxes II 404-438

From 198-63 B.C. The Syrian ruler Antiochus III captured Palestine in 198 B.C. Antiochus IV ("Epiphanes") tried to force Hellenistic culture down Jewish throats, even to supplanting their Yahweh with Greek gods. The Book of Daniel reflects this struggle between Hellenism and Judaism. Guerillas under the Maccabees fought the Syrians (the Seleucids), finally defeating them in 142 B.C. The Maccabees ruled Palestine until 63 B.C., when they lost their independence to the Romans. See Wright and Filson, *Westminster Atlas, The Interpreter's Bible* (The History of Israel), Volume I, and "The History of the Religion of Israel" in *I.B.* (*Interpreter's Bible*), pages 292-348. See Bibliography for additional references.

GEOGRAPHY OF PALESTINE: A SKETCH

RIVERS: *Euphrates*: (Hebrew = *Perath*) The Euphrates is one of the great rivers of western Asia; it arises in Armenia near Mt. Ararat, runs westerly for a while and then breaks through the Taurus Mountains to run southerly and then southeasterly to form the western boundary of Mesopotamia (the country between the Tigris and Euphrates Rivers, excluding the mountainous region where the rivers originate and excluding the low-lying plain of Babylonia lying in the opposite direction). The Tigris unites with the Euphrates at about latitude 31°N., longitude 47°E., and continues to flow on for 90 miles more to empty finally into the Persian Gulf. It is about 1800 miles in length, and formed a kind of boundary between the east and west, between Egypt and Assyria-Babylonia. It formed the boundary of the Seleucid kingdom as well as the eastern limit of the Roman Empire. The greatest city on its banks was Babylon; Carchemish, the old Hittite capital, also lay on its course.

Tigris: (Hebrew = *Hiddekel*) The Tigris arises in Armenia and goes east-southeast through the Kurdistan Mountains and flows in that direction until it finally joins the Euphrates just before emptying into the Persian Gulf. The great city of Nineveh once lay on its banks, and the city of Baghdad is split in two by its flow. It is 1146 miles in length.

Nile: (Hebrew = *Shihor*) The Nile, because of its vastness, is sometimes called a sea in the Bible. It arises in central Africa and flows northerly for about 3670 miles until it empties into the Mediterranean at Rosetta and Damietta. It brings fertility along its banks, although the Arabian desert lies to its east and the Sahara desert to the west.

Jordan: (means "descender" in Hebrew) The Jordan is the most important river in Palestine. Its largest source is Tell el-Kadi (probably the ancient Dan), and it flows into the Sea of Galilee (which is 13 miles long) after which it continues south for 65 miles until it empties into the Dead Sea. From Banias near the source to the Dead Sea it is 104 miles long. Alone among all the world's rivers it flows for the greater part of its course below sea level! At the Sea of Galilee it is 682 feet below sea level and when entering the Dead Sea it is 1292 feet below. The famous biblical associations lie along its southward course between the Sea of Galilee and the Dead Sea. The southern part of the Jordan is tropical and fertile, which is why Lot chose it for his home (Gen. 13:8-13). Near Jericho the river is so rapid that swimming is dangerous. Here Joshua and his soldiers crossed to take Jericho. An eastern tributary of the Jordan, the Jabbok, was forded by Jacob on his way back from Mesopotamia (Gen. 32:22).

Sea of Galilee: This is a fresh-water lake fed by the river Jordan, and is about eight miles wide and thirteen miles long. It is rich in fish.

Dead Sea: This is called the Salt Sea in the Bible. It is fed by the Jordan and is 1300 feet below sea level. It is rectangularly shaped and is about 47 miles long and 10 miles wide, approximately. Its maximum depth is about 1300 feet. It is so salty that eggs will float on its surface and organic life in its depths is virtually absent.

Along the eastern coast of the Mediterranean there is a narrow fertile strip. In the central area of the strip rises the Lebanon mountains. The Philistines occupied the southern coastal strip, while the Hebrews occupied the northern coastal area known as the Plain of Sharon. The Negev area is a desert and lies in the extreme southerly border area. The Jordan Valley is green and fertile, especially to the east. Bashan, Gilead, Ammon, Moab, and Edom lie to the east of the Jordan; they are areas that stretch from north to south in the order given above. The area of Palestine west of the Jordan is either hilly or mountainous and is divided into three main areas from north to south: Galilee (north), Samaria (central), and Judah (south).

Fertile Crescent: This is a huge arc of land crowning the Arabian desert; it begins in the Persian Gulf area and follows the courses of the Tigris and Euphrates upstream (northwesterly) until it veers southwesterly to include the fertile, coastal Mediterranean plains. This was a richly productive flat area along which great ancient civilizations flourished: Its name comes from its semicircular shape. Palestine lay directly in the trade route path which followed the Crescent and formed a kind of bridge between the western and eastern areas of the Crescent.

CLIMATE: Palestine (a rectangle about 50 by 150 miles) is subtropical in climate, much rain falling in the winter. (See the *Westminster Atlas* cited in the Bibliography.)

THE LITERATURE OF THE OLD TESTAMENT

The books of the Old Testament are grouped into seven classes: Prophecy, Legal Literature, Historical Narrative, Literature of Revolt, Wisdom Literature, Devotional Literature, and Apocalyptic.

1. PROPHECY: Books of prophecy are those in which God reveals his will to certain favored men; these oracular sages claimed an intermediary position between God and man. Ecstatics or dervishes were the first prophets. In the eleventh century B.C. they roamed in groups and through music worked themselves up into frenzy or trance. They carried no real moral or religious messages. To the great eighth-century B.C. reformers they were "false prophets." Before writing was known to the Hebrews (pre-literary prophets), *Samuel* became the first great prophet (about the eleventh century

B.C.). He urged a united front against Hebrew enemies. He is believed to have begun the united monarchy under Saul. *Elijah* (ninth century B.C.) was the greatest of the pre-literary prophets. He declared Yahweh victorious over Baal and other Canaanite deities. He also is the first of the "doom" prophets. *Elisha* followed Elijah; he forcibly established Yahwehism as a religion of strict formalism. *Amos* (eighth century B.C.) was the first of the literary prophets. His book is the first written book of the Old Testament, chronologically speaking. He is often known as the Prophet of Righteousness, who called the Jews to a more ethical and less formal religion. *Hosea,* the Prophet of Love, spoke of the inclusive and insistent love of God; spoke boldly of steadfast love "and not sacrifice"; the knowledge of God, rather than burnt offerings. *Isaiah* (late eighth century B.C.), the Prophet of Faith, saw God as transcendent and holy, and like his predecessors condemned extreme formal religious ritualism. It was Isaiah who predicted a Messiah (or saviour-king) would one day usher in a reign of peace and plenty. He initiated the doctrine of Messianism upon which Christianity so strongly rests. *Micah* (700 B.C.) was a kind of summary of his literary predecessors. *Jeremiah,* the Prophet of Personal Religion (626-586 B.C.), saw religion as intensely subjective and personal. The New Covenant of the heart will supplant the paper one. External laws are insufficient; man's heart is the center of his faith. *Ezekiel,* the Prophet of Individualism (592-570 B.C.), is unique. Every man is his own priest, and everyone is singly and individually responsible to God alone. Every man will be judged in terms of his own actions: inherited guilt or merit is nonsense! It was Ezekiel who held the Jews together in Babylonian exile and prepared their return to Jerusalem. To Ezekiel *sin* is ritualistic defilement, and *holiness* is non-contamination. Here is a reactionary swing away from the prophets. Deutero-Isaiah, the Prophet of Universalism (late sixth century B.C.), was an anonymous author who saw Israel as the "Suffering Servant" and looked forward to the Messiah. He called for the entire world to be saved—hence, the universal prophet.

Haggai, Zechariah, and *Malachi* represent the decline of prophecy; they renew post-Exilic legalism and exclusiveness, which makes them more priestly than prophetic. In summary, the prophets saw religion as not mere ritual but founded on ethical behavior and good morality. They made their religion more rational and useful in terms of social progress. They made their religion permanent by freeing it from narrow ritualism and parochialism.

2. LEGAL LITERATURE: The *Book of Deuteronomy* (621 B.C.) was written to set up specific rules of behavior. The good life came as a result of following concrete ritual formulas of contamination. The purpose was to offset a bit the influence of the great prophets and to unify more effectively the Hebrew people. The laws of the *Priestly Code* (fifth century B.C.) were aimed at preserving the sanctity of the Sabbath, the priesthood, circumcision, and the Temple. The laws of the Levites in this code dealt usually with sacrifice, offerings, etc. The Pentateuch, especially *Exodus,* also contains laws showing Babylonian influence via the Canaanites. The *Ten Commandments* (Exodus 20; Deuteronomy 5) most scholars find not to be written by Moses but come as a result of a long historical process. The Decalogue (the Ten Commandments) implies a farming civilization, not a nomadic one as pictured in Exodus, for example. The Mosaic laws are influenced by the prophets of the eighth century; hence their high ethical tone. See the section on

Exodus for further information on the authorship problem.

3. HISTORICAL NARRATIVE:

Early war songs, ballads, stories, legends, histories of kings, temple records, and post-Exilic editorializing make up some of the forms the historical writings take. Stories of the Patriarchs take up the *Book of Genesis;* especially great is the story of Jacob's favored son Joseph. *Exodus* and *Numbers* tell of the Jews' escape from Egyptian bondage. The stories dealing with the conquest of Canaan are recited in *Judges.* The united monarchy offers stirring biography in the lives of Saul, David, and Solomon (*I, II Samuel; 1 Kings*). Nehemiah and Ezra tell of post-Exilic times: the rebuilding of the Temple, the walls of Jerusalem, the city itself, the new ritualistic conformity, and the building of the second Temple. *I, II Chronicles,* written in late post-Exilic times (about 300 B.C.), edit previous history and give it all a priestly slant. There is a great amount of "white-washing" of black deeds committed by heroes like David and Solomon. On the whole the Chronicles are unreliable; history is manipulated to suit the priestly view.

4. LITERATURE OF PROTEST:

The Book of Ruth (about 400 B.C.) is a short story preaching tolerance for the foreigner. It protests against narrow exclusivism. *Jonah* (fourth century) is a satiric parable ridiculing exclusiveness and sectarianism. God's love is universal, says this great allegory.

5. THE WISDOM LITERATURE:

Greek culture influences Jewish writing in the third century B.C. Common sense, prudence, morality, individualism, humanistic values, and an exalted philosophy of life form their core. *Job, Proverbs,* and *Ecclesiastes* are the titles of the wisdom literature.

6. DEVOTIONAL LITERATURE:

The *Psalms* are the Hebrew hymns, poems, prayers and praises of Israel. They form the chief source of Christian hymnology. Some of the poems and songs reach the highest levels of spiritual aspiration, and others breathe fire and vengeance. Most are timeless and universal in their appeal as, for example, Psalms 1, 18, 19, 23, 43, 84, 90, 91, 103, and 139.

7. APOCALYPTIC:

The Book of Daniel (168 B.C.) was written to give courage to the Jews in their resistance to Greek influence, pressures, and desecrations. The author foresees "the Son of Man" ruling a new Kingdom of God of eternal peace and joy. He sees grand visions of things to come, the enemy defeated, and the righteous rewarded in heaven. Daniel is the only book of the official Bible expressing apocalyptic (revelations and visions of things to come) hopes. Only *Joel* expresses (fourth century B.C.) similar ideas.

See Julius A. Bewer's *The Literature of the Old Testament,* and Fred Gladstone Bratton's *A History of the Bible;* both are listed in the Bibliography.

OLD TESTAMENT CANONIZATION

1. THE LOST LIBRARY: Religious literature grew normally from oral traditions to writings, but in addition there was a selective process that operated to establish certain parts of that literature as sacred and authoritative canon. The word *canon* (cane) meant a rod, which later was used in measuring things to see that they were up to standard. The biblical canon is those writings that fill the criterion for sacred and authoritative scripture. There seems first of all to have been a lost library of Hebrew folklore which is freely quoted in the Old Testament. References are made to a book called "The Wars of Jehovah," to one called "The Book of Jashar," etc. This body of writings is completely lost, but the oral traditions continued from generation to generation.

2. THE MAKING OF THE PENTATEUCH:
The Greek word *pentateuchos* means "the fivefold book," and refers to the first five books of the Old Testament supposedly written by Moses; but scholars long ago have pointed out self-contradictions and discrepancies that prove such authorship impossible. Such authorities as Spinoza (seventeenth century) pointed out the internal contradictions that precluded Mosaic authorship; Simon (seventeenth century) found two different accounts of the Creation in Genesis and two contradictory flood stories; Jean Astruc, physician to Louis XV, noticed that God is called *Yahweh* in some sections and *Elohim* in others, thus pointing to two different authors. De Wetter pointed out that the Book of Deuteronomy dates from the seventh century B.C. and could not have been composed by Moses. Today, the most acceptable solution is the Documentary Theory of Graf and Wellhausen, two great scholars of the nineteenth century. They say that the Pentateuch is a compilation of materials written at different times by different authors; these authors are four in number and designated as J, E, D, and P.

J = the oldest document, written about 850 B.C. J consistently uses the name Yahweh for God. His writings are called the Bible of Judah (the southern kingdom). The author has a primitive, naive conception of an anthropomorphic God (a God who behaves like a human being).

God (for J) does everything in a perfectly natural way; J writes picturesquely and dramatically.

E = the next oldest document, written about 750 B.C., and is the Bible of Israel (the northern kingdom). This author uses the name *Elohim* for God consistently, and pictures God as a refined and spiritualized being who creates miracles and mighty works. He corrects and refines the older, more primitive conceptions and shows greater moral sensitivity than J. Even the vocabulary and style of the two writers differ. J and E are found in scattered places throughout the Pentateuch (Genesis, Exodus, Numbers, Leviticus, Deuteronomy).

D = the third document, dating from 621 B.C. in the eighteenth year of King Josiah. A "Book of the Law" was discovered while the Temple was being repaired. The book (i.e., scroll) was declared divine (see II Kings 22) and made the law of the land. This scroll was the Book of Deuteronomy, the first Jewish *official* Bible. It is filled with specific regulations, a bewildering array of complex laws on sacrifice, diet, non-defilement, etc. But it is also our first clear example of monotheism (see the *Shema* in Deut. 6:4ff.). The only place to worship God was now in the Temple in Jerusalem; the local sanctuaries and high places were declared invalid and illegal. This book was passed off as being written by Moses in order to give it prophetic authority and divine inspiration.

P = the fourth document dates from about 500 B.C. and is called "The Book of the Priests." This book contains stories of the Creation, the Deluge, the patriarchs, the Exodus, and the conquest of Canaan under Joshua. Its main theme is the divine rule and authority of God, and the codified laws on holiness. Religion is identified with ceremonial ritual and purity. The authors are extremely nationalistic, exclusive, formalistic; in sum, they are theocrats. Robert Pfeiffer calls the Priestly Code one in which regulation replaced spontaneity and discipline stifled freedom. See his authoritative *Introduction to the Old Testament* (New York, 1941), pp. 256-260.

J and E combined in the seventh century.

D(euteronomy) soon added to JE.

P interwoven into JE by a group of redactors or editors.

JEDP (plus the redacted material) = the first canon of the Jewish Bible by the end of the fifth century B.C. More exactly the dates are between 450 and 400 B.C. for the canonization of the Torah (i.e., the Pentateuch). The canonicity of the Torah is witnessed in all of the post-Exilic writings of the O.T. Moreover, the editors of the Septuagint (the Greek Old Testament, translated between 250 and 150 B.C..) take great care in translating the Torah but are relatively careless in their translations of the Prophets and the Writings. To them the Torah was the one and only authoritative Bible.

3. THE PROPHETS: In the Book of Ecclesiasticus (180 B.C.) the Prophets are given equality with the Law or Torah. This would indicate a fully canonic date by approximately 200 B.C. The New Testament considers the Law and Prophets as fully canonical also.

The Hebrew canonical order of the Prophets is as follows:

Former Prophets: Joshua, Judges, I and II Samuel, I and II Kings.

Latter Prophets:
Major: Isaiah, Jeremiah, Ezekiel.
Minor: The Book of the Twelve: Hosea, Joel, Amos, Obadiah, Jonah,

Micah, Nahum, Habbakkuk, Zephaniah, Haggai, Zechariah, Malachi.

Joshua, Judges, Samuel and Kings are listed as prophets because they contained stories of the early prophets like Elijah and Samuel. Besides, these books were considered to be written by prophets. *Major* prophets and *minor* ones refer only to the size of the scroll, not to their relative importance: the "twelve" for example were included on a single roll. Originally Joshua was joined to the Pentateuch but later was separated.

4. THE CANONIZATION OF THE WRITINGS: The third canon after the Law and the Prophets is "the Writings," Hebrew = *Kethubim*. They are so called because of their unrelated and varied character. The Writings are canonized into three groups:
1. The Poetical Books: Psalms, Proverbs, Job.
2. The Five Rolls: Canticles (Song of Solomon), Ruth, Lamentations, Ecclesiastes, Esther.
3. The Remainder: Daniel, Ezra, Nehemiah, I and II Chronicles. Most of the above books date from the fourth century B.C. The *Psalms* were canonized for their devotional and liturgical value. The *Proverbs* were ethical, wise sayings of a non-religious nature and were attributed to Solomon, just as the Psalms were supposedly written by David. *Job* is one of the most profound philosophical dramas in all literature. *Ruth* preaches tolerance; *Song of Solomon* or *Canticles,* is an oriental collection of erotic love poems, canonized because it was supposedly composed by Solomon, and allegorized as Yahweh's love for Israel. Popularity, antiquity (indicated by anonymous authorship), and other reasons justified canonization. Final, official canonicity occurred at the Council of Jamnia (90 A.D.). After the destruction of Jerusalem in 70 A.D. the Jews decided to close their canon of

scripture. The increasing popularity of the Septuagint version of the Old Testament among the Christians made it imperative for the Jews to establish an official text. They upheld the Hebrew list of 24 books (the Septuagint has 38). Samuel, Kings, and Chronicles were listed as one book, and Ezra and Nehemiah were considered one book, as were the twelve minor prophets:

1. *The Law*: Genesis, Exodus, Leviticus, Numbers, Deuteronomy = 5 books.
2. *The Prophets*:
The Former Prophets: Joshua, Judges, I and II Samuel, I and II Kings = 4 books.
The Latter Prophets:
Major: Isaiah, Jeremiah, Ezekiel = 3 books.
Minor: The "Twelve" = 1 book.
3. *The Writings*:
The Poetical Books: Psalms, Proverbs, Job=3 books.
The Five Rolls: Canticles, Ruth, Lamentations, Ecclesiastes, Esther = 5 books.
The Remainder: Daniel, Ezra, Nehemiah, I, II Chronicles = 3 books.
Total = 24 books.

In 250 B.C. the Old Testament was translated into Greek for the benefit of Greek-speaking Jews of the Diaspora (non-Palestinian). Latin *septuaginta* = 70; according to tradition 70 scholars worked for 70 years on the translation. The Hellenistic Jews were more tolerant in canonicity than the Palestinian Hebrews, and so there are 14 books (the *Apocrypha*) included in the Septuagint not to be found in the official canon of the Hebrews; they are *I and II Esdras, Tobit, Judith, Esther* (the remainder), *The Wisdom of Solomon, Ecclesiasticus* or *the Wisdom of Sirach, Baruch, Susanna, The Song of the Three Children, The Story of Bel and the Dragon, The Prayer of Manasseh, I and II Maccabees. Apocrypha* is Greek for hidden (mysterious, spurious). They are all anonymous and written by Jews. The rabbis at Jamnia rejected them because either they were in Greek or too recent in composition. See below for a further description of these books outside the Hebrew canon, the Apocryphal books. Eighteen books outside the Septuagint canon are called the *Pseudepigrapha* (false writings, writings under assumed names); but the Roman Catholic Church calls these books the Apocrypha while the Protestant Church calls them the Pseudepigrapha. These books are predominantly apocalyptic in nature, that is, the revelation of last things, predictions of a catastrophic end of the world, and the rise of a new heaven and a new earth. They were mostly written in the first century B.C. and are often quoted in the New Testament. They include *Enoch, Jubilees, The Testaments of the Twelve Patriarchs, The Testament of Job, The Life of Asenath, The Psalms of Solomon, The Secrets of Enoch, The Sibylline Oracles, The Assumption of Moses, Baruch, III and IV Maccabees, The Letter of Aristeas,* and *The Ascension of Isaiah.* See R. H. Charles' *The Apocrypha and Pseudepigrapha*, 1913.

THE DOCUMENTARY THEORY: A SKETCH

J DOCUMENT—about 900 B.C.
Uses "Yahweh" for God always.
Begun in Judah about 1000 B.C.; revised about 900.
History beginning with creation.

Informal, colloquial, dramatic, primitive, vivid.
Anthropomorphic God (human attributes).
Interested in the beginnings of things.

E DOCUMENT—about 750-700 B.C.
Elohim for God until Moses and the burning bush.
Written in Israel (Ephraim).
Begins history with Abraham.
Formal, devout, moralistic.
No crude anthropomorphisms.

D DOCUMENT—about 650 B.C.
The core of Deuteronomy, the Law found during Josiah's reform.
J-E: Combined into one story, about 600 B.C. in Judah.
Genesis (JEP); Exodus (JEP); Lev. (P); Num. (JEP); Deut. (DP).

P DOCUMENT—about 550-450 B.C. (Various Priests)
1. A History: formal, begins with creation, explains the origins of religious practices.
2. Law Collection: carefully codified, though founded on earlier laws. Ethics superior to D's, concerned with ritual cleanliness and priestly rights (more so than D).
3. Genealogies and Chronologies: carefully worked out, interest in racial purity, ties 4 documents together.
4. Editorial Work: Often called R (redactor); combined all 4 documents into Torah, then Pentateuch.

THE PENTATEUCH: AN INTRODUCTION

Pentateuch (Greek = *pentateuchos*, consisting of 5 books) is pronounced PEN tah tewk; it consists of the first 5 books of the Old Testament: Genesis, Exodus, Leviticus, Numbers, and Deuteronomy. The word does not occur in the Bible but is referred to as the Law, or the Law of Moses, or Book of the Law, etc. The five books were originally conceived as one, but it is the Septuagint translation that first adopted the fivefold division. The Mosaic authorship is not generally accepted by critics, although a surprising number of reputable critics of the more orthodox Protestant schools still attest to the Mosaic authorship, as do many Jews and Roman Catholics. The objections to Mosaic authorship are the following:

1. Reference to times after the death of Moses, "And the Canaanite was then in the land" (Gen. 12:6, that is, the Book of Genesis, chapter 12, verse (line) number 6). Reference is made to the town of Dan (Judg. 18:29), which is a post-Mosaic town. "Before there reigned any king over Israel" (Gen. 36:31) refers to a monarchy unknown in the days of Moses. The death of Moses is referred to in Deut. 34:5-12, a patent absurdity! The Documentary Theory of Graf-Wellhausen is explained above under "Old Testament Canonization." Some critics divide J into J^1 and J^2 or L; sometime around 650 B.C. a redactor (editor and reviser) combined J and E into JE, not by rewriting his sources but by dovetailing selected material from the two documents, hence making detection of the two sources relatively easy. About the middle of the sixth century the Holiness Code (H) adopted from Ezekiel was incorporated into P (the Priestly Code), which is the latest document in the Pentateuch composed sometime during the Exile. The third main stage in the redaction of the Pentateuch was the joining of P to JED, and again sources were not rewritten but combined. The foundation document, then, of the Torah is P supplemented by an editor with JED about 400 B.C. Needless to say, orthodox scholars object to the Documentary Theory on such grounds as its denial of the credibility of the Torah and of recent archaeological findings. Oddly enough, archaeological evidence is used to solidify orthodoxy in spite of the fact that liberal scholars point out that the reverse is true! *However,*

there are some objections to the Graf-Wellhausen hypothesis: 1. It is too formal and too exactly precise to be entirely right. Even phrases and words are supposedly identifiable as to authorship among J, E, D, and P. The scholars R. Kittel, Pedersen, and Gehman, for example, strongly object to the entire theory. A possible compromise position is that of a school of critics who accept JEDP but find the material considerably older than the time given; some find the four authors to be more representative of certain schools rather than persons—thus the Kadesh, Shechem, Shiloh, and Jerusalem schools, for example. W. F. Albright, a liberal scholar of great repute, places the Deuteronomic movement in the seventh century B.C., a movement reflecting a similar impetus throughout the Near East.

SUMMARY OF THE BOOK OF GENESIS

INTRODUCTION

Genesis (JENN uh sis) means *origin* in Greek, the name being borrowed from the Septuagint (the third century B.C. translation of the Hebrew Old Testament into Greek for the benefit of non-Hebrew speaking Jews living outside of Palestine, the Diaspora). It is the very first book of the O.T., and the very first word is *Bereshith* (Hebrew for "in the beginning"). It is divided into three natural sections: 1. The history of the universe, God's relation to it, and an introduction to human history (Chaps. 1:1 to 2:3). 2. A sketch of human history before Abraham, showing God's relation to mankind, and beginning the history of the chosen people of God, the Hebrews (Chaps. 2:4 to 11:26). 3. The history of the Hebrews who made the covenant (contract) with Yahweh down to the descent into Egypt (Chaps. 11:27 to 50:26).

Section 1:
a. The History of the Universe
1:1—2:3
Section 2:
a. Creation of Man; His Original Condition 2:4-25
b. The Fall 3
c. The Progress of Sin 4:1-15
d. The Worldly Race 4:16-24

e. The Godly Line 4:25—5:32
f. The Increase of Wickedness 6:1-8
g. The Flood 6:9—9:17
h. Repeopling of the Earth 9:18—10:32
i. The Tower of Babel 11:1-9
j. The Descendants of Shem 11:10-26

Section 8:
a. Abraham, His Call; His Sojourn in Canaan 11:27—25:10
b. The Life of Isaac 25:11—27:40
c. The Life of Jacob 27:41—35:29
d. The Descendants of Esau 36
e. The Early History of Joseph 37
f. Judah's Sin and Shame 38
g. Joseph in Egypt 39—45
h. Jacob and Family in Egypt 46—49
h. The Death of Jacob and Joseph 50

THE HISTORY OF THE UNIVERSE 1:1—2:3

"In the beginning God created the heaven and the earth. And the earth was without form, and void; and darkness was upon the face of the deep. And the Spirit of God moved upon the face of the waters. And God said, Let there be light: and there was light. And God saw the light, that it was good: and divided the light from the darkness." On the first day (a day is considered from evening to morning, as it still is among Orthodox Jews) Day and

Night are created; on the second day the firmament (the sky pictured as a dome with windows in it to let out floods or rain); on the third day the seas and earth, grass, vegetation, seed plants ("herb yielding seed"); on the fourth day the sun, moon and stars; on the fifth day living creatures: birds, great sea monsters ("great whales"), fishes, and "winged fowl after his kind" (winged birds according to their nature); on the sixth day cattle, creeping things, "beasts of the earth," and finally man: "Then God said, 'Let us make man in our image, after our likeness,'" and let him rule the fishes and birds and cattle and every "creeping thing" on earth. God created male and female in His own image, blessed them, and told them to be fruitful and multiply. On the seventh day God rested from His work and blessed the seventh day, "and sanctified it."

This account of the Creation is by P; he gives it sublimity. majesty, and solemnity; the Deity is omnipotent and invisible, gigantic in his cosmic sweep. He creates by decree, His power being limitless. P's aim as always is primarily religious: How did the world come about? How and when was man created? Man is God's image, the ruler of earth, the blessed and most beloved of God's creations in the golden age of Paradise. Most important is P's objective: to show that the Sabbath is the most sacred of all observances, instituted by God Himself! We shall see that Sabbath observances among the Hebrews are held to be peculiarly sacrosanct. The account is religiously motivated, much of it taken from legend and myth (see section on archaeology); he is not writing a geological tract. Attempts to show the ludicrousness of creating light on the first day and the sun on the fourth, of the impossibility of a 6-day creation, of the silliness of the "firmament" sky, of the gaucherie of the "creeping things," etc., reveal only the ignor-

ance of such attacks. P's conception of the cosmos in the eighth century B.C. is legendary, monotheistic, and supernatural. He has no conception (nor could he have) of scientific "truth"; to him all truths are bound in religion, and all history is merely the revelation of God's purposes in terms of man himself. In Hebrew, man = adam (his name Adam was given to him by tradition) and P has him created after birds, fishes, animals, and worms—on the sixth day, the climax all creation.

CREATION OF MAN; HIS ORIGINAL CONDITION; THE FALL: 2—3

In this second account of creation man is created before vegetation; he is formed by God of the "dust of the ground" and the breath of life is breathed into his nostrils, "and man became a living soul." Then God planted a garden "eastward in Eden" with the tree of life and the tree of knowledge of good and evil. Four rivers flow through Eden [Hiddekel (Tigris), Euphrates, Pison, and Gihon]. Man is placed in the garden to "dress it and to keep it," but he is forbidden to eat of the tree of knowledge of good and evil on pain of death. Eve is created from man's rib to serve as his help-meet (helper). Adam gives names to all the animals and birds. Man is called Adam and woman is called "Woman, because she was taken out of man." Man shall leave his father and mother for his wife, "and they shall be one flesh." Although both were naked, they were not ashamed of their nakedness. The serpent, "more subtile than any beast of the field," tempts Eve to eat of the fruit of the tree of knowledge of good and evil; she gives the fruit to Adam and he eats of it also. They sew fig leaves to cover their nakedness. God, who is "walking in the garden in the cool of the day," calls out to Adam, "Where art thou?" Adam answers that he and Eve were hiding because they were naked. God asks how he knew that he was naked. Adam blames Eve who blames the serpent. God curses the serpent to henceforth eat dust and crawl on its belly; the woman He curses by endowing her with birth-pains and domination by her husband: "and he shall rule over thee." Adam is given an earth that is unproductive; he shall sweat to earn his bread from it, "till thou return unto the ground; for out of it wast thou taken: for dust thou art, and unto dust shalt thou return." Then the Lord God makes coats of skins to clothe them, but lest man eat of the tree of life and become like "one of us, knowing good and evil," he is driven from Paradise.

Note the primitive conception of the Deity here: God *forms* man from dust, *breathes* into his nostrils, *plants* a garden, *walks* in the garden in the cool of the day, and *makes* clothes for Adam and Eve. J is the author here; this ninth-century author visualizes a very human Deity (anthropomorphic), more like a stern father than a God. The style is concrete, terse, and vivid. There is drama packed in every word. J is a master story-teller and master psychologist. Character is conveyed by means of dialogue and objective description, which is kept to a minimum. In short, J possesses those qualities inherent in folktale but sharpened to a great acuity by art. Another word for man is *ish*—woman is *isha* (note the cleverness of the pun, J being very fond of puns and other plays on language that are ordinarily missed in translation). Of course the entire account is mythical and folklorish with its miraculous creations, its speaking serpent, its flaming cherubim (angels), etc.; but J is writing religious history, attempting to answer vital questions such as the causes for an unyielding earth, man's eternal need to sweat and labor, the pangs of birth, the cause of death, etc. This account provides answers to all these questions; naive, primitive ones, yes, but suitable for their time and not without their sublimity. On

the other hand, since millions take these passages verbatim and have done so for three thousand years, it behooves us to note that woman is not inferior and subordinated to man because of God's curse, nor did Adam name the animals (imagine his naming the syphilis spirochete!), nor is anesthesia forbidden to women in childbirth, etc. It is the fundamentalists, seeing these words as literal and divinely inspired truth, who object to any interpretation but the literal one. Much harm is possible (the Bible says, "Thou shalt not suffer a witch to live!") unless a proper understanding of the milieu and sources of the Bible is obtained. This need not destroy (rather it amplifies) the nature of its divine inspiration and magnificently sublime religious doctrines.

THE PROGRESS OF SIN; THE WORLDLY RACE; THE GODLY LINE: 4—5:32

Eve gives birth to Cain and Abel, and later Abel the shepherd's offering is accepted by the Lord and Cain the farmer's offering rejected. Cain slays his brother, and in answer to the Lord's question as to Abel's whereabouts, Cain replies, "Am I my brother's keeper?" Cain is cursed by the Lord, a fugitive and vagabond on the face of the earth. To protect Cain from being killed by avengers, the Lord sets a mark on Cain, "lest any finding him should kill him." Cain then knew (had intercourse with) his wife and bore Enoch, whose name he also gave to a city he had built. Later Lamech, a descendant of Cain, introduces an irrelevancy (the subject was the beginnings of civilization) by swearing vengeance seventy-seven times on Cain: "If Cain shall be avenged sevenfold, truly Lamech seventy and sevenfold." Lamech's poem shows ancient origins.

Seth is born to Eve after Cain and Abel, and to Seth a son called Enos. A long genealogy follows, among whom is Methuselah who lived "nine hundred sixty and nine years;" and there was his son Lamech who died at 775 years, and his son was Noah, who begat three sons Shem, Ham, and Japheth when he was 500 years old.

The Cain and Abel story reflects a preference for semi-nomadism (Abel the shepherd) as against agriculture. The tale accounts for certain wandering tribes who carried signs of their tribal origins on their foreheads or arms. Or again, Cain might have carried the sign of the smith trade, since he was the father of a race which made considerable progress in the mechanical arts (4:1-25). Since the story is legendary the problem of where Cain got his wife need not arise (legends defy logic!); but Cain builds the first city and names it after his son. This accounts for the cities all over the world. The tale accounts for the reality the Hebrews saw and knew every day. Picturesque tales accounting for habits, customs, and beliefs, the whole permeated with the presence of God, abound in Genesis. Cain gives rise to various trades followed by his sons, such as cattle-keepers, musicians, and workers in clay and metals. These are the descendants of a murderer; evidently the author reflects dislike of cities and their trades. P's genealogy (5) differs from J's (4) in order to efface the Cain line. P's genealogy exaggerates the longevities to give an effect of great passage of time. "Enoch walked with God: and he was not; for God took him" still mystifies the scholars. Did he arise into heaven? The apocalypticists made Enoch a prominent character in their writings. Finally, note that there are ten generations from Adam to Noah.

THE INCREASE OF WICKEDNESS; THE FLOOD 6—9:17

When the earth was getting well populated, the "sons of God saw the daughters of men that they were fair" and took them as wives; there were "giants in the earth in those days," and the children became mighty men of renown. The sons of God are a mythical race of giants called the *Nephilim*. There was a belief that early man was gigantic in stature and semi-divine. J found nothing wrong in this mariage, but P made such unions evil and infamous; P also adds' the "giants in the earth" part to indicate the giants were not divine in origin.

God saw how wicked and evil men had become, and so He decided to destroy all living things except for the good and just Noah and his three sons, Shem, Ham, and Japheth (JAH feth). God found the earth also corrupt and decided to loose a flood. God gives Noah precise instructions on how to build an ark (a kind of houseboat): it is to be made of gopherwood, 300 cubits long and 50 cubits wide (a cubit is 18") and 30 cubits high—that is, 450' by 75' by 45'—three stories high, with a window and a door. God says He will release a flood to drown all mankind except Noah's family (his wife, the three sons and their wives). A male and female of everything living is to be saved. But a few lines later the Lord tells Noah to save seven pairs of all "clean animals," male and female, and a pair of unclean animals. The flood lasts for forty days, drowning all living things except the ark's inhabitants. After 150 days the waters lessen and leave the ark stranded on top of Mt. Ararat. A raven is released and then a dove to see if the waters are lowering, "but the dove found no rest for the sole of her foot" and returned. The next time, the dove returns with an olive leaf, and the third time finds a perch elsewhere and does not return. When the dry land reappears, Noah builds an altar in gratitude to the Lord and makes burnt offerings. The Lord smells the sweet savor (note the primitive concept of a God battening on the smell of the sacrifice = J) and promises never to curse the ground nor smite every living thing as He had done. He promises regular seasons "while the earth remaineth." Noah and his sons are blessed and a covenant is established (sacred contract between man and God), the terms of which are that there will be no more world-wide floods; and as a sign God sets His "bow in the cloud" as a token of the bargain. See the Babylonian original account of this mythical flood story in the archaeological section. Most scholars feel that this is a possible borrowing by J, for the resemblances are close indeed. Archaeological findings have shown evidences of a great flood at about the same time. Such a story could have mingled mythical and historical elements. The dove's olive leaf indicates the trees are poking their heads above water, although Gunkel (an O.T. scholar) believes the dove and olive have mythological meanings. The flood story is confused: J's version with seven pairs of clean animals and one unclean pair entering the ark is altered by P to one pair each of both impure and pure (they both assume the reader would know what a clean or pure animal is; the laws on purity will be dealt with in Deuteronomy, but for now purity has nothing to do with an animal's hygienic habits). P gives us the precise time in days as well as the dimensions of the ark. J's account as usual is dramatically vivid and spontaneous, while P's interpolations are planned and precise. The Gilgamesh epic of Babylonia in which a god Ea saves a man named Utnapishtim by directing him to build an ark has many similarities to the Flood story. The resting on the Armenian mountain called Ararat rather than on a Palestinian mountain indicates the foreign origin of the myth, which P has considerably refined. P uses the rainbow as a token of God's covenant with Noah; a safe enough bargain for P not to gamble on another world-wide flood!

REPEOPLING OF THE EARTH 9:18—10:32

Noah plants a vineyard, the first tiller of the soil on the unpeopled earth. He gets drunk on wine and lies uncovered in his tent when Ham (the father of Canaan) "saw the nakedness of his father" and tells his brothers. Walking backwards, eyes averted, Shem and Japheth cover his nudity. Noah wakes and curses Ca-

naan (not Ham!): Canaan shall be a slave unto his brothers, Shem shall be blessed in his descendants and Canaan shall be his slave. Japheth too is blessed, and given Canaan as his slave. Noah dies at 950 years of age. This story tells how the world is repeopled (P is the author). First P quotes a J legend on Noah's drunkenness; the names again really represent tribes, and one can readily see how the Canaanites were fitted only to be slaves to the Shemites (Semites). Since the Canaanites were abhorred by the Hebrews for their sexual licence and sodomistic practices, perhaps Ham's action involved more than staring at his father's nakedness. Verse 24 says that Noah "knew what his younger son had *done* to him"; besides, it is very likely the primary, popular form of the tale included the sodomistic act, but J omitted it out of delicacy. It is P who inserts "Ham the father of" before the word Canaan in order to harmonize a later genealogy showing Egyptians as descended from Ham. Since Africans are descendants of Ham, and God cursed Ham's descendants to be enslaved by his white brothers, it follows that all Negroes are destined by God as slaves to their white betters —for so the Bible says! This is the reasoning behind many a sermon from the lips of a bigoted Southern minister, one who can cite scripture to suit any devilish purpose. This will not be the first time the Bible is used to justify evil and wrongdoing, especially when ignorance is afoot! The many descendants of the three sons are given in Chapter 10.

THE TOWER OF BABEL; THE DESCENDANTS OF SHEM 11: 1-26

The whole earth speaks one language, but the peoples of the earth decide to build a tower to reach heaven. The Lord comes down to see the city and tower. He is furious: "Now nothing will be restrained from them"; so He confounds their language to make them unintelligible to one another. He then scatters them on the face of the earth, and the tower is left incomplete. That is why the tower is called Babel (*Babel* = Babylon, popularly derived from *balal,* "to mix," "to confuse": note the pun!). This curious legend accounts for the varied languages of the earth; but in addition it shows how man in his vain pride aspired to defy the Deity—and the punishment is swift. Eve too sought to be like God in knowledge, and her punishment too was swift and severe, as was Adam's. The gods jealously guard their sacred superiority. Chapter 11 indicates the descendants of Shem (the Semites), and is a long "begat" list of names, the last of which are Terah and his son Abram.

ABRAHAM; HIS CALL; HIS SOJOURN IN CANAAN 11:27—25:10

Abram's wife Sarai is barren, that is, without children. And Terah took Abram, his grandson Lot, and Sarai, and left Ur of the Chaldees (city near the northern end of the Persian Gulf at the southwestern tip of the Fertile Crescent) for Haran (in northwest Mesopotamia, a great center of moon-god worship, and then later a center of Aramaean culture; see Gunkel's *Genesis,* and Skinner's *Genesis*). The Lord had said to Abram that he should leave his relatives and seek a certain land, "And I will make of thee a great nation, and I will bless thee." Abram leaves with Lot and his wife and arrives in Canaan. Here the Lord apears to him and says, "Unto thy seed will I give this land." Near Bethel Abram builds an altar unto the Lord. This section combines J and P, but the actual facts of Hebraic history do not substantiate an eastern origin for Abraham or any other patriarch of the Jews, although there is some archaeological evidence pointing to the presence of Jewish names in Ur at that time. Oddly, Abraham (or Abram) is unmentioned in the pre-Exilic prophets, but the post-Exilic prophets were proud of their eastern contacts; hence P would "discover" an origin for the Jews in the east. Abram is the first and most ancient patriarch of the Jews: *ivri* means

one who crosses or perhaps *merchant* (*ivri* = Hebrew); sometimes it is transcribed as *habiru* or *apiru.* Perhaps then the *habiru* mentioned by the ancient Egyptians and Hebrews are identical. Perhaps! Perhaps Abram is a derivative of *ivri.* Perhaps again! The cycle of stories around Abraham is scattered and unrelated, and their unity is mainly genealogical. We must remember that Abram is to be considered a national symbol, the Father of the Hebrews. God's gift of Canaan to Abram proves that the later invaders and occupiers of Canaan, the Hebrews, have a divinely ordained right to the territory. Yahweh's compact with Abram, the first Hebrew, proved their right to the territory.

Now famine was in the land and so Abram went down to Egypt with Sarai. When they reached Egypt, he begged Sarai to pass as his sister for safety's sake. The Pharoah takes Sarai "into his house" while generously heaping gifts upon her "brother" Abram. But the Lord afflicts the Pharaoh with plagues because of Sarai, and the ruler complains to Abram: "Why didst thou not tell me that she was thy wife?" And so Abram and Sarai are allowed to leave Egypt unharmed. The original tale reveals Abram as a man of lies and a crafty opportunist; moreover, in the original, Sarai was very likely the Pharaoh's concubine. P "whitewashes" the episode to cast Abram in a much better light by making Sarai his "half-sister." But we do get glimpses of primitive ethics at work. In another episode Abram rescues his brother Lot from enemy capture, scoring a great victory. "And Melchizedek (mel KIZZ uh deck) king of Salem brought forth bread and wine: and he was the priest of the most high God." He is probably a priest-king of Jerusalem (Salem) of the Zadokite priesthood; these were priests who accepted Yahwism (Hebrew monotheism) when David captured the city and refused to deal with the Levitical priesthood (see Exodus). The Christians make a great deal of this episode of Melchizedek's greeting of Abram, allegorizing the patriarch as a kind of pre-Christ accepted as God's chosen. Melchizedek blesses Abram, and Abram gives him tithes of all (a tenth of everything) he owns. This reflects how dutiful Abram is in paying his just share to the support of the priests, the tithe being required as a kind of "tax" for church support. In a vision Abram complains of his childlessness, having only Eliezer of Damascus as his heir. The Lord promises him Canaan, and tells Abram that his descendants shall be as numberless as the stars in heaven. (Incidentally, on the clearest of nights only some 3000 stars are visible to the naked eye!) But certainly this legend intends numberless Hebrew descendants of Abram. A young heifer, a she-goat, a ram, a dove, and a pigeon are slaughtered and all but the birds are cut in two. That night a smoking furnace (fire-pot) and a burning lamp pass between the carcasses (God is the pot and lamp; He is sealing the covenant with Abram in this primitive manner). God, in a dream, tells Abram of the future: the slavery in Egypt, how Abram will die of old age. The same day the covenant is stated: the land from the Nile to the Euphrates is given to the seed of Abram, the land now occupied by the Kenites, Hittites, Perizzites, Amorites, Canaanites, Jebusites, etc. The childless Sarai tells Hagar, her Egyptian maid, to lie with her husband in order to produce a child. Hagar is made pregnant and mocks the barren Sarai. Hagar is forced to flee because of Sarai's wrath, but the angel of the Lord tells her to return, predicting that her son Ishmael "will be a wild man; his hand wil be against every man, and every man's hand against him." Hagar does give birth to Abram's son, Ishmael. In Chapter 17 the Lord changes Abram's name to Abraham (verse 5); and again re-establishes the covenant, adding that "every man child among you shall be circumcised" as a token of the covenant. Circumcision was a widespread primitive practice; the Egyptians circumcised, for example; it was performed at puberty as a sign of attained manhood. The Hebrews adopted the practice perhaps from the Canaanites (see Exodus 4:25 for its Mosaic origin). So Abraham circumcised all the males of the house on that very day. On the plains of Mamre three men suddenly appear before Abraham, and he addresses one of them as "My Lord." The Lord promises a son to Sarai (her name is changed too, to Sarah, which means the *mother* of the Hebrews); she laughs cynically to herself at the thought, considering her advanced age. An interpolator has changed the story here as a visit by Yahweh to "three men." Sarah's skeptical laughter explains why the child is called Isaac (*laughter* in Hebrew).

The Lord now declares his intention to destroy the wicked cities of Sodom and Gomorrah (guh MORE uh), but Abraham persuades the Lord not to destroy the cities should there be 50 (by clever pleading Abraham reduces the number to ten) good men in the cities. The two angels visit Lot in Sodom, and they are most inhospitably treated. The Sodomites collect at Lot's house and demand his two guests for carnal use; Lot offers his two virgin daughters instead. The angels smite the Sodomites with blindness. The decision is made to destroy the cities; it is evil and depraved and deserves destruction. Lot escapes with his two daughters while the two cities are destroyed with fire and brimstone; his wife had been forbidden to look back, but when she does so, she is turned into a pillar of salt. Israelis are fond of pointing out a salt mass near the Dead Sea resembling a woman to this very day! The narrative is obviously mythical, and just as obvious are the moral lessons: evil practices and sin will ensure destruction; hospitality is the greatest of virtues; God's wrath is monumental in the face of wickedness. There are rationalists who see here an actual volcanic destruction of Sodom and Gomorrah, since the Bible says they were destroyed with fire and brimstone. Such an explanation of miraculous and mythical material only takes the wonder from the miracle, and few believe the rationalist explanation anyway. Besides, there is no evidence of volcanic activity anywhere near the Dead Sea.

Lot stays in a cave with his two daughters, who plan to make him drunk with wine so that they can lie with him. Their purpose is to continue the race. The result of their incestuous acts are the descendants of Lot and his daughters: the Moabites and Ammonites, the deadly and perverted enemies of the Hebrews! Thus, this quaint (!) tale accounts for the fierce enemies of the Hebrews. A similar tale was that of Ham and Noah. Such acounts are part of the historicizing process.

The Abraham-Abimelech story is a doublet (a repetition with variations) of the Abraham-Pharaoh story, but here (Chap. 20) Sarah's virtue is protected and Abraham becomes truthful. The same kind of rewriting occurs at Isaac's birth, where the laughter issues from the surprise of the neighbors and not from Sarah's skepticism. Isaac is circumcised on the prescribed eighth day after birth (21:1-21), and here Yahweh tests Abraham's fidelity by requiring the sacrifice of his first-born, Isaac.' The incredibly faithful Abraham prepares to knife his son on the block when Yahweh's angel stops him and offers a ram instead. This is P's reshaping of a primitive tale of human sacrifice of the first-born, which must have been a practice of the early Hebrews. The moral is changed from the necessity of human sacrifice to the deity, to obedience to Yahweh. Here is P's later, more highly developed morality and monotheism at work on the more primitive sacrificial features of early Yahwehism. In Chapter 22 we are told also that Abraham moves to Beersheba in northern Palestine. In 23 (1-20) we are told of Sarah's death at Hebron at the age of 127. Abraham bargains with the Hittites

for a burial place, the cave of Machpelah (mock PEE lah). Ephron the Hittite turns shrewd: "The land is worth four hundred shekels of silver; what is that betwixt me and thee?" ["A bit of land worth fifty pounds (about $300), what is a trifle like that between me and you?" in the Moffatt tr.] Abraham pays the price and buries Sarah there (also buried there later are Abraham, Isaac, Rebekah, Leah, and Jacob). Next (24: 1-61) Abraham sends his servant to Haran in Mesopotamia (the land of his relatives) in search of a suitable bride for Isaac his son. The beautiful Rebekah (daughter of Bethuel and sister of Laban) is met at a well, where her conduct convinces the servant she is the ideal Hebrew bride for Isaac. The family's consent is obtained and Rebekah leaves for distant Canaan. It is a case of love at first sight, and Isaac immediately conveys her into his mother's tent "and she became his wife; and he loved her" (24:62-67). We obtain an insight into marriage practices as well as a glimpse of the lovely character of Rebekah at the well. The servant did not fear to find a bride, but to find one who would leave for distant Canaan. Mesopotamia (land between rivers) meant to the Romans all the area between the Tigris and Euphrates with the exception of the headwaters and southernmost lands adjoining these rivers; but to the Hebrews it represents a vaguely described area centering around the Hittite city of Haran in the northwestern corner of the Fertile Crescent.

At 175 years Abraham dies and is buried by his sons Isaac and Ishmael with his wife Sarah in the cave of Machpelah (25:7-10). Ishmael is designated as the father of "twelve princes," who are the heads of twelve desert tribes; in brief this makes the Semitic Arabs descended from the rejected Ishmael (see above).

THE LIVES OF ISAAC AND JACOB 25:11—35:29
Rebekah gives birth to twins, Jacob

and Esau; Esau (hairy) issued first
from the womb, tawny and hairy
(note the pun!), and Jacob followed
holding on to Esau's heel. The basic
tales surrounding Jacob are ancient
indeed. His name means "cheater,"
the aptness of which is shown on his
issuing from his mother's womb trying already to supplant his elder
brother! Ankle is *aqeb* in Hebrew,
hence his name: Heel-catcher (25:
26). The primitive, uproarious folktale is reshaped as usual by the
Priests (P) to give the tales more
morality and seriousness; but the
process is never successful enough to
obliterate their folk and legendary
origins. Esau became a skillful hunter
and a favorite of Isaac, while Rebekah's favorite Jacob was a "plain
(quiet) man dwelling in tents." Again
we see tribal groups represented:
Jacob is agricultural and Esau a hunt-
ing nomad, rough and barbarous, and
simple enough to sell his birthright
for a mess of red pottage. (*Edom*
sounds like *adom* = red, a popular
pun since the Edomite tribes of the
desert areas descend from Esau, and
the superior Israelite people from
Jacob; Israel becomes his name
later.) One sees immediately the
country bumpkin and the city sharper
in the stories of Jacob and Esau. The
trade of birthright for red lentils
(pottage) gives the rights of first-
born inheritance (primogeniture) to
the younger son Jacob. Esau, a sim-
pleton indeed, is fleeced of his birthright by the clever Jacob. Primitive
peoples would find nothing unethical
about the use of such cunning; on
the contrary, it would be laudable
indeed. Twentieth-century morality is
ridiculously inept when applied to
primitive ethics. Now the father's
blessing is all-important, for upon
the blessed son and his descendants
would pass God's favor and covenant
promises. Jacob secures his father's
blessing by a trick (with his mother's
help), which is to dress like Esau and
pose as his brother at his dying
father's bedside. Isaac (ironically?)
says, "The voice is the voice of Jacob, but the (hairy) hands are the
hands of Esau." The *midrash* (Jew-

ish embellishment-explanation) on
this episode explains this as a contrast between spiritual strength (Jacob's voice) and animal power
(Esau's hands). Such tendencies to
explain and allegorize are for theologians only and have no place here.
Esau swears revenge and Jacob flees,
but later P inserts a more com-
mendable motive: Jacob leaves to
find a bride (27:46—28:9). Note
three stages in Jacob's character:
1. the folktale sharpster; 2. the Hebrew ancestor; 3. the idealized and
virtuous ancestor.

Another folktale appears in Jacob's
dream that he saw a ladder (a flight
of stairs?) reaching to heaven with
God's angels ascending and descend-
ing it. Yahweh appears and again
promises numerous progeny and the
land of Canaan. Jacob awakes and
changes the name of the place from
Luz to Beth-el, vowing to give tithes
(this is the second mention of tith-
ing: see 14:18-20).

At a well near Haran Jacob meets
Rachel, the daughter of Laban (the
brother of Rebekah, Isaac's wife,
hence Jacob's uncle). A bargain is
made for Jacob to work seven years
for his uncle in exchange for permission to wed Rachel, but Laban
welches by playing a crafty "bed-
trick," in which he substitutes the
dull-eyed ("tender-eyed") older
daughter Leah for the beautiful
younger one. Jacob is forced to work
another seven years for Rachel. Reuben, the oldest son of Jacob and
Leah, is sent to gather mandrakes
["love-apples" resembling a plum,
believed to promote conception; the
American mandrake (*Podophyllum
peltatum*) is a different plant]; and
for the price of a few love-apples
Rachel consents to let Jacob sleep
with Leah that night. The love-apples
prove effective in the barren Rachel,
for she gives birth to Joseph and
later Benjamin. Laban ("white" or
"smooth" in Hebrew) is outwitted by
Jacob who, when about to leave, asks
only for the spotted and speckled
animals, which Laban promptly hides

away. But Jacob takes poplar branches and peels white streaks in them, laying them near the water-troughs of the animals. By sympathetic magic the drinking animals breed on the spot and gave birth to spotted and streaked young! Another hilarious incident is that of Rachel's theft of her father's gods (note the primitive non-monotheistic touch), known as *teraphim,* good-luck household gods resembling the Roman *lares* and *penates.* The pursuing Laban discovers her sitting on the gods (statuettes, really), which Rachel has concealed in this way. She apologizes for not rising in her father's presence since "the way of women is upon me (i.e., menses)"! Laban leaves Jacob alone and returns home after God intercedes for Jacob.

From now on Jacob will be the beloved, virtuous, and respected ancestor; no sign of "the cheater" will be visible. In fact, this is a different Jacob, the reshaped one of the Priests, the respected Father of his race. At the Jabbok River (*he-abeq* = wrestling match; *yaboq* = Jacob— naturally, a punning place-name) Jacob wrestles all night with an angel who finally blesses him and changes his name to Israel. The change of name had also occurred to Beth-el in a similar episode. (Jacob = supplanter, to Israel = perseverer with God!) The change in name accompanies his change in character. A final incident shows the renewed friendship of the two brothers (33: 1-16). Dinah, Jacob's only daughter, is raped by a Hivite prince (34:1-5), but her brothers Simeon and Levi treacherously slay *all* the men of Shechem, to Jacob's great anger at his bloody avenging sons. Note that the Priest shows his indignation at the old revenge blood code in the words of Jacob's wrath. Chapter 34, in the language of J, is indescribably brutal, but the sophisticated P makes everything turn out all right.

Reuben, the oldest son, loses his birthright by committing incest, and that is why Judah will head the great-est of the Hebrew twelve tribes. It is Judah's line that leads to David and Jesus. Isaac is buried by his sons Esau and Jacob just as Isaac and Ishmael had buried Abraham.

THE DESCENDANTS OF ESAU, 36.

Chapter 36 gives a long genealogy of the families of the descendants of Esau.

THE STORY OF JOSEPH 37—50

Jacob's favorite son is Joseph (Rachel, his favored wife's son) and for him he makes a coat of many colors. The father's partiality and Joseph's insulting dreams (he dreams that his brethren bowed down before him) make the brothers (all 11 of them) conspire to kill him; but taking Reuben's advice they cast him in a pit instead (37:12-24). Then they propose to sell him to a band of Ishmaelites, but after the brothers leave him in the pit, Midianite merchants kidnap Joseph and sell him to the Ishmaelites! Both the Ishmaelites and Midianites are credited with selling Joseph into Egypt. Showing a "bloody" (i.e., goat's blood) coat to the father, they say a wild beast has devoured Joseph. The Joseph novelette is a skillful masterpiece of a basically moralistic author. It is a masterpiece of narration, unified if complex in structure, and containing magnificent characterization! "We follow Joseph from priggish adolescence, through misadventure, temptation, and ordeal, into triumph and magnanimity" (Samuel Sandmel, *The Hebrew Scriptures,* 1963, p. 368).

Joseph is sold for 20 pieces of silver to Potiphar, an officer of Pharaoh. Very likely this Pharaoh was one of the Hyksos who ruled from about 1720 to 1550. Joseph was probably in Egypt around 1700 (if we accept Joseph as a historical character, which is the orthodox position). Potiphar's wife attempts to seduce our virtuous hero but fails (note the hand of P!), and Joseph is cast into prison. By corectly interpreting the dreams of the royal butler and baker (40) he is brought to the Pharaoh's attention. For correctly interpreting the Pharaoh's dream of seven lean kine and seven fat kine (seven lean years, seven years of plenty), Joseph is made viceroy of all Egypt, second to the Pharaoh himself! Famine drives Jacob and his sons to go to Egypt for food; Joseph recognizes them, accuses them of spying, detains and then releases them, urging his brothers to return bringing Benjamin (his youngest and only full brother) with them. Simeon is held as a hostage while the brothers return to Palestine (still not having recognized Joseph). They return with Benjamin, and Joseph treats them most favorably. On leaving the second time, Joseph's silver divining cup is found in Benjamin's sack (planted there by Joseph), and the bewildered brothers are marched back to Joseph in the palace. Judah's tenderly eloquent plea that Benjamin be not detained is effective: "We have a father, an old man, and a child of his old age, a little one; and his brother is dead, and he alone is left of his mother, and his father loveth him" 44:20); who could resist such a plea as this? Now Joseph reveals his identity, and there is great joy. Jacob is brought down to be reunited with Joseph, and the family moves to a fertile area of Egypt near the delta, known as Goshen. Jacob blesses his sons Joseph, Ephraim, and Manasseh, and dies (he is buried in Machpelah in Canaan next to the other two great patriarchs, Abraham and Isaac). All is forgiven, and Joseph assures them that their evil was meant by God to effect good, "to bring to pass, as it is this day, to save much people alive . . .

And he comforted them, and spake kindly unto them."

Joseph's method was to exchange grain for money until the famished people ran out of money, at which time he accepted cattle, and then land, which was called "crown land"; it was then rented to the people on the basis of giving to the ruler one-fifth of the yield, the rest being kept by the renter. Such was the wise agrarian policy of Joseph, for which the modern term is the *ever-normal granary*. Note that Jacob in the Joseph story is the venerable patriarch, righteous and just, a far cry from the early "cheater." The story of Joseph is primarily didactic: a picture of a man unceasingly faithful to God; a picture of God's unceasing care and love for his faithful ones; a picture of God's providence in using evil to bring about good. The story is sophisticated and complex, unlike any folktale, certainly most unlike the tales surrounding the three patriarchs Abraham, Isaac, and Jacob. We have in this novelette a gifted, thoughtful author. Finally, the romantic notion that all Jews are descendants of the twelve sons of Jacob is mere folklore, not history. Besides, the full list would total 14 tribes if we add Machir and Gilead (Numbers 26:29-30). But it is true that the tribes of Israel did have a sense of confederation. By means of the Joseph story the Priestly editor accounts for the presence of Jews in Egypt, thus preparing us for Exodus.

EXODUS: AN INTRODUCTION

Exodus, "The second book of Moses" rivals Genesis in importance and in religious and historical interest. Like Genesis it is a compilation of J, E, and P (see chart on Documentary Theory and Introduction on Canoni-

zation). The book makes often for confused and difficult reading because of the many parallel variants, wholesale changes of order and placement, editorial interpolations, expansions, and "linkage-work." Yet, basically the structure is sound. We have seen from our examination of Genesis that biblical history is encrusted with legend and myth, and yet close examination of Exodus will reveal valuable evidence as to past history. Here and there one finds a surprising kernel of fact amidst the saga, the folktale, and the legend. Moses reduces the other characters in this book like Jethro, Joshua, Nadab, and Abihu into midgets. Other stories deal with the tribes of Israel, their increase, enslavement, and persecution; their thrilling escape from the Egyptians; their covenant with God at Sinai; their heathenish failings; their quarrels and complaints, and their early struggles and conflicts.

Exodus is also a book of origins, supposedly recounting how various religious customs and institutions arose, as for example the authorship by Moses of *all* Hebrew codes of law. The book is divided into three parts: 1. Israel's flight in Egypt, Moses' mission, and the authenticating wonders attending it (1-12:36). 2. The Exodus, Red Sea crossing, desert trials (12:37-18). 3. The giving of the Law, the Sinai Covenant, the sanctuary (19-40).

SUMMARY OF THE BOOK OF EXODUS

Exodus comes from the Greek *exodos* (exit, departure) and refers to the departure of Israel from Egypt in the time of Moses. Most of the events can be traced to the time of Ramses II and his son Merneptah (13th century B.C.). The best books on Exodus are those by Albright, Buber, Driver, and Meek (see Bibliography).

OUTLINE OF EXODUS
I. After Genesis (1-2)
II. Birth and Call of Moses (2—4:16)
III. The Plagues (4:17—13:16)
IV. The Red Sea (13:17—18)
V. Sinai (19—24)
VI. The Tabernacle (25—27)
VII. Priesthood, Sacrifice, etc. (28—40)

AFTER GENESIS 1—2
From 70 Hebrews in Jacob's day the number of Jews in Goshen (Egypt) in approximately 400 years are enough to fill the land! A new king (Ramses II? about 1301-1234) arises, fears their great numbers, and enslaves them to prevent their giving aid to Egyptian enemies. Israel's lot is hard, with harsh taskmasters overseeing their work, culminating in the order of the king to slay at birth all Hebrew males. The midwives refuse to execute the orders (there are *two* midwives in all of Egypt!) and so God rewards them with houses (1:21), which means giving them a long line of descendants. Then comes the order to cast the male infants into the Nile because of the midwives' refusal to cooperate.

BIRTH AND CALL OF MOSES 2—4:16
Moses is the son of Levites and the brother of Aaron and Miriam. His mother sets him as an infant afloat in a basket (ark of bulrushes) on the Nile. He is rescued by the Pharaoh's daughter, who later adopts Moses as her son. She calls him Moses because he has been drawn from water. This is popular etymology (invariably wrong), in spite of the fact that Mosheh (Moses) sounds much like *mashah* (to draw out). Our punning author again! The first act of Moses in his manhood is to slay an Egyptian who had struck a Hebrew (2:11), so Moses flees to

Midian to dwell with Jethro, the priest of Midian. There he keeps sheep and marries Jethro's daughter Zipporah (the Midianites were descended from Midian, the son of Abraham and Keturah (Gen. 25:1-4). At either Mt. Sinai or Horeb (Neither Sinai nor Horeb has been identified with certainty. Some find it in Midian, some in Paran.) God addresses Moses from a burning bush (the bush burns but is not consumed, denoting supernatural presence). Such appearances of the Deity are termed *theophanies*. Moses hides his face and removes his shoes because he is on holy ground. Yahweh at this stage is a tribal god of fear, awful power (fire, lightning, thunder: perhaps a sky or mountain god) whose presence brings death and destruction if taboos are violated. It was forbidden to stare at His person, to be shod in His presence, etc. God tells Moses to free his people from bondage and gives His name to Moses as I AM, or I AM THAT I AM (3:14). The name intends to imply self-existence. The divine name YHWH in Hebrew is often translated as *Lord,* and among orthodox Jews is still forbidden to be written; the euphemism *Adonai* is used instead. The name is so powerfully sacred that orthodox Jews dare not write G-d in full! God gives Moses two signs that the people would heed him: 1. His rod cast upon the ground becomes a serpent. 2. His hand becomes leprous when placed on his breast, but it comes out well again, just as the serpent once again becomes a rod when picked up. In answer to Moses' objection that he was not fluent enough of tongue (did Moses stutter?), God or Yahweh (His name henceforth according to E) gives him Aaron, his eloquent brother, as his spokesman. It is important to recall that Aaron is a Levite like Moses and Miriam.

THE PLAGUES 4:17—13:16

A strange incident now occurs: Moses is taken critically ill (perhaps because he failed to have his son

Gershom circumcised). "The Lord met him, and sought to kill him. Then Zipporah took a sharp stone, and cut off the foreskin of her son, and cast it at his feet, and said, Surely a bloody husband art thou to me." This is an etiological (why things occur as they do; doctrine of causes) story which is different from the account in Genesis 17 (P's). The flint knife indicates ancient ritual, but infant circumcision is much later than pubertal. Problems: The demonic element, Moses addressed as a bridegroom when he is the father of two children, Zipporah herself performing the rite, etc. Probable good answers: Zipporah the Midianite circumcises to indicate the rite originated with the Midianites; in an earlier version she circumcised Moses and *not* the son; the occasion *was* on the bridal night, and her aim was to save Moses from a demon who denied him possession of the bride. The demon is appeased by the touch of the foreskin and her words, "Surely you are a bridegroom of blood to me!" (See George Beer and Hugo Gressmann in Bibliography).

When the Pharaoh refuses to permit the Hebrews to go for three days into the desert (wilderness) to offer sacrifices, the Hebrew slaves are forced to gather their own straw for making bricks (the straw was mixed with the mud to give consistency and strength to the bricks). In 6:1-13 God renews His promise to deliver Israel. Moses and Aaron beg the king to free the Jews but his heart is hardened. Aaron casts his rod before the Pharaoh and it becomes a serpent; but the king's enchanters (magician-priests) perform the same deed of magic. Aaron's rod then swallows up their rods! (The power of the Hebrew God is stronger than the Egyptians'.)

Now follow nine plagues from God to humble the Pharaoh: 1. The Nile is turned to blood. 2. Loathsome frogs infest the land. 3. Lice (or gnats in RSV) infest the land. 4. Flies (perhaps dog-flies common in

Egypt). 5. A murrain (epidemic) in the animal flocks and herds. 6. Boils among the men and cattle. 7. A terrific hail (Goshen is spared; in fact all the plagues spare the Hebrews). 8. Locusts. 9. A three-day darkness. Still (with variations) the Pharaoh is hard-hearted (perhaps deliberately made so by Yahweh). The slaves "borrow" silver and gold jewels (ASV* and RSV* have "ask"), while for the last plague (number 10) Yahweh slays all the firstborn of the Egyptians, both men and animals. On the night of the tenth plague (Hebrew *Abib* or *Nisan,* which is about the time of the Christian Easter) the Passover is instituted. The Hebrews escape the plague by slaughtering a lamb and smearing its blood on the door posts. Yahweh, seeing this sign, *passes over* (= Passover) the Hebrew homes. Passover (*Pesah*) is a very sacred holy day to the Jews, a memorial to Yahweh's freeing of them from Egyptian bondage.

THE RED SEA 13:17—18
The Hebrews are chased by the troops of the Pharaoh, but by a miracle the Red Sea parts, allowing the Hebrews to cross; then it descends upon the Egyptians to drown them. Much scholarship is wasted on the Red Sea miracle. Rationalists say, for example, that a "strong east wind" caused the shallow sea to back up, etc. But a more credible way is not to rationalize a miracle taken from legend but to accept it as legendary and yet miraculous in terms of faith in God.

The song of the Red Sea, a famous song of triumph follows, and is sung by "Moses and the children of Israel" (15:1-18). It describes God's victory over the enemy and is a poetic masterpiece. Incidentally, Miriam leads the women in singing and dancing for joy.

*See section on translations below.

Now begins the long journey across the Sinai peninsula (attempts to trace their route in the desert of Sinai are guesswork mainly, since the details are imprecise and bare). In their hunger they are supplied miraculously with manna (perhaps a sap-like exudation from a tree; the tamarisk tree, say the rationalists, but in Hebrew the word means "What is it?"). To satisfy their complaints of hunger, Moses smites a rock with his rod and water gushes forth freely. (See a doublet in Num. 20:1-13.) The Amalekites attack the Hebrews; Moses watching from the crest of a hill raises his arms, at which the battle goes in his favor, but when he lowers them the reverse occurs. To offset this, his arms are held up by two men and the battle is won.

Jethro (Moses' father-in-law) arrives with Zipporah and her two sons. Jethro blesses Moses' God, declaring Him to be "greater than all gods" (18:9-12). This indicates the subordination of the Midianite gods to the Hebrew Deity. Moses is told by Jethro to appoint judges to assist him, thus sharing responsibility more efficiently.

SINAI 19—24
The Hebrews reach Mt. Sinai (precise location still unknown on the third month after leaving Egypt. God calls Moses to the top to assure Moses that if the Hebrews will keep the covenant, He would make them a "kingdom of priests, and an holy nation" (19:3-6). The people heartily assent. Thunder and lightning, clouds, smoke, and fire betoken the presence of God, who has summoned Moses to the top of Sinai. Moses is handed the Ten Commandments during the theophany (God-appearance) on Sinai (see 34:28, where the expression Ten Commandments is used). The Israelites are terrified and beg Moses to be their mediator lest they die by contact with the awful God. Scholars conjecture that Yahweh in the beginning was a mountain god or perhaps a volcano god of some local area in Sinai who was later adopted by the Hebrews as their single God; His vol-

canic, sky, and mountain associations will gradually be shed as the Hebrews develop more sophistication in their originally crude monotheism.

The Ten Commandments (or *Decalogue*, Greek for ten words), along with a few fragments of other laws, comprise the Book of the Covenant, the oldest existent code of Hebrew laws. Some scholars believe the Ten Commandments represent a kind of digest of the Book of the Covenant. Much of the rest of the Pentateuch is but an amplification of the Law given here. The laws refer to images, altars, offerings (20:22-26); to slaves (21:1-11); to capital crimes such as murder, kidnaping, and the cursing of parents (21:12-17); laws of personal injury and property damage (21:18-33 and 22:15); miscellaneous laws involving morals and ritual (22:16—23:19). God then promises to guide his people to the Promised Land, sending before them a guiding angel, and hornets to help against the enemy. A historicizing factor (framing historical episodes to account for customs and traditions) uses the Sinai episode to explain a multiplicity of customs which have taken hundreds of years to formulate. The laws are made up of royal decrees (*huqqim*, or "inscriptions"), judgments (*mishpatim*) or judicial decisions, commandments, and "revelations," or injunctions from priestly oracles. Many scholars believe the Code of Hammurabi (about 1728-1686 B.C.) influenced the Decalogue strongly (See Introduction). To call Moses the author of Pentateuchal legislations runs against all the findings of scholarship. Through the historicizing process early and very late legislation is depicted as issuing from God in a single episode! What is wonderful about the episode is the skill with which Moses is depicted in literary terms (his wrath, stubbornness, his loyalty to his people, etc.). Oddly, the prophets looked back upon the Sinai days as ideally golden, but we know that there was much murmuring, complaining, even rebellions and apostasy! The making

of the Golden Calf is rank apostasy, causing the wrathful Moses to break the tablets of stone in two; the idolworshippers would have been slain then and there had not Moses intervened. Anthropomorphic elements appear, as when Moses sees the "back parts" of God but not his face (33:18-23); yet the Pentateuch rises to sublime heights in these passages. The second set of tablets given to Moses are unlike the first, being more ritualistic and less ethical and religious than the first set. The primitive laws can be discerned beneath the more sophisticated additions and interpolations, such as that requiring all first-born males as sacrifice, and the prohibition against boiling a kid in its mother's milk, etc. Frazer (*Folk Lore in the Old Testament;* see Bibliography) finds this to mean that primitive peoples in many areas looked upon goat's milk as precious, sacred, and life-sustaining; hence, its use to boil meat (a particularly succulent dish) would be taboo. Each of the laws has a complex sociological and ethnological history for which there is little room here—but see the Bibliography for further references. To indicate the complexity involved, scholars have found the tradition in the "Book of the Covenant" (21:1—23:19) very much differing from both the early accounts of the two tablets of stone inscriptions; these differ from the latest accounts, which assume there were two tablets. Beyond this 24:1, 9-11 is still a different account in fragmentary form! Summary:

1. First there was a primitive ancient account of Sinai which is used by later editors as a *second* narration (the Golden Calf incident separates them).
2. A long legal section implying the covenant was recorded not in stone but on paper.
3. A fragment exists stating Moses, Aaron, and Aaron's sons also climbed the mountain to receive the Decalogue.
The Decalogue known as the ethical or prophetic one, which is in con-

trast to the earlier ritual versions, is also a more sophisticated and ethical set of laws (See 20:2-17).

PRIESTHOOD, SACRIFICE, ETC. 28—40

We are informed that Aaron and his sons are the first Israelites to be consecrated to the priesthood (the house of Levi, hence the popularity of Levy and Levine as Jewish surnames). Then we are given a minute description of their vestments, their ornaments, the Urim and Thummim (stones used to determine guilt or innocence?), the ceremony for priestly ordination, the daily sacrifice, the altar, the conditions of the poll tax for the support of the Tabernacle services, the special recipes for making anointing oil and sacred incense (30:23-38; 37:29). The skilled Bezaleel of the tribe of Judah superintends the building of the Tabernacle. The Sabbath is explained as a day of rest, a *sign* that the observers are in a covenant relationship with God (circumcision also). Most of Chapters 35 to 40 is repetition of information given in 25 to 31, but there are omissions, additions, and changes; the interested student should examine and compare both in detail.

What must be remembered is that the narration in Genesis through the first half of Exodus is a preparation for the climax to the whole story: the Laws; these were of central interest to the compilers of the Pentateuch. To the devout Jew what one *does* is as important as what one *thinks.* In fact, in late Judaism *action* and *conduct* implicitly implied belief. Without this supposedly dull list of laws, there would be very little understanding of Judaism and Christianity. No wonder then that the Jew looks upon the Torah or Law as the most sacred section of the *Tanak* (Old Testament)!

LEVITICUS: AN INTRODUCTION

Leviticus means "relating to priests," and is concerned principally with sacrifice and priests. The title really is not indicative of the contents, since only two verses (25:32-3) speak about the Levites as an official body of priests. Actually, the book has to do with one small branch of the Levite family, the descendants of Aaron (the Aaronic priesthood). The title then can apply to the priestly Aarons if thought of in this special sense. Certainly, all priests were Levites (descendants of Levi, the third son of Jacob and Leah), but we shall see that not all Levites were priests. The Book of Leviticus is simply a kind of manual of laws meant primarily for priests and worshippers. What little narrative there is is imbued with a legal setting. The priestly style is monotonous and legalistic, with the result that the modern, disinterested reader is likely to find the book heavy-going and dull. For the scholar the book contains great antiquarian interest; and for the scribe and rabbi it has cultic features of outstanding importance— a guidebook to ritual and law. Exodus and Numbers were concerned with the accoutrements of cult, but Leviticus gives the obligations of the Hebrews to their religion, and accents what one must do when offering sacrifice, etc. Chronologically, the book is correctly placed: Numbers left off with the building of the Tabernacle in Sinai, and now Leviticus' priestly laws logically follow. The next book (Numbers) will be narrative on the wanderings in the wilderness after Sinai.

SUMMARY OF THE BOOK OF LEVITICUS

The Book of Leviticus can easily be divided into five sections:
I. Laws Relating to Sacrifice (1—7)
II. Consecration of Priests (8—10)
III. Laws Relating to Uncleanness and Purification (11—16)
IV. The Laws of Holiness (17—26)
V. Vows and Tithes (27)

The title of the book derives from the Latin Vulgate translation of the Old Testament (*Liber Leviticus* = the book pertaining to the Levites, which is the Latin rendering of the Septuagint title; for Vulgate and Septuagint see Introduction). Chapters 28—9 of Exodus had described Aaron as high priest, and the beginning of Leviticus should have described his investiture (ceremony in assuming office)—but it does not. Chapter 8 is actually the point where Leviticus should have begun, while the first seven chapters distinguish types of sacrifice.

LAWS RELATING TO SACRIFICE 1—7

The burnt offering is the first sacrifice to be considered. The animal was cut in pieces and burned entire upon the altar. Thus Isaac was to be sacrificed as a burnt offering (Gen. 22:2). The skin became the property of the officiating priest. The "meat" offering was made up of vegetables, better translated as "meal" or "cereal" offering. Only a handful of the meal was burnt, the remainder being eaten by the priests. The peace offerings were made in three categories: the thank offering, the votive, and the free-will offerings (7: 11-16). Here only a small portion was burned, the rest of the animal being eaten by the priests, the offerer, and his family. The peace offering was really a thank offering and symbolized peace and harmony between God and the offerer. Of interest is the fact that clean wild animals were never offered in sacrifice since they were already God's property and could not then be offered as gifts to Him. The sin offering was made to atone for sins committed unawares, in ignorance. The rules were complex, but of interest is the fact that the poor might substitute birds for animals, and the very poor need offer only a tiny portion of flour. One can readily see the need for the sin offering in view of the highly complex and multifarious laws attendant upon the religious Hebrew. Finally, there is the trespass offering (guilt offering): this was offered for sins deliberately committed and is very difficult to distinguish from the sin offerings except by the expert. Sin was conceived of as violation of ritual law; the reader is warned to keep this constantly in mind while reading the Pentateuch. The sections 6:8—7:38 deal with the procedure for priests during offerings. Note that tail fat and internal fat (like blood) were considered as the seat of life, hence forbidden eating. Also forbidden eating was any animal torn by beasts or which had died of itself.

THE CONSECRATION OF PRIESTS 8—10

Chapters 8 and 9 describe the investiture of Aaron and his elevation as the first of the high priests. While Aaron and his sons are being consecrated, Moses performs the priestly office. At the close of the first ordination service we see Aaron's benediction, a famous one:: "The Lord bless thee, and keep thee: The Lord make his face shine upon thee, and be gracious unto thee: The Lord lift up his countenance upon thee, and give thee peace" (9:22-3). Nadab and Abihu are slain by God because they offer "strange" (unholy) fire before the Lord. Strange fire might mean coals brought from an unapproved source. Nadab and Abihu were the two oldest sons of Aaron, and the text implies they were drunk also (10:8-10).

LAWS RELATING TO UNCLEANNESS AND PURIFICATION 11—16

These laws relate to uncleanness of meats, dead bodies, leprosy, and "discharges," such as sexual secretions, menses, and after-birth. Important: which animals are "unclean"? Those which did not have a cloven hoof and chew the cud; hence, most large quadrupeds are ceremonially "unclean," except oxen, sheep, goats, and certain deer (the rock badger, not a cud-chewer, looked as if it were, hence it was considered clean). Aquatic animals of the unclean variety: those lacking fins and scales, like eels, shrimp, lobster. Birds of prey and carrion-eaters (among birds) were unclean, including the bat, which is here considered a bird. Small quadrupeds and tiny creeping things were also unclean. Among insects, those not resembling grasshoppers (i.e., with leaping legs) were considered unclean. Contact with dead bodies was unclean. Leprosy (really skin disceases like ringworm, although genuine leprosy might have been present) is the one type of uncleanness most thoroughly covered. Leprosy of garments might merely have been mildew. Purification was by shaving, bathing, and by following a complex religious ritual (14). A mother after the birth of a son had a 40-day period of ritual uncleanness, and a girl involved double that number. Mary, the mother of Jesus, made an offering of two birds after the birth of her son following the period of her purification (Luke 2:24). Finally, the sexual discharges of men and women are considered; perhaps the "issues" of gonorrhea were also considered here (15). Chapter 16 describes the most sacred of Jewish holy days, Yom Kippur, the Day of Atonement; here is described the ritual of the scapegoat (a very ancient folklore rite). The goat for Azazel was sent into the wilderness. Azazel might have been an evil spirit

of some sort. There is much legislation connected with atonement. Note the change: the Tabernacle (tent of meeting in the Wilderness) is now entered into its holy of holies (the inner part separated by a veil from the antechamber) only on the Day of Atonement; but in earlier writings the "Holy of Holies" is freely entered at any time. This change, among others, signifies later redaction by priests.

LAWS OF HOLINESS 17—26

This section contains the oldest priestly materials in Leviticus. This section emphasizes holiness and insists that Israel be holy, "Ye shall be holy: for I the Lord your God am holy" (19:2); hence it is known as the "Holiness Code." The style of this section is less dry and legalistic than the rest of Leviticus; indeed, it is the highest literary level the book reaches. The section (known as "H" by scholars) dates from about 530 B.C.; a similar section in Ezekiel 40—48, dates from about 540; and P (as we have already seen) dates from about 400 B.C. In H we find the laws more ethical in import, such as the famous chapter 19 where the well-known Golden Rule is found (19:18): "thou shalt love thy neighbor as thyself." This injunction is commonly found in ancient literatures; certainly, Jesus (Matthew 7:12) is repeating in his sermon a hoary rule of conduct well known in ancient times. What we should remember is that it was the priests who taught the Golden Rule. To say that they emphasized ritual only to the harm of high ethical conduct is to distort. To the priests religious law and high ethical conduct were bound inseparably together. Chapter 23 summarizes the Hebrew sacred calendar: the Sabbath, the Passover and unleavened bread, First Fruits, Feast of Weeks, Feast of Trumpets, Day of Atonement, and Feast of Booths or Tabernacles. Sandmel's book on the Old Testament has a useful and interesting discussion on the development of the calendar (see Bibliography) in his Appendix II. The Holiness Code ends with a promise of blessing if the laws are kept, and threatens curses should any one of the complex set of laws be violated.

VOWS AND TITHES 27

Persons could redeem themselves in the matter of vows and tithes by cash payments (gauged accordingly to the wealth of the redeemer). Tithes could be commuted by money payment also. Much cash revenue came in for the support of the sanctuary in this manner. Had Jephthah lived later, for example, his daughter could have been money-commuted (Judg. 11:39-40).

NUMBERS: AN INTRODUCTION

This fourth book of the O.T. derives its title from the censuses mentioned in the book. These were taken for military and political purposes. Notwithstanding this, the title is misleading since the numberings are relatively few: more inclusive are the adventures of the Hebrews "in the wilderness," a phrase occurring in the first verse. This is the second phase of the escape from bondage, the events from Sinai to Jericho in Palestine. The next phase (entry and partial conquest of Canaan) is described in Joshua. The religious import is to teach the discipline of delay, the dependence on God for daily bread, divine leadership, the organization of religious life, and character sketches of Caleb, Joshua, Miriam, Aaron, and Moses. The authorship and date have been already discussed. The book can easily be outlined into three major sections:
I. Last Days of the Encampment at Sinai, 1—10:10.
II. Period of the Wilderness Wanderings, 10:11—22:1
III. Encampment on the Plains of Moab, 22:2—36:13.

The census occupies much of the first four chapters, but much space is still spent on the Levitical duties and privileges. Levi, as we already know, was strongly rebuked in Genesis 49. Yet here the family is exalted. The confusion is possibly due to the use of priestly titles read into a much earlier historical period.

SUMMARY OF THE BOOK OF NUMBERS

LAST DAYS OF THE ENCAMPMENT AT SINAI 1—10:10

The first census results in a grand total of 603,550 men able to bear arms (not including the Levites)! Obviously such figures are legendary exaggerations, but in basic historic terms the actual number of Israelites is impossible to determine. The Levites were excluded because they were in charge of the Tabernacle. All four of Aaron's sons were ordained as priests, but, as pointed out earlier, Nadab and Abihu were killed by the Lord for their "strange fire." The Levites were divided into the priestly caste (Levites descended from Aaron) and the non-priestly Levites. Ezekiel attached other limitations, making them the descendants of Zadok only, an Aaronic descendant. The non-priestly Levites assisted the priests. The camp itself was kept clean by removing the "lepers," all persons with an "issue" (discharge of some sort), and those defiled by contact with dead bodies. Trial by ordeal in cases involving marital jealousy is especially interesting: the wife is forced to drink water mixed with floor dust:

if her belly swells, guilty; if not, innocent! Such rituals are ancient indeed, and common among primitive peoples. (*Ordeal*: a form of judicial procedure subjecting the accused to a painful test believed to be under God's control.) Chapter 7 is famous for its length: the longest in the Bible (only Psalm 119 is longer, and it is not a chapter in the biblical sense). The object lesson of the longest chapter is a plea for generous support of public worship.

Chapter 8 deals with the purification and presentation of the Levites. In presenting the Levites to the Lord, the people laid their hands on them (perhaps symbolically). The phrase is often found in the New Testament in similar situations. A pillar of cloud by day which becomes a pillar of fire by night now guides the Israelites in their march away from Sinai and towards the Promised Land. We have the first mention of "silver trumpets," used for summoning the twelve tribal leaders (one blast), and for summoning the whole congregation (two blasts). When they finally reach Canaan, the silver trumpets will be used for battle calls. The cloud and fire pillars are of course symbolic of God's guiding presence.

PERIOD OF THE WILDERNESS WANDERINGS 10:11—22:1

The first wilderness the Israelites enter is the wilderness of Paran (wide wastelands northeast of Sinai). Much attention is paid to the order in which the tribes march, but more important is the fact that Moses' father-in-law perhaps acted as a guide. [(Is his name Jethro, Reuel, or Hobab? Is his tribe the Kenites or the Midianites? Did he leave Moses' camp (Exod. 18:27) or did he stay (Num. 11:29)? Multifarious confusion of contradicting facts serves to make many parts of the Bible hopeless reading for the beginner, but an understanding of the process of compilation will serve as an aid to comprehension (see Introduction above).] Tiring of manna, the Israelites long for fish, leeks, cucumbers, and melons—recalling their previous life under the Egyptians. God provides quail in such numbers that two days and a night are spent in bagging the elusive quarry! The slowest poke amongst the gatherers collects a minimum of a hundred bushels! Rationalists explain the quail-miracle by actual freak migratory flights that still occur over Egypt; but as previously explained such rationalistic naturalism merely tends to ridicule and "demiracalize" the miracle! No migratory flight can cover the ground a yard deep for miles! (11:18-20, 31-34) In a curious episode Moses' sister Miriam and brother Aaron defy his authority (out of envy perhaps), but their actual charge was that he had married an "Ethiopian woman" (perhaps the Cushite Zipporah). Miriam is struck with leprosy by the Lord, Aaron left unharmed. She is healed after Moses prays in her behalf. The Paran period includes Chapters 13-19. In Chapters 13 and 14 twelve spies (one from each tribe) are sent to "spy out" Canaan and bring back samples of its fruit, soil, and reports on the inhabitants and their defenses. Figs, grapes, and pomegranates are brought back to indicate the fertility of the Promised Land, one flowing "with milk and honey." All twelve spies agree on the land's fertility, but only two (Caleb and Joshua) file a minority report encouraging attack. The ten of the pessimistic majority report are "smitten by the Lord" (14: 36, 37) whereas Caleb and Joshua are the only two of the first secular census allowed to enter the Promised Land. The rest of the adults of that census never did get to enter Canaan, even after 40 years (a legendary round number) of desert wanderings. Historically, the period of infiltration through Arabian deserts and into Canaanite lands must have taken many decades and many generations of Israelites. The conquering of Canaan itself must have been a long process (never quite completed) of infiltration, border raids, military victories and defeats, eventual conquest and inter-penetrations of the two Semitic cultures. Chapter 15 concerns ritual, garments, and Sabbath breaking (death penalty by stoning!). Curious item: the law of tassels and borders concerns the fastening of tassels or fringes on the hems of certain garments (at the four corners?), which served to remind the wearers to keep the Decalogue. Orthodox Jews still use the *talith*, an oblong, tasseled cloth worn in synagogue worship.

Chapters 16—18 concern rebellions in camp and the portions due priests and Levites. Korah rebels against Aaron and his sons (he claimed priesthood for all Levites); he and his followers (250 of them) are slain instantly by the Lord (by fire)! Dathan and Abiram rebel against Moses' authority in civil matters (they claim leadership as descendants of Reuben, Jacob's eldest son); and they and their families sink into a hole "as the ground clave asunder that was under them!"

Next, Aaron's rod blossoms and bears ripe almonds as a sign that his descendants are chosen by God to serve in the sanctuary. Important: Aaron's name was written upon the rod of Levi. A summary of priestly duties ends the eighteenth chapter.

Chapter 19 deals with purification (the Ritual of the Red Heifer), and Chapters 20 through 22 deal with the closing events of the wilderness wanderings.

Miriam is buried at Kadesh; Moses procures sparkling water from repeated striking of a rock with his rod (see the doublet of this miracle in Exod. 17:4-7). In some way Moses offends God (either by striking more than once or by claiming credit for himself), and the result will be that God forbids his entering Canaan; the same is true for Aaron, who dies on Mount Hor, on "the edge of the land of Edom," wherever that is. According to Deut. 10:6, Aaron dies at Mosera. Eleazar succeeds his father as priest.

Israel secures her first victory over the Canaanites at Hormah in southern Palestine. Israel's probable line of march from Kadesh in the wilderness to the plains of Moab is in this wise (probably): a. Circle northeast of Kadesh for about 50 miles; b. Then due south to Ezion-geber, a town on the Red Sea; c. Refused permission to take the "king's highway" through Edom, they go northward to the southern end of the Dead Sea; d. Then southeast along the Zered River (between Edom and Moab) for about 30 miles; e. Then north through Sihon to a point opposite the city of Jericho (See *Westminster Bible Atlas* for the most accurate scholarly layout of the routes through the Wilderness). God sends fiery serpents to sting the complaining Israelites for their "murmurings"; and Moses is commanded to make a serpent of bronze and raise it on a pole, thus healing those bitten by their gaze upon the bronze image. "Brazen" in KJV is either copper or bronze. This serpent symbol reveals serpent-worshipping Israelites in ancient times. An Amorite king, Og, is defeated and his territory goes to the tribe of Manasseh (Bashan lay between the Jabbok river and Mt. Hermon).

ENCAMPMENT ON THE PLAINS OF MOAB 22:2—36:13
The story of Balak and Balaam (22:2—24-25) is famous: Balak was a king of Moab (the Moabites, like the Ammonites, were descendants of Lot's incestuous union with his daughters; see above) who was in mortal fear of the Israelites. He requests the prophet Balaam of Mesopotamia to curse Israel, but he refuses (the Lord had forbidden him to curse the "blessed" Israelites.) While Balaam is riding on his ass, the angel of the Lord blocks the way, thus bringing the ass to a stop. Balaam does not see the angel, so he beats and curses the animal: this for three successive refusals by the poor animal! Had not the ass turned aside, the angel would have killed Balaam. This ass and the talking serpent in Genesis are the only

two animals that are allowed to speak in the Old Testament. Obviously this is a religious motif tied on to a very old folk-tale. The result is a blessing of Israel by Balaam, much to the annoyance of Balak, who, as an enemy of Israel, is cursed by Balaam! The account blends two story layers: Balaam as serious prophet, and Balaam as wily rogue, as in the ass incident. "The Balaam episode is one of the comic highlights of the Tanak," says Sandmel in his *The Hebrew Scriptures*. A famous Messianic prophecy is uttered by Balaam: "There shall come a Star out of Israel . . ." (24:17).

Whoredom with the Moabite women and Baal worship are some of the sins committed by the Israelites on the plains of Moab; for this their leaders are executed (25:27).

In the second secular census we obtain a total of about 1800 less than the first one. In a forlorn passage God commands Moses to prepare for his death (27:12-14), but for his actual death we must wait for Deut. 34. Joshua is chosen to succeed Moses as leader of the Israelites.

Chapters 28 and 29 deal with a quantitative table for use in public offerings, and a section on the validity of vows (30). Chapter 31 shows how

Moses defeats the Midianites, killing all their men and taking as captives their women and children. Tribal plunder in those times included exterminating the fighting males and taking captive the women and children, as well as confiscating all portable cattle and goods. Crude stuff, but those were primitive times, with tribal codes of behavior, and with tribal gods of vengeance and battle. Even God at this stage is a tribal war god, exulting in aggressive acts and bloody spoil. More of this is in the final chapters of this book. One half of the war spoil was given to the soldiers, the other to the congregation (31:25-47).

Chapter 32 deals with the allotment of territory (as it was conquered): the trans-Jordan (see Introduction) is given to the tribes of Reuben, Gad, and Manasseh (a half-tribe, since he was not the *son* of Jacob, but his grandson). Chapter 33 gives the itinerary of the march from Egypt to the plains of Moab (33:1-49). Chapter 34 is largely concerned with instructions pertaining to boundaries, heiresses, and the settlement of Canaan. Chapter 35 cites six cities of refuge for asylum purposes (accidental homicides could find refuge from death-punishment in these cities). Intentional homicide always resulted in the death penalty.

DEUTERONOMY: AN INTRODUCTION

The title of this book is taken again from the Septuagint translation of 17:18 which reads *To Deuteronomion touto* ("this copy of the law"), an inaccurate translation of the Hebrew meaning a "copy of this law." The English translations simply anglicize the Greek term *Deuteronomion*. Verse 18 of Chapter 17 mentioned above refers to the Hebrew king's necessity for transcribing to his personal use *a copy* of the Deuteronomic law in order to make

its teachings the center of his life.

The book is the fifth and last book of the Pentateuch, and really the first book of a long narrative extending through Kings; but in spite of this it was detached and affixed to the *Tetrateuch* (first four boks of the Pentateuch) to make up what is called the Pentateuch. Two views are necessary: 1. As the first part of a long narrative extending through Kings, and 2. As the last book of the Torah (Pentateuch).

The contents are varied: it reformulates laws already given; it interprets those laws and adds new one; there is much historical reminiscing, exhorting, and prophecy. Structurally, it is made up of three discourses suposedly by Moses, plus a kind of introduction and conclusion. As literature the book is of the first rank.

Like the rest of the Pentateuch the story of its composition is similar. The original Deuteronomy cannot be later than 621 B.C., when Hilkiah the high priest discovered it (he said) in the house of the Lord. Hilkiah's find is nearly identical with most of Deuteronomy (see 2 Kings 22:8). Most important is the strong stress laid on the *ethical* greatness of God.

SUMMARY OF THE BOOK OF DEUTERONOMY

INTRODUCTION AND MOSES' FIRST DISCOURSE 1—4:49
In the plains of Moab "on this side Jordan" in the eleventh month and fortieth year of the Exodus, Moses makes his first discourse. He reminds them of their lack of faith in Yahweh, as shown in their reception of the spy report (see Numbers 13—14). This is principally why the entire Wilderness generation (including Moses) will be barred from entering Canaan. Then Moses goes over the march from Kadesh towards the Gulf of Aqaba and then northward (the route conflicts with that in Numbers). When near the Promised Land, Moses had begged to be allowed to enter, but Yahweh is angry over Israel's disloyalty. Moses is directed to climb Pisgah (a pass between mountain peaks), which some declare to be a mountain named Pisgah, Nebo, or Ebarim, depending upon which section of Deuteronomy one happens to be reading (for the variants see 32:19, 34:1, 3:13-29). From Pisgah Moses views the Promised Land.

Chapter 4 is made up of Moses' exhortation to keep the law and shun idolatry. He predicts the Exile if the Israelites prove lax and forget God (the Exile is dated in the sixth century; see Introduction). The chapter also contains a second introduction (4:44-49) and again military victories are rehearsed.

MOSES' SECOND DISCOURSE; THE TEN COMMANDMENTS 5—28
Chapter 5 declares that the Horeb (or Sinai) Covenant was based upon the Ten Commandments, and declares also that no previous covenant had been made with patriarchs Abraham, Isaac, and Jacob! The chief differences between the Commandments here and those in Exodus 20 are the following: :
1. An additional reason is given for honoring one's parents.
2. More reasons are given for keeping the Sabbath.
3. Inclusion of "ox" and "ass" in the command concerning the Sabbath.

Chapter 6 deals with Israel's relationship with God; obedience is the purpose of the law. We are given the Jewish confession of faith subscribed to by Jews of all sects, the *Shema* (Hear!), which has become for Jews a predication of the singleness and unity of God: "Hear, O Israel, the Lord our God, the Lord is one," 6:4. There is a tradition that this verse was repeated by the sons of Jacob at his deathbed; pious Jews recite the verse when dying (or they may listen to it while dying). Of 6:5, concerning man's principal duty to God (to love Him), we are reminded of Jesus' saying that "This is the first and great commandment" (Matt. 22:37-8). Of Deut. 6:13, 16, we have Jesus quoting it in his second and third temptations by the devil, "Thou shalt not tempt the Lord thy God," and "Thou shalt worship the Lord thy God, and him only shalt thou serve" (Matt. 4:7, 10). Man's love for God should be total and unreserved, and God alone is worthy of Israel's loyalty, since God had brought them out of bondage in Egypt (this is constantly mentioned in the latter part of the Pentateuch). In Chapter 7 Moses urges intolerance and non-compromise with the heathen; their symbols of worship must be demolished lest Israel be led by them into idolatry (7:1-5). In verses 6-8 God is said to have chosen the Israelites because He loved them and because of His oath to the patriarchs to redeem Israel from Egypt; God promises (says Moses) to bless and protect Israel *if* they keep the law, His Comandments.

From Chapters 8 through 28 there is much variegated material: Moses warns against unrighteousness and self-sufficiency (8-10:11), and exhorts them to love and obey God; he describes the Promised Land as one of hills and valleys flowing with milk and honey, blessed with rain, fertile in grain, wine, oil, and cattle pasturage. Rain will fall if God holds them in favor; if not, there will be drought (11:10-17). Chapter 11:13-21 is also part of the *Shema* and makes one of four such passages memorialized in phylacteries (leather boxes about a cubic inch square containing such passages; they are worn on various parts of the body). Of interest is 12:8-14 in which a central sanctuary is established in the Promised Land as soon as Israel becomes established there (see Introduction). Those Israelites seduced by idolatry are to be stoned to death (12:29—13:11).

Chapter 14-15 deals with dietary laws, tithes, debts, and the release of slaves. Chapters 16 and 17 deal with the law of judges (civil judges served the tribe in each locality within each tribe), and kings (kings are permitted but not required by Deuteronomic law).

Chapter 18 again takes up laws concerning the Levites, priests, and prophets (the last, prophets, was a new office to establish a mediator between the fearsome God and the people). Then there are laws concerning criminals, manslaughter, the conduct of wars (in battle *all* Canaanites are to be destroyed; among non-Canaanites the men only are to be slain, the women and children enslaved, and cattle and spoils to be saved; obviously tribal concepts are at work here: see Introduction, 19—21:14.) There follows some forty or so miscellaneous laws (e.g., An unruly and intractable son is stoned to death!) dealing with humans and animals (humane treatment is prescribed). Chapters 27, 28 concern rituals interspersed with exhortations and solemn declarations, ending with Moses' final curse should the Israelites fail to keep the Deuteronomic laws: they shall be made sick and be scattered to the ends of the earth; and the Lord will rejoice at their woe (28:58-68)!

MOSES' THIRD DISCOURSE 29—30

Moses cites in retrospect the Egyptian and Wildnerness years as a basis for keeping the covenant; if not kept the land would be destroyed, as was Sodom and Gomorrah (29:22-29). In the event of Exile only sincere repentance will return them home. Moses concludes his third and last discourse with an appeal to heaven and earth as witnesses to his giving the Israelites a choice between "life and death, blessing and cursing" (30:15-20).

APPENDIX: LAST DAYS OF MOSES 31—34

God chooses Joshua to be Moses' successor, and Moses predicts splendid victories for him in Canaan. To the priests and elders he entrusts the Deuteronomic laws, to be kept in safekeeping "by the side of the ark of the covenant" (31:24-26). In a cloud pillar the Lord appears to Joshua and swears to be with him through the conquest of the Promised Land. Moses' song follows: its theme is the contrast between the justice and rightness of God versus the instability of the Israelites. Israel is pictured as a fat ox that manifests no gratitude to his master, but kicks him instead (Jeshurun = Israel). If the Israelites fail, they will be tortured with hunger, heat, beasts, serpents, and destruction by the sword, but in the end God will not abondon His people, and will grant them vengeance upon their enemies (32: 34-42). His song ends with a congratulation to Israel for having so merciful a God as her Lord.

Chapter 33 contains Moses' blessing of the tribes (just as Jacob had blessed the original ancestors of each tribe at his dying bedside).

From Nebo (Pisgah) Moses views the Promised Land in all directions; and it is here where he dies and is buried at the age of 120 years: "his eye was not dim, nor his natural force abated . . . but no man knoweth of his sepulchre unto this day (31:2; 34:6-7)." Note that Moses' life divides neatly in three periods of 40 years each: 1. In Egypt 2. In Midian 3. From Egypt to the Jordan in Palestine. Deuteronomy concludes, ranking Moses as the greatest of all the prophets: "There arose not a prophet since in Israel like unto Moses, whom the Lord knew face to face" (34:10-12).

In summary: There are unmistakable signs of the postexilic period in this book (see Sandmel, pp. 414-5); the legislation is not genuine (much is found in the midst of discourses); and this is proved by the non-legal form of much of the law, such as the odd requirements for the conduct of wars (20); or how to recognize false from true prophets (18:18-22). The book is kind to the priesthood but it is not a writing by priests. The purity insisted on is ritualistic, not priestly. In fact, the priests are spoken of in the third person, whereas in P the priests are referred to as "us." They keep insisting that God reveals Himself in history: obey His laws and He (history) will work for the Israelites. The authors present the work as if written by the great Moses but containing a contemporary message. Their regard for other great figures like Joshua, Samuel, David, and Solomon is shown in the books after Deuteronomy. The material on the priests represents an earlier stage than P (who thinks of priests as a family within the Levites). Very likely Deuteronomy comes to us by way of P, who in turn edited D. The book is a masterpiece of literature, stirring, humane, ethical, and passionate. The impersonal narrative is turned into a stirring concluding sermon in this last book of the Pentateuch.

THE BOOK OF JOSHUA

The Book of Joshua is the first book of the second large division of the Bible, the Prophets, the others being the Pentateuch (also known as the Torah or the Law) and the Writings. Joshua belongs to the first part of this grouping, the part known as the Former (i.e., earlier) Prophets. While on the surface Joshua does not seem to be a prophetic book, it is placed in this category because it views Israel's history from a prophetic point of view. This is also true of the other books of the Former Prophets —Judges, I and II Samuel, and I and II Kings. The Book of Joshua is a largely Deuteronomic work which tells the story (in chapters 1-12) of the three battles by which Israel conquered Canaan. The style of the Deuteronomists is again evident in chapter 23. (The intervening chapters are largely concerned with listing various kinds of geographical information.) As in the other Deuteronomic works (Deuteronomy through Kings) there are in Joshua three levels of composition: first, ancient tales and historical accounts; second, the reworking of this material by the Deuteronomists; and third, the P author's version of the Deuteronomic works. P appears frequently in Joshua and much less often in the other Deuteronomic books. (For further discussion see Sandmel, *The Hebrew Scriptures,* in Bibliography.) The account of the conquest of Canaan given by the Deuteronomists is not considered to be historically accurate. It is more than likely that Canaan was not conquered in one short series of great battles, but was taken by the Israelites as the result of many military engagements. (The conquest was also aided by intermarriage.) However, it has been established that sometime in the thirteenth century B.C. the Israelites did defeat the Canaanites and thereby gained possession of a very large section of upland territory; it was during the thirteenth century that the events in the Book of Joshua were supposed to have taken place. In all probability, the Deuteronomists surrounded this event with other victories in order to emphasize the power of a Yahweh-loving nation under the direction of an Yahweh-inspired leader. The great disparity between the account of hte Conquest given in Joshua and the account given in the Book of Judges—one says the conquest of Canaan was immediate, the other says it was slow and gradual—may be due in some measure to this Deuteronomic desire to exalt Yahweh. The truth about the speed with which the Conquest was made probably lies someplace between the two accounts: that is, parts of it came about at once and other parts extended over many years.

SUMMARY OF THE BOOK OF JOSHUA

PREPARATIONS FOR THE CONQUEST OF CANAAN, 1. Moses dead, the Lord now turns to Joshua to lead the children of Israel. The Lord renews with him the covenant He had made with Moses. Joshua is told that if only he will be strong and courageous, the land across the Jordan, its people, and their property will be given to the Israelites. The Lord tells Joshua to obey the Divine word and nothing can withstand him and his people: "Have I not commanded thee? Be strong and of good courage; be not afraid, neither be thou dismayed: for the Lord thy God is with thee whithersoever thou goest." Then Joshua gives the command to move toward the Jordan. He tells the tribes of Reuben and Gad, and half the tribe of Manasseh, not to cross but to remain in their lands on this (the eastern) side of the river, as Moses had ordained. All the people express willingness to obey Joshua.

THE SPIES SENT TO JERICHO, 2. Joshua sends two men ahead to Jericho to gather intelligence about the city. They lodge at the house of a harlot named Rahab who hides them when the authorities come to search for them. She tells them that the news of the Israelites' miraculous escape from Egypt has become known in Jericho, and everyone is now afraid of what the Israelites will do. She asks the spies to spare her and her family during the invasion because she has hidden them. They agree, telling her to hang a scarlet thread from the window as a sign. The spies make their way back to Joshua and tell him that the people of Jericho are terrified, and that the city may be taken easily because the Lord has given the place into their hands.

ISRAEL CROSSES THE JORDAN, 3. The entire people comes down to the river and camps there for three days.

They are told to follow the priests carrying the Ark as an indicator of the the route, but not to approach the Ark itself.

The Lord tells Joshua that when the priests carrying the Ark reach the river they will be able to stand in the river and not be washed away by the water. Joshua tells the people that God is with them, and that when the priests bearing the Ark shall step into the water, the river will dry up (as the Red Sea did during the Exodus). This is exactly what happens, and the entire nation crosses the river on dry land.

THE TWELVE STONES, 4. When the Israelites have completed the crossing, the Lord tells Joshua to choose one man from each tribe and to command each of them to take one stone from the river bed, where the priests had stood. They are to take these stones and set them up as markers at their campsite as a memorial to future ages of the miracle the Lord has performed. This is done and the editor tells us that the stones "are there to this day." After the twelve stones have been gathered, the priests with the Ark cross the river, and the waters resume their normal course. The Israelites make camp at Gilgal, the place directly on the western side of the river, and there the twelve stones are set up as a monument.

CIRCUMCISION AND PASSOVER, 5. The Amorites, the people living on the western side of the Jordan, are terrified when they see how the Lord has dried up the river so that the Israelites might pass over. At this time the Lord commands Joshua to circumcise the children of Israel once again, and the editor explains the reason for this command. All the males who had come out of Egypt, and had been circumcised, had died out; meanwhile, the males born during the wandering in the wilderness had not been circumcised. It was these men whom Joshua circumcised. After

the ceremony is performed, the people rest until everyone is well again. The Lord tells Joshua that, in circumcising the men born in the wilderness, He has rolled (the meaning of the name Gilgal) the wickedness of Egypt off the shoulders of the people. The people celebrate Passover at Gilgal. The manna the Lord has sent for food ceases once the Israelites begin to eat from the grain growing within the Promised Land. At that time Joshua, while near Jericho, meets a man with his sword drawn. Joshua asks him whether he is friend or foe. The man responds that he is "the captain of the host of the Lord" (i.e., an angel). Joshua prostrates himself before the man and asks what he must do. He is told to take off his shoes because the spot he is standing on is holy ground, and he does so.

THE BATTLE FOR JERICHO, 6. The Israelites besiege the walled city of Jericho. The Lord informs Joshua how the city must be taken. The people are to march around the city once a day for six days, and seven priests shall march before the Ark blowing seven ram's-horn trumpets. On the seventh day the people shall march around the city seven times, and the priests shall blow on their trumpets. Then as the priests blow a long blast on the trumpet the people are to give a great shout. At this shout, the walls will fall, and the army will be able to enter. The Lord's instructions are carried out, and the walls fall according to plan. Joshua orders the troops to spare Rahab's house and its inhabitants. He also tells them to gather the silver and gold for the treasury of the Lord, but otherwise to destroy the city completely. Jericho is burned to the ground, and the spot is cursed forever.

THE SIN OF ACHAN, 7. One of the Israelites, Achan, disobeys Joshua's order not to take anything from Jericho, and therefore the Lord is angered. Joshua sends scouts ahead to report on the city of Ai, the next place to be captured. The scouts say that a small force will suffice to take

Ai, and so Joshua sends only three thousand men. The men of Ai defeat the Israelites, and Joshua is sick at heart because he knows that the defeat means that the Lord is angry. The Lord says to Joshua that the people have broken their promise to obey God: they have stolen forbidden goods and lied about it. He tells Joshua to command the people to sanctify themselves, because the Lord has declared that there is an "accursed thing" (i.e., "accursed" because Jericho and all its contents were cursed) among them. Then all the people shall come before Joshua, tribe by tribe, and family by family, and the Lord will indicate who is the guilty one. The criminal and his family and property shall be burned. Joshua does as the Lord has said, and he comes to Achan. He knows (because the Lord has told him) that Achan is the guilty one, and Achan admits his guilt. The treasure is found, and then Achan and all his people and goods are first stoned to death and then burned and buried under a great mound of stones. (It was customary to kill people by stoning because that way no one person was guilty of the death.)

THE CONQUEST OF AI, 8. The Lord says to Joshua that His anger is lifted, and that Ai may now be seized. This time the Lord permits the Israelites to keep the treasure of the city. Ai is to be taken by surprise attack. Joshua is to select thirty thousand men and station them behind the city, but far enough away to be out of sight. Then he, with the rest of army, will attack Ai from the front. The Israelites will pretend to retreat before the defenders, who will pursue them, thinking they have won another victory. Then the second force will come out of hiding and descend on the city and capture it. The capture of Ai takes place in exactly this way. All the inhabitants of the place are killed, and the king of Ai is captured. The city is plundered and then burned to the ground (which, the editor tells us, it still is "to this day") and the king of Ai is hanged. Then Joshua

builds an altar to the Lord at Mount Ebal, and he makes sacrifices there. Joshua makes a copy of the Law of Moses in the presence of the entire people, and reads to them the whole of the Law.

THE GIBEONITES, 9. All the peoples of the area (the chief of which are Amorites) form an alliance to fight against Joshua and the Hebrews. The inhabitants of Gibeon, however, adopt a different course of defense. They send ambassadors dressed in their oldest clothes to Joshua at Gilgal. The Gibeonites say that they are from a faraway nation. They have come because they have heard of the wonders the Lord has performed for the Hebrews, and they wish to become their allies. They say that their ragged condition results from the great distance they have had to travel. The Israelites do not ask counsel of the Lord but instead make the agreement. After the alliance is made, the Hebrews learn the real identity of the Gibeonites. They are extremely angry at the trick the Gibeonites have played, but they do not dare break their oath. Joshua says that the Gibeonites will be spared, but because of their trickery they will become the slaves of the Hebrews.

DEFEAT OF THE AMORITE ALLIANCE, 10. When the Amorite alliance learns that the Gibeonites have made peace with the Hebrews, they decide to make war on the Gibeonites. The Gibeonites send to Joshua for help. The Lord assures Joshua that he will defeat his enemies. Joshua wins a great victory over the armies of the alliance. The enemy flees, and in order to pursue them more effectively, Joshua (with the help of the Lord) makes the sun stand still, thus giving the Hebrews more daylight in which to fight. (The editor remarks that this miraculous event is recorded in the old chronicle, the Book of Jasher.) The five kings of the Amorites are found hidden in a cave. Joshua commands that a great stone be rolled into its mouth. After the killing of the enemy comes to a halt, Joshua orders that the kings be brought out. He tells his officers to place their feet upon the necks of the kings, thus symbolizing the supremacy they have won through their courageous fighting. Then the kings are killed and their bodies are thrown back into the cave, which is again sealed up. Joshua leads the Israelites to further victories at Libnah, Lachish, Eglon, Hebron, and Debir (i.e., over all the allies of the Amorites). After all these enemies have been destroyed, Joshua and the people return to Gilgal.

THE DEFEAT OF JABIN'S ALLIANCE, 11-12.
When news of these Isrealite victories spreads to the neighboring peoples, they decide to band together in the hope of vanquishing the Hebrews. The great armies of this alliance, led by King Jabin of Hazor, meet the Hebrews at Merom. There the Lord gives them over into Joshua's hands, and the Hebrews win a great victory. Joshua then proceeds to destroy all the cities whose armies he had crushed at Merom. In every case the Israelites slay the inhabitants and enrich themselves with plunder. Thus Joshua takes the land for the Israelites and destroys the native population. Chapter 12 lists those kings who had been defeated by Moses and those who had been defeated by Joshua. (Despite the conquests and victories described in Joshua up to this point, it should be noted that there is no description of an attack on a major Canaanite military base. One reason for this, besides that mentioned in the introduction, is that Israel was incapable, at that time, of successful combat with people already advanced into the Iron Age. While in the Book of Joshua, the inability to make such an attack or attacks does not prevent Joshua from conquering Canaan, in reality the weapons of the Iron Age must have been formidable obstacles to a complete victory. This is one more reason that the conquest of Canaan must have taken place over a much longer period of time than is allotted to it in Joshua.)

THE LAND YET TO BE POSSESSED, 13.
Joshua is now old, and the Lord tells him that there is yet much of the land to be conquered. From 13:2 to 13:14 is a list of the localities that remain to be subdued. The rest of the chapter gives in detail the territory that Moses had assigned to the tribes of Reuben and Gad and half to Manassaeh, the tribes whose land lay on the eastern side of the Jordan.

CANAAN DIVIDED BY LOT, 14.
The land of Canaan is divided up by lot, and in this way the various tribes (with the exception of the two and a half that had settled on the eastern shore of the Jordan, and of the tribe of Levi, which was to serve the Lord and be supported by contributions by the other tribes) get their inheritances. At this time Caleb comes to Joshua and reminds him that he had served, forty-five years earlier, as one of the spies sent out by Moses to Canaan, and that he had given a true report while the others had lied (see Num. 13 and 14). At that time Moses had promised him as an inheritance the land his feet had walked on. Joshua confirms Moses' promise, and gives Hebron to Caleb and his children.

THE TERRITORY ALLOTTED TO THE VARIOUS TRIBES, 15-19.
The first twelve verses of chapter 15 give the boundaries in detail of the territory of the tribe of Judah. There then comes an account of the conquest by Caleb of Hebron and Debir. The narrative then resumes with a list of the cities of Judah, followed by long lists defining the boundaries of Ephraim, Manasseh, and the rest of the tribes.

THE CITIES OF REFUGE, 20.
The Lord tells Joshua to appoint cities of refuge (see Num. 35:6-32). These cities are places of sanctuary for those who have killed someone accidentally. Such persons previously would have been killed by the relatives of the slain man and would never have received a trial. Now, such a man may go to one of the cities of refuge and there be safe until he is judged

by the authorities. Then if he is judged to have killed by accident he shall be permitted to return to his native town. Six such places of refuge are established, three on either side of the Jordan.

THE CITIES OF THE LEVITES, 21.

Although the tribe of Levi (the Levites) had no territory like the other tribes, it nevertheless required a place to live. Therefore Joshua allots them forty-eight cities, chosen by lot, within the territories of the various tribes, and these are listed. The editor closes this chapter by saying that the Lord has thus given into the hands of the Hebrews all of the land that He had promised.

THE ALTAR BY THE JORDAN, 22.

Joshua calls the two and a half tribes whose land lies east of the Jordan and praises them for having fought with the rest of the Israelites (even though their own lands had already been won) and tells them that they can now go back home. He bids them always follow the word of God, gives them his blessing, and they depart for their territory. They proceed to build a great altar right at the Jordan. When news of this altar becomes known throughout the nation, the other tribes are horrified. They prepare to wage war on them because they think that the altar has been raised to a deity other than Yahweh. However, before attacking, the other tribes send a group of chiefs and priests to their brethren living across the river to find out why the altar has been erected. These ambassadors reproach the eastern tribes, saying that the transgressions the people had committed in the Wilderness were sufficient. Why, they ask, have they turned away from the Lord anew? Do they not remember what happened to those who turned away in the past? Then the eastern tribes answer that their countrymen have misunderstood completely. They intended no impiety in building the altar; rather the reverse. They were afraid that, living separated from the rest of the people, their children

would grow up thinking that Yahweh was the God only of those who lived on the western side of the river. To prevent future generations from losing touch with the rest of the people, and thereby forgetting their God, they have constructed the altar not for sacrifice but so that "your children may not say to our children in time to come, 'Ye have no part in the Lord.' " When the leaders of the western tribes hear this explanation they are happy; they return to their tribes and inform everyone. The people are pleased that they there will be no civil war, and it is decided to leave the altar standing "as a witness between us that the Lord is God."

JOSHUA'S CHARGE TO THE PEOPLE, 23.

When Joshua grows very old he calls the leaders of the various tribes together. He makes it clear to them that their present position is wholly due to the goodness of the Lord, who has seen fit to fight for them. It is He, and He alone, who has given them what they have. Joshua says that if they continue to follow the word of God, then all will be well: The Lord will watch over and protect them, and the nation will prosper. But they should beware that if they stray from the word of God, He will give them over into the hands of their enemies.

JOSHUA'S FAREWELL ADDRESS, 24.

Joshua gathers all the people and addresses them. He briefly traces the history of the Israelites from Abraham to the present, dwelling on how the Lord has caused everything to happen. Now He has given the people a fine country in which they may live happily if they heed His word. The people acclaim his words and pledge fidelity to Yahweh, "for He is our God." Then Joshua repeats that their choice is a serious one because Yahweh is a severe and jealous God, punishing harshly those who turn away from Him. The people again swear to follow Him. A third time Joshua tells the assembled masses to turn their hearts to the Lord, and a third time the people swear that they will be true to Him. Joshua then writes a covenant between the people of Israel and the Lord, and he sets a stone near the sanctuary at Shechem as a reminder of this covenant. (It has been suggested by one scholar [Professor Anderson in **Understanding the Old Testament**] that this ceremony was more than a repetition and renewal of covenant allegiance. Anderson holds that the ceremony may have marked the first incorporation into the Israelite community of Hebrew tribesmen who had not taken part in the descent into Egypt. He theorizes that the people of Shechem, where the covenant ritual takes place, were just such Hebrews and that at this time they put away their pagan gods and turned to Yahweh.) Then the people return to their lands. Joshua dies, at the age of a hundred and ten. The bones of Joseph, which were brought out of Egypt, are now buried. And lastly, Eleazar, the son of Aaron, dies and is buried.

THE BOOK OF JUDGES

It is now thought that the twelve tribes into which the Israelites were loosely divided formed a confederation around the time they first settled in Canaan. Before this, the people had followed one divinely inspired leader. With the settlement in Canaan this leadership passed to what we have come to call "Judges." It should be understood, however, that the term did not have the primarily legal meaning to the Hebrews that it has to us today. The Hebrew word for judges (shoftim) can also be translated as "rulers," and a better title for the Book of Judges might be the "Book of the Great Deliverers." These great deliverers presumably ruled Israel one after another, but the occasions on which they aroused Israel to concerted action were not many. In other words, they could not, in general, rule Israel as had Moses or Joshua, and unified action by all the tribes was the exception rather than the rule. The Deuteronomic editors of Judges were very much against this (to them anarchic) state of affairs, and they advocated the rise of a kingship (this attitude is reversed in the later Deuteronomic books) which, they felt, would once more unite the people absolutely. The Book of Judges, then, recounts the events which took place between the leadership of Moses and Joshua,

who were both prophet and ruler, and the rise of divinely ordained kings. While the Book of Judges lists twelve "deliverers" (of which only five are discussed in detail) there are really thirteen—Samuel being the last. It is thought that the D editors provided exactly twelve deliverers in order to coincide with the number of tribes of the confederacy. (Samuel is excepted not for this reason, but because he provides the necessary link to the monarchy.)

The Book of Judges is a series of five stories which bear no direct relation to each other. They have been brought together by the compilers of the book to illustrate the view that the people needed a king and that only because they were without one did the need for deliverers arise. Generally speaking, the pattern can be described as follows: the people live happy and contented lives, but as they prosper they turn from the worship of the Lord to the worship of various pagan deities. God punishes them for their infidelity by giving them into the hands of a foreign power. Then there arises a deliverer, also sent by God. Under the deliverer prosperity is restored. The people again turn away from God, and the entire pattern repeats itself. The Deuteronomists felt that this could not have happened had there been kingly rule. A good king (unfortunately, most of the rulers in I and II Kings are bad) would subject the people to his infallibly just will and thereby prevent them from following their all too fallible instincts. Although some of the material in Judges may be historical, much of it consists of folk tales. Professor Sandmel points out that the moral and teaching value of the book lies not in the stories themselves, but rather in the Deuteronomic commentary which surrounds them. The folk stories were concerned with exciting accounts of heroes and their deeds, and not with ethical or religious significance. The Deuteronomists preferred to leave the stories intact and accomplish their purpose by interweaving moralistic interpretations into the fabric of the tales themselves. The last part of Judges (chapters 17-21) is not properly of a piece with the rest of the book. The material given here is more historically reliable than that given elsewhere in the book, and, moreover, these chapters mark a departure from the tales of the great deliverers. The stories told here, however, are generally like the others in that they are modern retellings of very ancient matter. Perhaps the most important story is that of the alliance of the other tribes against the tribes of Benjamin. We see here that the general system of ethical beliefs under which the Israelites lived could serve, when necessary, to unite them in action against a wrongdoer even when the offender was one of themselves. Thus we see that even though technically they were bound together in only the loosest way, the covenant relation the tribes bore to each other was able to supersede their essential separateness, even when there was no deliverer to unite them.

SUMMARY OF THE BOOK OF JUDGES

TRIBAL CONQUESTS, 1:1-2:5. These verses are an account from a very primitive chronicle of the conquests made by the various tribes and are not properly part of the narrative of the Book of Judges, which may be said to begin at 2:6.

DEATH OF JOSHUA, 2:6-3:6. Joshua's death is mentioned for the third time (also in Josh. 24:29-30 and Judg. 1:1). There follows a statement of the theme of this book (as well as that of Samuel and Kings —see Introduction). The children of Israel forsake the Lord and worshsip idols (Baalim, the Canaanite fertility god). The Lord punishes them by permitting various enemy peoples to oppress Israel. Then He causes a judge to arise, who aids the people in its time of need. When the judge dies, the pattern repeats itself.

OTHNIEL DELIVERS ISRAEL, 3:7- 3:11. Othniel, the first of the judges, delivers the people from the hands of the Mesopotamians.

EHUD AND SHAMGAR, 3:12-3:31. Once again the Israelites do evil, and God gives them into the hands of the Moabites. Then Ehud stabs the king of Moab to death and leads his people to victory over the Moabites. Shamgar fights against the Philistines.

DEBORAH AND BARAK, 4-5. The children of Israel again stray from the true path, and again the Lord permits an oppressor (this time the Canaanites) to rule over them. After twenty years of Canaanite rule, the prophetess-judge Deborah and the warrior Barak stage a revolt. They win a victory over the Canaanite forces, and the Canaanite general, Sisera, flees. Sisera thinks he has found refuge in the tent of Jael, but she kills him by driving a peg through his head while he sleeps. Chapter 5 is the victory song of Deborah and Barak. This is thought to be the oldest piece of writing in the Old Testament and is believed to have been written by an eye-witness to the events described, or even by a participant in them. The events and the song of Deborah date from the last quarter of the twelfth century B. C. It praises the Lord for having given them the victory and exults in the destruction of the enemy. (Some of the text is not understood at the present time.)

GIDEON, 6-8. Once again the Israelites do evil in the sight of God and are punished by being bound over, this time to the Midianites. The Lord chooses Gideon to save the nation. Gideon throws down the idol of Baal in his town. Then he gathers a large force to oppose the Midianites. The Lord performs several miracles to show that He is with Gideon. Then He tells Gideon that his army is too large; when Israel shall defeat Midian, it will be with only a small group of men, so that it will be clear to all that the victory has been brought about by God and not by men alone. Gideon pares down his forces to three hundred men (against the many thousands of Midianites). He conquers the enemy through a surprise night attack. The Ephraimites are angry with Gideon for not having called them in on this glorious victory, but Gideon appeases them with soft words. He and his small force pursue the Midianites and capture and kill the Midianite kings. Gideon makes an ephod (it is not known what this was, but it seems to have been an object used in religious services) out of the gold taken from the Midianites. This is a mistake because the Israelites rush to worship it. Gideon becomes judge and rules for forty peaceful years. When he dies, the Israelites go back to worshiping false gods.

REIGN OF ABIMELECH, 9. Abimelech, Gideon's son, slays all his brothers except Jotham and proclaims himself king. (Abimelech's abortive kingship is the first attempt recorded in the Bible to establish a strong central government, and it therefore foreshadows the rise of the monarchy. Jotham's parable (9:7-15) is similar in meaning to the view of the kingship presented in the first chapters of Samuel—that it is undesirable. Only the bramble, a thorny and worthless plant, consents to rule over the trees, for the trees of value are not interested in being king. Jotham is here characterizing Abimelech's brief reign.) Abimelech's main support comes from the men of Shechem, his mother's home town. After three years, the Shechemites plot against him. He crushes the revolt and destroys Shechem. In another battle Abimelech is killed in action (as a punishment for having killed his brothers, so the editor says).

TOLAR, JAIR, AND JEPTHAH, 10-12. Tola and Jair are mentioned as judges but hardly anything else is said of them. After Jair, the people again leave the true God to follow false deities, and God allows the Philistines and the Ammonites to subdue them. The Ammonites mass their forces in Gilead, and the leaders of the Gileadites look for a general to conduct the war against the Ammonites. They ask the mighty warrior Jephthah to lead them, and he consents when they assure him he will become their chief if he wins. First Jephthah tries to persuade the Ammonites that they have no business in Gilead, but the Ammonites refuse to listen. Then Jephthah is filled with the spirit of the Lord and vows that if the Lord gives him the victory he will sacrifice the first thing that comes out of his house to greet him when he returns. Jephthah battles and wins against the Ammonites. When he returns to his house, the first thing to issue from his door is his only daughter. He is heartbroken, but he knows he cannot break his vow, and his daughter agrees. She only asks that she be allowed two months "to bewail her virginity" (that is, to mourn because she will never have any children). When the time had passed, Jephthah sacrifices her as he had vowed. The Ephraimites are angry with Jephthah (as they were with Gideon) because they were not called in against the Ammonites. Jephthah does not turn them away with soft words but instead beats them on the field of battle. Jephthah becomes judge of Israel, and after his death he is followed by Ibzan, Elon, and Abdon, about whom we are told practically nothing.

SAMSON, 13-16. Once again the children of Israel leave the Lord and follow strange gods, and once again they are penalized; the Philistines subdue them for forty years. (The Philistines migrated from the Mediterranean island of Crete around the thirteenth century B.C. They settled in the coastal areas of Palestine, which was named after them.) At this time a woman who is barren is told by an angel of the Lord that she will have a child who shall be a Nazarite—that is, he shall drink no alcohol, eat nothing unclean, nor ever have his hair cut. The child is called Samson and is blessed by the Lord. (Samson is the typical folk hero, strong of body and weak of mind, and his story is probably the most legendary of all those told in Judges.) Although the Nazarites were supposed to serve God, Samson is certainly no model of holiness. He sees a Philistine girl whom he fancies. and he asks his father to obtain her for him as a wife. (Here the editor feels it necessary to explain that the Lord was using this intermarriage as an occasion to smite the Philistines.) Samson, unarmed, kills a lion on his way to see his beloved. When he goes to her again he finds that some bees have nested in the carcass of the lion, and he takes some of their honey. At his marriage feast he puts a riddle to his "companions": "Out of the eater came forth meat and out of the strong came forth sweetness." The companions cannot guess the answer and threaten his wife into getting it from Samson, which she does. He

is angry at their deceit, and kills thirty Philistines in revenge. His wife is given to someone else without Samson's knowledge. When he learns of it, he burns down the Philistines' crops. When the Philistines come to take him for what he has done, he kills a thousand of them. Samson becomes judge. After some time, he falls in love with Delilah, who is prevailed upon by the Philistines to find out the secret of Samson's strength. She finally learns that his power resides in his hair. She cuts it and thereby enables him to be captured by the Philistines. He is blinded and led prisoner to Gaza. His hair begins to grow back, and he prays to God that he may avenge himself on his enemies. Samson is brought out at a Philistine celebration and he pulls down the pillars holding up the building in which the festivities are taking place, killing himself along with three thousand Philistines. (Professor Anderson suggests that the difficulties with the Philistines depicted in the Samson narrative afford a valuable insight into Philistine-Israelite relations at this time (probably around 1100 B.C.). The minor skirmishes and antagonisms described here foreshadow the all-out war that will develop within the century.)

MICAH, 17-18. Micah the Ephramite steals eleven hundred shekels (silver coins) from his mother. She had intended the money to pay for a graven image, and when Micah restores the money to her, she has the image made. Micah makes one of his sons the priest in the sanctuary he erects to house this image. He makes a passing Levite into the head priest in this small temple, and he and his sons serve the Levite. In those days the tribe of Dan had no fixed territory, and therefore they sent out spies to find a suitable place for the tribe to settle. The spies recognize Micah's priest. They are attracted by the town of Laish and decide to capture it. On the way they stop at Micah's temple, take the images, and force the priest to come and serve them as religious leader. Micah can do nothing to stop them. The Danites capture and destroy Laish, which they rebuild and name Dan. Thus we learn how the Danites came to reside where they did.

THE LEVITE AND HIS CONCUBINE, 19-21. A Levite who lives in Ephraim has a concubine from Bethlehem in Judah. She leaves him and returns to her father's house. The Levite goes to fetch her and be reconciled with her, and her father keeps detaining them with feasting. Finally they leave and, instead of spending the night in Jerusalem (which is not an Israelite city), they move on to Gibeah, in the territory of the tribe of Benjamin. An old man takes them into his house. That night some hooligans surround the house, demanding that the farmer give over the Levite to them for homosexual purposes. The man offers them his virginal daughters but they do not want them. Finally, the old man pushes the concubine out, and the mob rapes and beats her throughout the night. By morning she is dead. The Levite takes the body home with him to Ephraim and there cuts

it up into twelve pieces, sending one to each of the tribes to incite them to do something in revenge for this disgrace. A huge number of people gather, hear the Levite's story, and demand of the Benjaminites that they hand over the scoundrels responsible for the crime. They refuse, and war breaks out. The Benjaminites repel two attacks, but the third attack is successful. They are defeated, and twenty-five thousand of their men are killed. The other tribes have sworn not to permit their daughters to marry the Benjaminites, and therefore there is a real danger that it will cease to exist as a tribe for want of wives for its surviving men. To prevent this, Gilead (which did not supply men to fight against Benjamin) is attacked, but the four hundred virgins captured are not enough. Then it is remembered that there is an annual festival at Shiloh, at which the girls of Shiloh dance. If the Benjaminites seized the girls, it would not be breaking the vow because that applied only to arranged marriages. And this is what is done so that the tribe might be saved.

THE BOOK OF RUTH

Some scholars regard the Book of Ruth as a historical document, i.e., one that recounts an actual event and is a reliable source of information about the time it describes. Their belief is that the book was written before the Babylonian exile. However, other students of the Bible feel that it is post-exilic, that it is not historical but in fact an updated retelling of an ancient legend. These scholars argue that the book is primarily a didactic work intended to refute the doctrine advanced by Ezra and Nehemiah that it is morally

wrong to marry a gentile. According to this interpretation, the book was intended by its author to show his fellow Hebrews that marrying a non-Jew was by no means necessarily bad; the good gentile could be as exemplary a spouse to a Hebrew as one of his own faith and culture. Despite these differing scholarly views on Ruth, there is general agreement that the story it tells is one of great antiquity. No matter when the book was set down, the legend it narrates dates back to about 1200 B.C.

SUMMARY OF THE BOOK OF RUTH

RUTH AND NAOMI; RUTH GLEANS IN THE FIELD OF BOAZ, 1-2. At the time of a famine in Israel a man named Elimelech takes his wife Naomi and their two sons to the land of Moab. They live happily and the two sons marry Moabite women. In time Elimelech and his children die, and Naomi, heartbroken, decides to return to Bethlehem whence she and her husband had migrated so many years before. She bids her daughters-in-law return to their mothers and stands weeping with them on the road to Judah. Orpah, the first daughter-in-law, kisses Naomi and leaves, but Ruth refuses to part from her and says the most well-known words in the Book of Ruth: ". . . whither thou goest, I will go; and where thou lodgest, I will lodge: thy people shall be my people, and thy God my God." Thus they journey to Bethlehem and arrive in time for the harvest. Ruth decides to go to the fields to gather grain. (It was the custom among the Hebrews to provide for their poor by purposely leaving unharvested grain for them to glean.) It happens that the field she is working in is owned by a man named Boaz, who is a relative of Naomi's dead husband. Boaz comes to the field and, seeing her, asks his servant who she is. When he is told he answers her request for permission to glean by asking her to reap only in his fields and inviting her to eat the food he provides for his field hands. He explains that he does this because of her faithfulness to Naomi. When she leaves him to harvest more grain he instructs his men to let her glean even among the sheaves and to drop some of what they themselves have gathered so that she can glean that too. When Ruth returns home she tells Naomi where she has been and of Boaz's kindness to her. Naomi is heartened in her grief and they decide that Ruth should take advantage of Boaz's offer to let her work in his fields until the harvest is over.

RUTH AND BOAZ AT THE THRESHING FLOOR; BOAZ MARRIES RUTH, 3-4. Naomi is concerned for Ruth's happiness and wants her to remarry. She therefore tells Ruth to dress herself and to go to Boaz, who will be working on the threshing that evening (thresing was done in the evening because it was so much cooler then) but not to make herself known to him until, after eating and drinking, he lies down to sleep. At that time she is to go to him, uncover his feet, and lie down next to him. Boaz will then tell her what to do. (It was the Hebrew practice to have the brother-in-law of a widow marry her if she was childless, the point being to provide her with offspring. Whether this custom extended to relations other than brother-in-law is not known but if it did it would be very unlikely that such a marriage would take place merely to provide the widow with security. It is this which is at least partly implied in Ruth. However, because the legend is so old and the practices which it describes are therefore also old, and little is known about them, it is impossible to be certain. When Ruth uncovers Boaz's feet she is performing part of a ritual act which asserts her claim on him.) Ruth follows Naomi's instructions and when Boaz awakes and sees her next to him she affirms their kinship. Boaz is not at all displeased that Ruth wants him to marry her, for she is respected by the entire city. However, there is a man who is closer kin to her than he is and that man must have the first opportunity to claim the right to care for her. Boaz tells Ruth that he will arrange to see the man on the following day. Ruth stays the night and in the morning Boaz sends her home with six measures of grain. True to his word, Boaz goes in search of the man and finds him at the city gates. He gathers around him ten elders of the town. He speaks of Ruth, but says first that Naomi has "a parcel of land" which she wants to sell. The man is asked to redeem the land and take Ruth with it but he says he cannot and yields the right to do so to Boaz. As a token of this agreement and in keeping with ancient custom, the man then takes off one of his shoes and gives it to Boaz. Boaz then declares that he has this day bought of Naomi all her husband's land and her daughter-in-law Ruth to be his wife. Soon they are wed and shortly thereafter Ruth conceives and bears a son. Naomi is greatly pleased and becomes the child's nurse. The book ends with a genealogical table which reveals the important fact that Ruth was the great-grandmother of David. (This is to emphasize to the reader the point the author was trying to make, i.e., that the gentile Ruth was so worthy that she was made the ancestor to the greatest of the Hebrew kings.)

THE FIRST AND SECOND BOOK OF SAMUEL & THE FIRST AND SECOND BOOK OF KINGS

First and Second Kings and First and Second Samuel explain the religious importance to the Israelites of the monarchy under which they had come to live. At first the ruling power of the king seemed a highly desirable thing, and it was during this period of happiness (more particularly during the reign of the benevolent Josiah, late seventh century B.C.) that the Books of Samuel and Kings were first written. The stories told were the accounts of various kings under whom the Israelites lived, but there was much other material added; there is, for example, perhaps too much about David. Unfortunately, after Josiah died the Hebrews began to suffer under a succession of irresponsible and selfish rulers. The optimism and satisfaction of the early edition of Samuel and Kings had largely given way to discontent. There had been many battles and much privation and unrest, ending, finally, in exile. It was at this time that the second version of the books was put together. Although the new editors generally did not change the words of the first version they obviously felt a need to express the great reservations they now had about the kingship. They did this by interpolating long passages condemning kings and warning the people against desiring them, for they felt the latter to be contrary to the will of God. Because of the original viewpoint of the books and the nature of the insertions made so many years later (we do not know exactly how much later), there are many contradictions and inconsistencies in them. The result is that we often have side by side two completely different viewpoints of the monarchy.

SUMMARY OF I SAMUEL

THE BIRTH AND YOUTH OF SAMUEL, 1-3. An Ephraimite named Elkanah has a wife Hannah who is infertile. She vows to the Lord in the temple that if she be given a male child he will be dedicated to the service of the Lord. Her prayers are answered, and the boy, Samuel, is given over to Eli, the high priest. Samuel is brought up in Eli's house and assists him. Meanwhile, Eli's two sons are very wicked and will not reform no matter how often their father speaks to them. Eli is warned by a man of God that because of their sins, his two sons will be killed and that a new priest (not of his family) will be established. Eli grows old and his sight fails him. One night, when Samuel is asleep, the Lord calls to him. The young Samuel immediately gets out of bed and goes to Eli, whom he supposed has called him. Eli says that he has not called and tells him to go back to bed. The Lord calls again to Samuel, and again he goes to Eli, who once more tells him to return to bed. When the same event occurs a third time, Eli realizes that it is the Lord who is calling. (It is probable that the Lord must call Samuel three times because at this period in Israel's history people with prophetic gifts are uncommon; that is, because prophecy is not a familiar part of the world it does not occur to him—or to Eli—that he is having a prophetic experience, and that he is hearing the voice of God.) He tells the boy to return to bed, and if he is called to answer. Samuel lies down, and the Lord calls him. He tells Samuel that the prophecy against Eli will be executed because of the wickedness of Eli's sons. In the morning, Samuel tells Eli the words of the Lord. Samuel grows up and is recognized throughout Israel as a prophet of the Lord.

THE PHILISTINES AND THE ARK, 4-6.

Israel and the Philistines are at war. The Israelites are losing, so the elders devise a plan. They will bring the Ark of the Covenant out on the battlefield, and the presence of the Lord will help them. When the Ark is brought, guarded by the two sons of Eli, the Israelites are very encouraged. The Philistines are fearful of the power of the Lord, and they fight with the courage of desperation. They win the battle and capture the Ark as well. In the fighting Eli's sons are killed, and Eli himself dies when he hears the terrible news. The Philistines take the Ark back with them to their country. Wherever they bring it, a plague breaks out, and finally they decide to return it to the Israelites, along with a gift of gold and jewels to atone for their misdeed.

SAMUEL JUDGES ISRAEL, 7-8.

Samuel tells the Israelites that the Lord will protect them if they stop worshiping idols and return to the worship of the true God. Samuel establishes a time and a place where he will serve as judge over the people. When the people gather there, the Philistines plan to attack them. The people are very fearful, but Samuel tells them to pray and the Lord will save them. The Philistines are defeated, and Samuel becomes the judge over Israel. When he grows old, he sets his sons as judges over Israel, but they are wicked. The people protest to Samuel and ask that he choose them a king. At first he refuses, but the Lord tells him to do as they ask. Samuel tells the people what the Lord has said, but he also adds that they will regret having a king because he will be a tyrant. The people insist, and Samuel finally agrees to find a king for them.

SAUL CHOSEN KING, 9-11.

Saul is the son of Kish, from the tribe of Benjamin. The asses of Kish are lost, and Saul is sent to find them. He searches but cannot locate them. At last he and his men come to Zuph, where Samuel is residing. They think to go and ask him where they should go to seek the asses. Meanwhile, the day before, the Lord had told Samuel that the next day he would see the future king of Israel. When Saul approaches Samuel, Samuel hears the voice of the Lord saying that Saul is the man. Samuel tells Saul to come and dine with him. He anoints Saul and tells him that he has been chosen by the Lord to serve as king over Israel. Saul returns to his family, and Samuel calls the entire people together at Mizpeh. He then proclaims Saul to the people as their king. Saul is inspired by the spirit of God and leads the people to victory over the Ammonites. Saul is officially pronounced king.

SAMUEL'S ADDRESS AND THE WAR WITH THE PHILISTINES, 12-14.

The aged Samuel addresses the people. He reminds them that the Lord had been their king, but that they insisted on having a man as king over them. He warns them that no good can come from it unless they obey the commandments of the Lord. If they do, all will go well; if not, they will meet with disaster. There now begins a long series of misunderstandings and quarrels between Samuel and Saul. The first of these occurs when Samuel, who alone has the right to offer sacrifices, is late in arriving at Saul's camp. Saul goes ahead and makes the sacrifice himself. This is followed by a daring victory by Jonathan, Saul's son, over the Philistines, who are again threatening Israel. Saul has ordered all his men not to eat during the day that they are to fight the Philistines, but Jonathan disobeys because he has not heard the order. Saul is ready to put his son to death, but he is stopped by the people, who praise Jonathan for winning the battle. Throughout the reign of Saul the Philistines wage war against Israel.

SAUL'S DISOBEDIENCE AND REJECTION, 15.

Samuel tells Saul that the Lord has decreed that the nation of Amalek be destroyed completely, down to the last bit of their property. Saul crushes Amalek, kills all except one of its people, but does not destroy all its valuable goods. Samuel reproaches Saul for having disobeyed the command of God, and warns him that since he has rejected the word of God, God has rejected him as king and has chosen another. With these words he turns away from Saul.

(The Israelites were performing a religious duty in annihilating the Amalekites and everything belonging to them. The actions of the Amalekites during the Exodus (see Exod. 17:8-16) could not be forgiven and the time had come for them to be punished. They had offended God by injuring His people and it was through Israel that He was to be avenged. It was for this reason that the spoils of the battle were the Lord's and only the Lord's to do with as He willed. Therefore, when Saul disobeys His decree that everything of the Amalekites be destroyed as a sacrifice to Him, he is doing more than going against the word of God—he is also appropriating holy property and putting it to a use other than that for which it was ordained.)

DAVID IS CHOSEN, 16.

The Lord tells Samuel to find another king. Samuel is to go to the family of Jesse, of Bethlehem, and there he will find the new king. Samuel is told by the Lord that David, the youngest of Jesse's children, is the chosen one. He anoints David. Meanwhile Saul is troubled by an evil spirit. David is known to be a skillful harpist and is sent for. His playing on the harp is found to soothe Saul, and he stays at the court as the harpist and armor-bearer to the king.

DAVID AND GOLIATH, 17.

The Philistines attack the Israelites once again. The giant Philistine Goliath issues a challenge to fight any one of the Israelites, with the outcome of the combat to determine the entire war. All the Hebrews are terrified of Goliath, and no one will fight him even though Saul promises great riches to anyone who defeats the giant. David says that he will take up Goliath's challenge. He does not arm himself, but instead takes five smooth stones for his slingshot. Goliath laughs when he sees the small boy come out against him, but David slings a stone at him and hits him in the forehead. Goliath falls unconscious and David cuts off his head. The Philistines flee when they see what has happened.

DAVID AND JONATHAN, 18-20.

David and Jonathan become firm friends. Saul makes David a general, and all the people love him. The king becomes jealous of the young man because of his great popularity. Saul seeks to kill David but is unsuccessful. David marries Michal, the daughter of Saul. Jonathan persuades his father to promise not to try to kill David, but Saul soon breaks his promise. David escapes Saul's trap and goes to Samuel, to whom he tells all that has occurred. David returns and meets Jonathan, who tells him he will do anything he can to help him. He tells David he will find out what Saul intends to do and will warn him of any danger. He sees that Saul is set on killing David, and lets David know. David leaves the court for the last time during Saul's reign.

SAUL PURSUES DAVID, 21-24.

David goes to Nob. He asks Abimelech, the priest there, for food and arms. Abimelech gives him the sanctified bread from the altar of the Lord, and the sword taken from Goliath. David then goes to Achish, king of Gath. He is afraid of being taken prisoner or of being killed, so he pretends to be insane. He goes to the cave at Adullam, where he assembles an army made up of debtors, men in trouble with the law, and others who are unhappy with Saul's government. Saul learns that David has been in Nob. He thinks the priests there are conspiring with David, and so he has them all killed (one son of Abimelech named Abiathar escapes and joins David). The Philistines' attack Keilah, and David defeats them with the help of the Lord. Saul hears of David's victory and attempts to besiege him at Keilah, but David escapes. He and his force remain in the wilderness, and Saul cannot find them. Saul pursues David and is about to suround him when news is brought that the Philistines are attacking once more. Saul goes off to fight the Philistines and then returns to pursue David. David has a chance to kill Saul at Engedi but refuses to kill the Lord's anointed king. Saul recognizes David's mercy in sparing him and promises not to harm him further, but David stays fast in his stronghold in the wilderness.

DAVID AND ABIGAIL AND THE FURTHER PURSUIT OF DAVID, 25-31.

Samuel dies and is buried at Ramah. David goes to the wilderness of Paran. He asks a rich man named Nabal to give him and his men some food and assistance. Nabal refuses in a very brusque manner. David decides to take forcibly what has not been offered him, and he is riding on Nabal's house when he is met by Abigail, Nabal's pretty young wife. Abigail gives David what he asked for, and no blood is shed. When Abigail tells Nabal what she has done, he dies (from shock) and David takes her as his wife. He also marries Ahinoam, Saul, meanwhile, has given Michal, David's first wife, to another man. Saul continues to pursue David. David again has a chance to kill Saul, and again he refuses. David decides that his best plan is to go into the land of the Philistines because there Saul will not follow him. He stays with Achish at Gath, and he is accepted there because Achish thinks that David and Saul are irreconcilable enemies. Therefore, when the Philistines mount another invasion of Israel, Achish asks David to fight with him. Saul opposes the Philistine advance. He is afraid, and he hopes that the Lord will declare Himself to be on the side of Israel. But the Lord is silent. Saul goes to a trance medium (the witch of Endor) and asks her to summon up the spirit of Samuel. Samuel tells Saul that the Lord has departed from Israel because of the sins of Saul, and that therefore the Lord will give the victory to the Philistines and Saul and his two eldest sons will die. In the Philistine camp, the leaders are unhappy with Achish for bringing David to fight against Israel. They are afraid that he will turn against them, and David is sent back to Philistia. On his way back he finds that, in his absence, the Amalekites have destroyed his camp. He pursues them and completely crushes them. Meanwhile the battle between the Israelites and the Philistines has gone exactly as Samuel prophesied. The Philistines win, and Saul and his two eldest sons are killed.

(Although, technically, with the advent of Saul Israel had a king, it was not until David's accession to the throne that a substantial difference in the ways of the Israelite community came about. Under Saul, life for the Israelites was essentially the same as it had been under the Judges. He was a dynamic leader whom the people obeyed because of his emotional power and their love for him. Under David, the nation changed from a loose tribal confederacy to a small empire. Power now resided in the king *because he was a king* and not because of the strength of his personality. For example, although David was a very popular king, he would have suffered little lessening of power had he not been one. Thus it is in David's reign that the change from the old ways to the new really takes place. Because Saul kept one foot in the past and one foot in the present, and in fact was in spirit closer to the time of the Judges than to the kingdom, he was not a success as a **king**. Alienated from the past (Samuel) and the future (David) he experienced failure of the most bitter kind—that of rejection by Yahweh.)

SUMMARY OF II SAMUEL

DAVID LEARNS OF SAUL'S DEATH, 1-4. David learns the outcome of the battle and mourns for Saul and Jonathan: "The beauty of Israel is slain upon thy high places: how are the mighty fallen!" Then David goes to the land of Judah, and the people there make him their king. Abner, Saul's general, takes Ishbosheth, one of Saul's surviving sons, and makes him king of Israel. Abner's forces meet those of David, commanded by Joab, and David's army wins; in the struggle, however, Abner kills Joab's brother. David's six sons by his various wives are born at Hebron. The war between the house of Saul and the house of David continues. Abner has a quarrel with Ishbosheth and decides to make an alliance with David. David is agreeable, but he demands that Michal, his first wife, be restored to him. This is done, and Abner and David become friends. Meanwhile, Joab and his men return to Hebron and learn of the new alliance. Joab decides to take the law into his own hands. He lures Abner back and kills him because Abner had killed his brother. David mourns for Abner. Ishbosheth is killed by two of his own generals.

DAVID IS MADE KING OF ISRAEL, 5-7. David is made king of Israel. He captures Jerusalem, which is known thereafter as the city of David. More children are born to him. David again triumphs over the Philistines. The Ark of the Lord is brought to Jerusalem. God makes a convenant with David. Through the prophet Nathan He instructs David to construct a temple, and He tells David that He will protect the people of Israel. David thanks the Lord for what He has promised, and vows that he will follow His commandments.

DAVID EXTENDS HIS KINGDOM, 8-10. David extends his kingdom, conquering the Philistines, the Syrians, and many other peoples. He inquires whether there are any of Saul's family left alive so that he might honor them because of the kindness shown him by Jonathan. He learns that Mephibosheth, the son of Jonathan, is still alive; and he restores to him all the lands of Saul. David defeats the Ammonites and the Syrians. (The description of David's court that extends from 9:20 through the first two chapters of I Kings is generally considered to be an excellent example of ancient historical writing. Most of the material concerning David is of high authenticity because it was probably written by someone close to the events described, perhaps even by a member of David's court.)

DAVID AND BATHSHEBA, 11-12.
David sees the beautiful Bathsheba as she is bathing and desires her. They sleep together, and she becomes pregnant. David writes to Joab to put Uriah, her husband, in the front lines, where he might more easily be killed. Uriah dies in action. After the period of mourning David marries Bathsheba, who bears him a son. But David's action has displeased the Lord, who sends Nathan the prophet to reproach the king. (Nathan is the first person whose sole function is prophecy — Moses, Joshua, and Samuel were leaders as well as prophets — to make an extended appearance in the Bible.) David recognizes that he has sinned, and Nathan tells him that God has pardoned him, but he adds that the child will die. Bathsheba bears another son, Solomon, whom the Lord favors. David conquers Rabbah, the capital city of the Ammonites.

AMNON AND TAMAR, 13-14.
David's son Amnon falls in love with his half-sister Tamar. He rapes her and then his love for her turns to hatred, and he sends her away. David is exceedingly angry, and Tamar's brother Absalom is full of hatred for Amnon because of what he has done. Absalom murders Amnon and flees the country. David mourns for Absalom. Joab sees that David wishes that Absalom would return, so he prevails upon David to permit Absalom to return.

ABSALOM'S REVOLT, 15-17.
Absalom sets himself up as a judge and soon becomes very popular with the people. David learns that Absalom is preparing to revolt, and he flees from Jerusalem. Shimei curses David, but David refuses to kill him. Absalom wants to pursue David immediately, but Hushai, who secretly sympathizes with David, counsels Absalom to delay. Meanwhile he warns David to beware of an attack. Absalom decides to attack David.

THE DEATH OF ABSALOM, 18-20.
There is a great battle, and David's forces triumph. Absalom is killed by Joab. David is glad when he learns of the victory, but when he hears of the death of Absalom, he mourns him: "O my son Absalom! would God I had died for thee, O Absalom, my son, my son!" Joab rebukes David for mourning over Absalom, who was an enemy. David returns to Jerusalem. Sheba revolts against David and is crushed by Joab.

THE AVENGING OF THE GIBEONITES, 21-24.
A famine breaks out which the Lord tells David is caused by Saul's having slain the Gibeonites. David asks the remaining Gibeonites how he can atone, and they demand that seven of Saul's sons be given over to them. David complies, and the famine is lifted and God returns to the land. There are more battles against the Philistines, which the Israelites win. There follows two of David's songs of deliverance sung to the Lord for having saved him from his enemies. Next comes a list of David's leading soldiers. Against Joab's advice, David orders that a census be taken. David understands that he has done wrong in numbering the people. (It is not explained why this is so but Professor Sandmel suggests that it may have been because of God's promises, throughout the Old Testament, to make the Isarelites innumerable, i.e., literally uncountable. He gives as an example Gen. 15:5. Under these circumstances, the taking of a census could be interpreted as distrust of God's word.) As a result a plague comes and kills seventy thousand. The Lord pardons David when he builds Him an altar and offer sacrifices.

SUMMARY OF I KINGS

(For introductory comments on I and II Kings see the introduction to the Books of Samuel.)

ABISHAG MINISTERS TO DAVID, 1:1-4. One day when David is old and weak with age he feels extremely cold. One of his servants suggests that he have a young and beautiful virgin, Abishag, cradle him to her bosom and thereby warm him. This is done (David does not make love to her).

ADONIJAH USURPS THE THRONE; SOLOMON MADE KING, 1:5-53. Adonijah, David's eldest son, decides that he wants to be king; he is too impatient to wait until his probable succession upon his father's death. He appeals to many of his brothers and to many of the powerful men of Judah to back him. A large number of them comply, but many do not. Among the latter is Nathan the prophet. Solomon does not know of Adonijah's plans. Nathan goes to Bathsheba, Solomon's mother, to warn her that her life and the life of her son are in danger. He tells her she must go to David and ask him why Adonijah is reigning when David has promised the throne to Solomon. Bathsheba does as Nathan tells her and, as a result, David promises her that no one but Solomon shall reign after his death. He instructs Nathan and Zadok the priest to take Solomon to Gihon and there to anoint him king of Israel and Judah. The anointing is accomplished and as they return, followed by many people dancing and piping in celebration, the sound of the festivities reaches the ears of Adonijah and his guests. He asks and is told the reason for the merriment. His guests are afraid of David and Solomon's wrath and they all leave. Adonijah also is afraid and he goes to a sanctuary and places his hands on the altar horns (anyone seeking safety who did this could not be taken away or harmed). When Soloman hears of this he decrees that only if Adonijah is found to be wicked will he be killed; if he is a good man he shall remain unharmed. (This may be said to be a foreshadowing of the great wisdom and sense of justice which was to be Solomon's.)

DAVID'S CHARGE TO SOLOMON; SOLOMON ESTABLISHES HIS KINGDOM, 2. Shortly before David's death he calls Solomon and charges him to behave as a man and to walk in the ways of God. He reminds him of God's promise (at the founding of the Davidic dynasty) to care for all of David's descendants who would succeed to the throne of Israel, providing they kept His ways. He also passes on to him information about particular enemies and people whose past disloyalties are to be avenged by Solomon. Then David dies, having reigned for forty years. One day Adonijah comes to Bathsheba and says that she knows that the kingship should rightfully have been his and would she therefore, as compensation, present a request of his to Solomon. He desires to marry Abishag. Bathsheba agrees to intercede for him, but when she asks this of Solomon he becomes furious with Adonijah and decrees his death. (Solomon is angry because since Abishag had been David's concubine, for Adonijah to have her would put him on a par with David.) Solomon then sets about obeying David's last commands and ridding the kingdom of some few traitors and disloyal or treacherous men.

SOLOMON MARRIES PHARAOH'S DAUGHTER; SOLOMON'S WISDOM AND PROSPERITY, 3-4. Solomon falls in love with Pharaoh's daughter, marries her, and brings her to Jerusalem. He prays to God and makes 1000 burnt offerings. God appears to him is a dream and asks "What shall I give thee?" Soloman tells Him that he is not capable of ruling so great a people as the Israelites and that therefore he would be grateful if God would give him an understanding heart, one which would enable him to "discern between good and bad." God is very pleased with Solomon for not asking for personal gain and so He gives him great wisdom, greater than any man has ever had, and also gives him wealth and honor. Then Solomon awakes and finds he has been dreaming. One day two women come to him, both claiming to be the mother of the same baby. The king decrees that the only way in which justice can be done is to cut the living child in two and give each woman half. One of the women protests this, saying she would rather give up the child than have it die, but the other woman is willing to have the child slain. Solomon then gives the child to the first woman, saying "She is the mother thereof." From that day all Israel fears Solomon's great wisdom. What then follows are two lists of names—of princes and of officers responsible for provisioning the royal household; this is followed by a list of all the supplies used by the king and his court. Solomon's wisdom is again exalted and it is said that he spoke three thousand proverbs (see the Book of Proverbs).

SOLOMON'S AGREEMENT WITH KING HIRAM; SOLOMON BUILDS THE HOUSE OF THE LORD, 5-6. Solomon asks King Hiram of Tyre to give him the wood of the cedars of Lebanon to build a Temple for the Lord. Hiram agrees to do this in exchange for food for his household. The men of Israel and the men of Lebanon work together to prepare the building materials for the Temple. All the materials are brought ready to be installed so that there will be no sound of construction within the Temple walls.

The word of God again comes to Solomon, saying that if Solomon keeps His ways He "will dwell among the children of Israel, and will not forsake [them]." The Temple is completed. It is carved all over and overlaid with gold. Its decorations are described in detail. Solomon takes seven years to build the Temple. (This Temple was destroyed in 586 B.C. by the Babylonians; a second Temple was built in 515 B.C. and destroyed by the Romans in 70 A.D.)

SOLOMON'S OTHER BUILDINGS; THE FURNISHINGS FOR THE TEMPLE, 7. It takes Solomon thirteen years to complete his own palace, which also is built of the cedars of Lebanon. It is fifty cubits (a cubit was 18 inches) long and thirty cubits high, and it is surrounded by three rows of hewn stones. Solomon then asks Hiram of Tyre, a talented worker in brass, to make various ornaments for the Temple. All the furnishings for it are made of gold. Also placed in the Temple are all the vessels David had dedicated of the nations he had vanquished (II Sam. 8-11).

THE DEDICATION OF THE TEMPLE; THE LORD'S COVENANT WITH SOLOMON, 8:1-9:9. When the Temple is finished Solomon says that the Lord has fulfilled His promise to David, for his son has built "a house for the name of the Lord God of Israel." He gathers the people around him and prays to God to look favorably upon Israel. He asks Him to listen to the prayers of the people, to do good to the deserving and to condemn the wicked, to forgive those who, having turned away from Him in error, wish to return to the fold, and to send rain or dispel famine if those who have sinned repent of their misdeeds. He also asks God to harken to the prayers of non-Jews who have come to love the Hebrew God, so that all the world may come to know His greatness. Solomon then turns to the people and asks them to obey God's commandments so that He will keep His convenant with them. God again appears to Solomon and tells him that all will be well if he is true to the Lord, but if he should turn away from Him in the slightest degree then He will forsake the Israelites.

SOLOMON'S FURTHER ACTIVITIES; THE QUEEN OF SHEBA VISITS SOLOMON; SOLOMON'S RICHES AND FAME, 9:10-10:29.

Solomon gives King Hiram twenty cities in Galilee; Hiram is displeased with them. Solomon raises a large levy of men (see I Kings 5-13-18) in order to build the Temple, to build his palace, and generally to improve the kingdom. He builds a navy which, with Hiram's men, goes to Ophir and brings back 420 gold talents (a vast sum of money). The Queen of Sheba hears of Solomon's wisdom and fame and decides to visit him to see for herself whether he is as great as he is reputed to be. They exchange wisdom and she realizes that he is even more than he is said to be. She blesses the God who set him on the throne of Israel. They exchange gifts and she returns to her own country. Solomon's wealth is described in detail. He is wiser and richer than anyone on earth, and people come from all over "to hear his wisdom." Solomon trades in horses and chariots (Solomon's stables at Megido have been excavated; they are believed to have been capable of holding as many as 450 horses; see I Kings 9:15, 19.)

SOLOMON'S APOSTASY AND ADVERSARIES; THE DEATH OF SOLOMON, 11.

(Here the Deuteronomist begins to render his personal negative judgment of Solomon.) "Solomon loved many strange women," women of the heathen nations with which God had forbade the Israelites to mingle. He has 700 wives and 300 concubines; many of the former are of foreign birth and impose their religious beliefs on Solomon's. He builds them places of worship and incurs the wrath of God. (It is this very "international" outlook for which the Deuteronomist condemns Solomon. It should be pointed out, however, that perhaps most of Solomon's marriages were political in origin. They created for Solomon military, cultural, and political ties with neighboring countries. Solomon, therefore, was not particularly concerned with his wives' manner of worship and, indeed, as he got older may have felt it would cement his alliances to allow them to worship in their own way. He no doubt felt that they had not influenced his own religious beliefs at all; nevertheless, he did introduce elements of pagan worship into the Mosaic tradition. The signs of this mingling of cultures had appeared long before this time, i.e., in the decor of the Temple, which showed marked Canaanite influence. While it is certainly true that the life of cosmopolitan Jerusalem was bound to absorb elements of surrounding cultures, it was exactly this which God had forbade to the Israelites. The "chosen people" were to keep themselves separate in every way.) God tells Solomon that because he has broken faith with Him, his kingdom will be taken from him, and only for David's sake will he be allowed to rule until he dies. His son will succeed him, and it is from his son that rule will be wrested. God sets against Solomon Hadad the Edomite (an old enemy of David's who has been living in Egypt), Rezon of Damascus, and Jeroboam of Zereda, whom Solomon had made "ruler over all the charge of the house of Joseph." One day Jeroboam comes upon the prophet Ahijah. Ahijah takes hold of Jeroboam's garment and tears it into twelve pieces, each of which symbolizes a tribe of Israel. He gives ten of the pieces to Jeroboam and tells him that God has decreed that rule over those ten tribes shall pass to him. Because of God's love for David, one tribe (actually two—Judah and Benjamin) would continue under the rule of Solomon's son. However, Ahijah says, the blight on David's seed will not last forever. When Solomon learns of this he tries to kill Jeroboam, but Jeroboam flees to Egypt and stays there until Solomon's death. (Jeroboam's accession to the throne of Israel about 922 B.C. will mark the beginning of the "divided kingdom.") Solomon dies, having reigned forty years, and he is succeeded by his son Rehoboam.

ISRAEL'S REVOLT; JEROBOAM LEADS ISRAEL INTO SIN, 12-13.

Rehoboam is anointed king. The Israelites ask him if he will be kinder to them than Solomon was, for only if he is will they serve him. Rehoboam, listening to the foolish advice of his young friends, tells the people that he will be much harder on them than Solomon was. As a result of his words all the tribes of Israel except Judah and Benjamin secede. Jeroboam is made king over the remaining ten tribes. Rehoboam tries to fight to recapture his kingdom but a prophet tells him it is God's will that things stay as they are, and Rehoboam gives up his plans. Jeroboam, afraid that his people will return to Jerusalem and the Temple unless he prevents them, introduces pagan practices to satisfy their religious needs. God, enraged at Jeroboam, sends a prophet to tell him that Josiah of the House of David shall destroy him. When Jeroboam tries to lay hands on the prophet his hand withers and the altar is split in two. Jeroboam begs the prophet to ask God to restore to him the use of his hand. The prophet does as he asks and his hands is restored. Meanwhile an old prophet who lives in Bethel hears what the other prophet has done that day and he sets out to find him. When he does he asks him to come home and eat with him. The prophet from Judah refuses, saying that the Lord has told him not to eat or drink in that country. The other prophet lies to him, saying that he too has had a vision in which God came to him saying that he was to bring the prophet home and give him food. The prophet of Judah believes him

and goes to the man's house and dines with him. God punishes him for his disobedience by keeping him from being buried with his family. As the prophet leaves to return to Judah he is killed by a lion, which does not eat him but stands quietly by the carcass. The other prophet goes to him and takes his body back to Bethel for prayers and burial. He asks his sons to see that he is buried in the same sepulchre as the dead prophet.

AHIJAH'S PROPHECY AGAINST JEROBOAM, THE REIGN OF REHOBOAM, 14.

Jeroboam's son becomes ill and Jeroboam sends his wife to the prophet Ahijah, who will be able to tell her the child's fate. Before she gets there the Lord comes to Ahijah and tells him what to say to her. When she enters, Ahijah tells her that because Jeroboam has not kept his promise to God, and has deserted Him for pagan deities, the entire house of Jeroboam will fall, including, of course, the sick child. Jeroboam reigns for twenty-two years and when he dies his son Nadab succeeds to the throne. In Judah, meanwhile, Rehoboam rules and the people of Judah grow wicked and worship pagan gods. Shishak, king of Egypt, invades Jerusalem and takes the "treasures of the house of the Lord." Rehoboam dies and his son Abijam reigns in his stead.

THE REIGNS OF ABIJAM, ASA, NADAB, BAASHA, ELAH, ZIMRI, OMRI, AND AHAB, 15, 16.

Abijam rules Judah for three years. He is as sinful as his father Rehoboam, but because he is a descendant of David's the Lord allows his son Asa to succeed to the throne. Asa reigns in Jerusalem for forty-one years, and he walks in the ways of the Lord, destroying all the pagan idols in the land. At this time Baasha is the king of Israel, and he tries to blockade the northern approach to Judah (Judah had been waging war with Israel since the kingdom was divided). Asa sends gifts to Benhadad, king of Syria, asking him to come to his aid. Benhadad agrees and marches into Israel and devastates many cities. Baasha flees to Tirzah. Asa dies and his son Jehoshaphat reigns after him. Nadab, the son of Jeroboam, begins to reign in Israel in the second year of Asa's reign over Judah. Nadab is wicked and is overthrown by Baasha, who proceeds to kill all of Jeroboam's family, thereby fulfilling Ahijah's prophecy. Baasha also is evil. The word of the Lord comes to Jehu; the Lord decrees that what has happened to Jeroboam's family will also happen to Baasha's. When Baasha dies his son Elah succeeds to the throne. Zimri, a military leader, conspires against Elah, murders him, and ascends the throne. He kills all of Baasha's family, again fulfilling a prophecy. Zimri reigns only seven days when the people overthrow him for his tyranny and make Omri, the captain of the army, their king. Zimri kills himself. Omri is worse than any king that has gone before him. When he dies he is succeeded by his son Ahab. Ahab also is said to be more evil than any who had ruled before him. His worst sin is that he marries the Baal-worshiping Jezebel, and that he too worships Baal. Hiel the Bethelite rebuilds the city of Jericho.

ELIJAH, 17-19. Elijah the Tishbite tells Ahab that there will be neither dew nor rain except at Elijah's command. The Lord then comes to Elijah and tells him to go to a certain brook and remain there. He is promised that the ravens will feed him. He goes and everything happens as the Lord said, but after a while the brook dries up because there is no rain. God comes to him again and tells him to go to Zarephath, where there is a widow who will care for him. He goes and, meeting the widow, asks her for something to eat. She says she can give him nothing for she has but a handful of meal and a drop of oil. He tells her not to worry but to make him a cake and bring it to him, and then make one for herself and her son. He explains that God has promised that she will have meal and oil "until the day that the Lord sendeth rain upon the earth." Then the woman's son falls ill and dies, and Elijah prays to the Lord to restore him to the living; the Lord hears Elijah and the boy revives. Then God tells Elijah to go to Ahab; when he does, God will make it rain. There is a terrible famine in Samaria, and Ahab and Obadiah, Ahab's chief steward and a very religious man, are out in the fields looking for a bit of grass with which they might save some of the animals. Obadiah, who fears the Lord, risked his life to hide and maintain one hundred of the prophets of Yahweh whom Jezebel tried to destroy. (Jezebel was a power-hungry, domineering woman who tried her best to drive the Hebrew traditions out of Israel. She tore down altars, brought in prophets of Baal, and killed the Hebrew prophets. Only those who could go underground, like the ones saved by Obadiah, could survive.) Obadiah and Ahab separate, and as Obadiah walks he meets Elijah, who tells him to find Ahab and tell him that he (Elijah) has returned. Obadiah is afraid to do as Elijah asks because Ahab has searched far and wide for Elijah. Obadiah is afraid that when Ahab returns with him to see Elijah, Elijah will have disappeared and Ahab, in anger, will kill Obadiah. Elijah, however, is determined to see Ahab, so Obadiah goes to Ahab and he comes to Elijah. Ahab accuses Elijah of troubling Israel, but Elijah says it is Ahab who troubles her. He tells Ahab to gather all of Israel and 450 of the prophets of Baal (he also tells him to bring 400 other prophets but these do not reappear in the story) and bring them to Mount Carmel. There is a contest between Elijah and all the prophets of Baal. Each chooses a bullock (young bull) to make ready for sacrifice to their respective gods, but they do not light a fire under the animal. Elijah will pray to the Lord God of Israel and the pagan prophets will pray to Baal to send the necessary fire. First the Baal prophets call upon their god, but their prayers and rituals do not avail them. Then Elijah calls upon the Lord. God answers his prayer by a burst of flame which consumes the stones of the altar along with everything else. The people then acknowledge Yahweh to be the only true God, the prophets of Baal are captured, and Elijah slays them all. (This did not, however, completely wipe out Baalism in Israel. In II Kings 10-21 we are told that Jehu calls together all the worshipers of Baal and that there are enough of them to fill a large Baal temple.) Elijah then prays for rain on the top of Mount Carmel, and when his servant tells him that he sees a cloud as small as a man's hand Elijah knows that there is going to be a deluge. He warns Ahab to leave the mountain immediately so that his chariot will not get bogged down in the mud. At this moment Elijah is so possessed of the spirit of the Lord that he begins to run down the mountain and is so fleet of foot that he passes Ahab and runs before him all the way to Jezreel. Upon hearing what Elijah has done Jezebel determines to kill him. Elijah fears for his life and flees into the wilderness where he prays to God that he may die because, like his fathers, he has failed to make the Israelites free of wickedness. But he does not die and instead is miraculously fed by an angel. This enables him to journey "forty days and forty nights unto Horeb [Sinai], the mount of God." When he arrives he takes up lodging in a cave and the word of God comes to him, asking what he is doing there. Elijah tells him of Jezebel's threat to his life, after which the Lord tells him to leave the cave and stand on the mountaintop before Him. He hears God not in the earthquake, or the fire, or the wind, but in a "still small voice." God tells him to anoint Hazael to be king of Syria and Jehu to be king of Israel. He also tells him to anoint Elisha to take his (Elijah's) place as a prophet, and that between them, Hazael, Jehu, and Elisha shall slay all the Baal worshipers in Israel. When this is

done there will be 7000 people left for God. (It is important to note that it is symbolically very appropriate that Elijah traveled to Sinai to speak with the Lord. It was on Sinai that the cornerstones of the Hebrew faith were laid and it is a return to this faith which the prophets were advocating.) Elijah leaves Mount Horeb and finds Elisha, who then follows and cares for him.

AHAB DEFEATS THE SYRIANS; AHAB AND NABOTH'S VINEYARD, 20-21. Ahab and Israel are attacked by Benhadad, the king of Syria. A prophet comes to Ahab and tells him that God will deliver the Syrians into his hands. This comes to pass but Benhadad escapes. The prophet again comes to Ahab and tells him to strengthen his army, for at the beginning of the following year there will again be war with Syria. The Syrians meanwhile tell Benhadad that the reason they lost was because the Hebrew God was God of the hills; they advised him to fight the next battle in a valley, for there they were bound to be stronger than the Israelites. When the two nations meet to do battle again the Hebrews are vastly outnumbered. A man of God comes to Ahab and tells him that once again the Syrians will be defeated by Israel because the Syrians have said that the Lord is not God of the valleys. Benhadad escapes but on the advice of his servants goes to Ahab to ask for mercy. Ahab grants him his life in return for the restoration to him of the cities Benhadad's father took from his father. (This disobeyed God's will, for Ahab was to slay Benhadad.) A prophet comes to Ahab after performing a series of symbolic acts and tells him that because he has allowed Benhadad to live, his life shall be taken for Benhadad's and his people's lives for the lives of the Syrians. Sometime after this Ahab goes to Naboth the Jezreelite to ask him to give him his vineyard for an herb garden. He offers to give him in its stead either a better vineyard or its worth in money. But Naboth refuses, saying "The Lord forbid it me, that I should give the inheritance of my fathers unto thee." (The land really was not Naboth's to dispose of, for according to Hebrew tradition it belonged to all of his ancestors. Religiously speaking, it belonged only to God, who had fulfilled His promise to give the Israelites a fertile land in which to live.) Ahab is very displeased and goes home to sulk. Jezebel promises to get the vineyard for him and accomplishes this by arranging for two men to bear false witness against Naboth, saying that he has blasphemed against both God and the king. Naboth is then stoned to death. Jezebel brings Ahab the news and he takes possession of Naboth's vineyard. While he is there Elijah comes to him and tells him that because of what he has done God has cast him out. It has been decreed that "in the place where the dogs licked the blood of Naboth" shall his blood also be licked. Jezebel will be eaten by dogs. At these words Ahab becomes truly contrite and humbles himself before the Lord. God, seeing this, is merciful and tells Elijah that because of Ahab's behavior He will not bring evil upon his family until after his death.

MICAIAH PROPHESIES THE DEFEAT OF AHAB AND JEHOSHAPHAT; THE REIGN OF JEHOSHAPHAT AND THE REIGN OF AHAZIAH OF ISRAEL, 22. Israel and Syria are at peace for three years. Then Judah and Israel join together to make war on Syria in order to regain a piece of territory, Ramoth, which they had previously lost to her. Jehoshaphat, the king of Judah, asks Ahab to ask the prophets if God favors their plan. They are told that Ramoth will be delivered into their hands. There is one prophet, however, who is not consulted because he always prophesies evil about Ahab. His name is Micaiah, and Jehoshaphat asks to hear his opinion about their venture. Micaiah prophesies that Ahab is doomed and that God, to make him go to Ramoth, put "a lying spirit in the mouth of all his prophets." Upon hearing this, Ahab throws Micaiah into prison. Ahab and Jehoshaphat proceed with their plans and both are defeated and Ahab is killed. In keeping with the prophecy, the dogs of Samaria lick his blood. Ahab is succeeded by his son Ahaziah.

Jehoshaphat (of Judah) is a good king, as was his father Asa, but he does not rid his kingdom of paganism. He makes peace with the king of Israel and he dies at the age of 60, having reigned for 25 years. His son Jehoram succeeds him. Ahaziah reigns for two years and he is a very wicked king.

SUMMARY OF II KINGS

THE DEATH OF AHAZIAH; ELISHA SUCCEEDS ELIJAH, 1-2. After Ahab dies the Moabites rebel against Israel. One day King Ahaziah falls out of his bedroom window and becomes very ill. He sends his servants to ask the Ekronite god Baalzebub (the Lord of the Flies) whether he will recover. On the way they meet Elijah, who has a message for them to take back to Ahaziah. The Lord has spoken to Elijah and instructed him to tell Ahaziah that because he has turned to a pagan god instead of to the Lord he will die. The servants return and tell Ahaziah what Elijah said. The king tries to capture Elijah, and three times he sends a captain and 50 soldiers to do the job. The first two times Elijah calls down fire from heaven and it consumes them. The third time, however, the captain is a religious and God-fearing man who asks Elijah to spare both his men and himself. The Lord speaks to Elijajh and tells him to go with this man. Elijah repeats God's message to Ahaziah. It comes to pass as God said, and Ahaziah dies. He is succeeded by Jehoram. Elijah and Elisha go to Bethel on God's instructions. They then proceed to Jericho and cross the Jordan on dry land when Elijah parts its waters. They are traveling to the city where Elijah's impending death will take place. Elijah asks Elisha if there is anything he can do for him before he dies, and Elisha asks for "a double portion" of Elijah's spirit. He is told that if he sees Elijah being taken from him it is a sign that his request has been granted. At that moment Elijah is taken to heaven in a whirlwind and Elisha, seeing him, cries out after him. He then pick up Elijah's cloak and going back to the Jordan tries to make the water part for him. He is successful and is recognized by the sons of the prophets to be Elijah's successor. The men of Jericho complain to Elisha of the fact that there is little water in Jericho and the ground is infertile. Elisha throws salt in a brook and tells the men that the Lord has said that the land will no longer be barren and that they will have plenty of water. He then returns to Samaria.

THE REIGN OF JEHORAM OF ISRAEL; ELISHA PREDICTS VICTORY OVER MOAB; THE WIDOW'S OIL; ELISHA AND THE SHUNAMMITE WOMAN, 3-4 Jehoram, Ahab's son, is king of Israel for 12 years. He is a wicked king but in a different way than his father has been, for he does not worship Baar. When Moab rebels against Israel, King Jehoram asks King Jehoshaphat to aid him in battling the Moabites. Jehoshaphat agrees and he and Jehoram, along with the king of the Edomites, begin to travel with their armies. They encounter a drought and, afraid that the Lord is against them, they consult Elisha as to His will. Elisha tells them that they are to dig ditches throughout the valley

and the Lord will, by filling them, provide the armies with water. He will, moreover, bring them victory over the Moabites. The Moabites prepare to fight and rise early in the morning to ready themselves. However, when they look over to the Israelite camp they see the sun shining in the pools of water and it appears to them to be blood. Thinking that the kings have fought among themselves and killed each other, they prepare to plunder the Israelite camp. When they cross to the camp the armies rise up and do battle with them, chasing them all the way back to their own country. The Moabites are badly beaten. A woman comes to Elisha and tells him that her husband is dead and, because she cannot pay him, her creditor is going to make bondsmen of her two sons. She tells Elisha she has nothing in the house but a pot of oil. The prophet tells her to go and borrow from her neighbors as many empty vessels as she can. She is then to fill as many of these as she can from her little container of oil. Through a miracle she fills them all and there is still oil in the pot when she is finished. She tells Elisha what has happened and he tells her to sell the oil and with money pay her debts and live happily with her sons. There was a Shunammite woman who was very good to Elisha and who kept a special room ready for him when he came to Shunem. He asks her if there is anything she wants in return for her kindness, and she tells him, through his servant Gehazi, that her husband is old and she has no child. Elisha calls her to him and tells her that she will give birth to a son. She thinks he is lying to her but time passes and she does give birth to a son. One day, when the boy is grown, he falls ill and dies. His mother leaves him in Elisha's room and goes in search of the prophet. She finds him and he gives Gehazi instructions for reviving the child. These do not work (perhaps because, as we learn later, Gehazi is unworthy). When Elijah arrives at the house he locks himself in his room with the boy and lies on top of him; the child's flesh begins to get warm. Elisha repeats this action several times and then suddenly the boy sneezes seven times and awakens. The Shunammite woman falls at Elisha's feet and, taking her son, leaves him to himself. Elisha goes to Gilgal, where there is a famine. He sends his servants to gather herbs for a dish of pottage (stewed vegetables) to be shared with the sons of the prophets. The servant accidentally picks a poisoned vine and includes it with the herbs in the pottage. As the sons of the prophets begin to eat they realize that "there is death in the pot" and they cannot eat their food. Elisha asks for some meal (ground grain) and throws it in the pot and thereby destroys the poison. A man from Baalshalisha comes to Elisha with a small gift of food. The prophet tells him to feed the people with it. The man objects, saying that there is nowhere near enough food to feed 100 men, but Elisha tells him that God has said that there will be more than enough and that there will even be some left over. And, of course, it is so.

THE CURE OF NAAMAN'S LEPROSY; THE AXE HEAD; ELISHA AND THE SIEGE OF SAMARIA, 5-7. Naaman, the commander of the Syrian army, is a very great man, but he suffers from leprosy. An Israelite girl, a Syrian captive who is Naaman's wife's maid, tells her mistress that she wishes Elisha were with her master for he could cure him of his sickness. This is told to the king, who then sends Naaman with a message to the Israelite king asking him to cure him. He is sent to Elisha and bidden to wash in the Jordan seven times. Naaman does this and his "flesh came again like unto the flesh of a little child." He tells Elisha that he will henceforth worship only the Lord God of Israel and offers to reward Elisha for his services to him. Elisha refuses and Naaman leaves. Gehazi, Elisha's servant, decides that

he will take from Naaman some of the gifts Elisha refused. He runs after the Syrian and tells him that Elisha has asked him to give to two sons of the prophet a silver talent and two changes of clothes. Naaman agrees and sends Gehazi away with the gifts which he, of course, takes for himself. When he comes home he tries to lie to Elisha about where he has been, but Elisha knows what he has been doing and as punishment turns him into a leper and decrees that all his descendants shall also be lepers. The sons of the prophets ask Elisha to journey with them to the Jordan where they will build themselves a place to live. Elisha agrees. When they arrive and are chopping beams, the head of one man's axe falls in the river. The man is distraught because it was borrowed, but Elisha merely throws a stick in the water where the axe sank and it rises to the surface. Syria and Israel are at war and Elisha warns the Israelite king of the location of the Syrian camp so that he will not go near it. When the Syrian king finds out about Elisha's warning he tries to capture him by surrounding the city of Dothan where Elisha is living. Elisha calls on the Lord to blind the Syrian army temporarily and he leads them into Samaria, the stronghold of the Israelite king, whereupon their sight is restored. They are fed and provided for and sent back to their king. Samaria is besieged by King Benhadad of Syria. His men surround the walls and there is a terrible famine in the city. The king of the Israelites curses Elisha and goes to his home to try to kill him. He is preceded by his messenger, to whom Elisha says that within twenty-four hours the famine will be over. Four lepers sitting at the city gate decide to go out to the Syrians in the hope that they will save them. If they kill them it will not matter because they are going to die of hunger anyway. When they arrive at the Syrian camp they are amazed to find it deserted. The Lord has caused the Syrians to hear the sound of chariots and approaching armies and they, thinking that Israel has enlisted the aid of the Hittites and the Egyptians, have fled. The lepers take some booty for themselves and then run and tell the king that the Syrians are gone. The king checks their story because he is afraid the Syrians have laid a trap for the Israelites. He discovers that the story is true, and the people go out and loot the tents of the Syrians.

THE SHUNAMMITE WOMAN'S LAND RESTORED; HAZAEL, JEHORAM, AND AHAZIAH, 8.

Elisha warns the woman whose son he had saved (II Kings 4:8-37) that there is going to be a seven-year famine in the land and that she and her family must live elsewhere for its duration. They live with the Philistines and return at the end of seven years. At this time the king of Israel is speaking to Gehazi, Elisha's servant, and Gehazi is telling him of the things Elisha has done. Naturally he tells him the story of the Shunammite woman's son. The woman comes to the king to reclaim her land (which she deserted to flee the country), and Gehazi recognizes her and tells the king that this is the woman he has been speaking of. The king then knows her claims are just and he restores her land to her. Benhadad, the king of Syria, is ill and sends Hazael to Elisha to ask if he will recover. Elisha says that Benhadad is capable of recovering but will die regardless. He will be succeeded by Hazael who will be a wicked, cruel king and who will persecute the children of Israel. Hazael returns to Benhadad and tells him that Elisha says he will recover. On the following day he murders him and succeeds him as king. Jehoram, the son of Jehoshaphat, rules Judah after his father's death. He is an evil king and is married to one of Ahab's daughters. During his time Edom and Libnah revolt. He reigns eight years and upon his death is succeeded by his son Ahaziah. Ahaziah reigns one year and is a wicked king. He is a descendant of Omri. With Joram he makes war against Syria in Ramothgilead. When Joram is wounded he returns to Jezreel and Ahaziah goes to visit him.

JEHU ANOINTED KING OF ISRAEL; JEHU KILLS JORAM, AHAZIAH, AND JEZEBEL, AND DESTROYS THE HOUSE OF AHAB; JEHU WIPES OUT THE WORSHIP OF BAAL 9-11.

Elisha instructs one of the sons of the prophets to go to Ramothgilead and there anoint Jehu, the son of Jehoshaphat, king of Israel. The prophet does as he is bidden and tells Jehu that the Lord has said that through Jehu He will destroy the house of Ahab. (At the moment of Jehu's anointment the Omri dynasty is terminated and with it all its dreadful evil, for Jehu will slay all of Omri's descendants.) Jehu takes his army and marches to Jezreel where the wounded Joram, Ahab's son, and Ahaziah are staying. Joram and Ahaziah go out to meet Jehu and ask if he comes in peace. Jehu says Jezebel's wickedness is too great for him to come in peace and he shoots Joram with an arrow, telling his soldiers to bury him in the field where Naboth is buried and thus fulfill the prophecy of the Lord (I Kings 21). Ahaziah is wounded, but manages to get to Megiddo before he dies. Jehu enters Jezreel and Jezebel paints her face and looks out of the window at him. He asks who is on his side and three eunuchs look out of a window and, at Jehu's bidding, throw Jezebel out. When they go out to bury her they find that nothing is left of her but her skull, feet, and the palms of her hands. Once more the prophecy of the Lord is fulfilled because Jezebel's flesh has been eaten by dogs (I Kings 21:23). Ahab has seventy sons in Samaria. Jehu writes a letter to the elders of Jezreel telling them to pick a king from among these sons and then fight to hold their master's kingdom. The elders refuse and say they will do whatever Jehu advises. He tells them to kill Ahab's sons and to bring their heads to him. The elders obey and send the heads to Jehu in baskets. Jehu then kills all the remaining members in the temple of Ahab's house. Jehu meets Ahaziah's brothers and slays them also. He then comes upon the holy man Jehonadab, the son of Rechab (Jer. 35), and takes him with him to wipe out what remains of Ahab's house in Samaria. Jehu calls all the worshippers of Baal together by deceiving them into thinking that he also is a pagan. When the servants of Baal enter the Baal temple to make burnt offerings and sacrifices, Jehu sends his soldiers in to kill them all. Then the temple and the idols are broken and burned. Although Jehu is a good king he is far from perfect, and God tells him that his children will rule Israel only until the fourth generation. (Again the Deuteronomist is making a judgment with the benefit of hindsight.) He does not break completely with the ways of Jereboam and allows the golden calves which have been erected in Dan and Bethel to remain. The editor says that in those days "the Lord began to cut Israel short: and Hazael smote them in all the coasts of Israel." Jehu rules Israel for twenty-eight years, and upon his death his son Jehoahaz ascends the throne.

ATHALIAH USURPS THE THRONE; THE REIGNS OF JEHOASH OF JUDAH, JEHOAHAZ, AND JEHOASH OF ISRAEL; ELISHA'S DEATH, 11-13.

Upon the death of Ahaziah, his mother, Athaliah, usurps the throne by killing all his children. However, his sister, unknown to Athaliah, hides one of her brother's sons, a child named Jehoash (also called Joash) and keeps him hidden for six years. At the end of that time, Jehoiada, the priest, calls together "the rulers over hundreds, with the captains and the guard" and shows them little Jehoash. Under Jehoiada's instructions they surround the Temple and Jehoash is anointed. Athaliah is slain. "And Jehoiada made a covenant between the Lord and the people, that they should be the Lord's people." The people then destroy the temple of Baal and escort the king home to his throne. Jehoash is a good king but he does not destroy the pagan idols in Judah, and pagan priests are still permitted to make sacrifices. Jehoash tells the priests to take the money which every man owes as his assessment (see Exod. 30:11-16), along with whatever money the people may want to give, and with these funds to repair the house of the Lord. The priests do not do this. Jehoiada then takes a box and sets it beside the altar. It is soon filled with donations from the people and given to artisans to repair the Temple. Hazael, king of Syria, determines to take Jerusalem, so Jehoash takes all the holy things and all the treasures and leaves. Jehoash is later killed by his servants and his son Amaziah reigns in his stead.

Jehu's son, Jehoahaz, rules Israel for seventeen years. He is a wicked king and, like Jereboam, makes Israel sin. The Lord, to punish his people, "delivered them into the hand of Hazael king of Syria," and later into the hand of his son Benhadad. Jehoahaz prays to the Lord for deliverance and his prayer is answered. Still the Hebrews are sinful. Jehoahaz dies and is succeeded by his son Jehoash (Joash) (of Israel), who reigns sixteen years. He too is sinful. He has a son named Jeroboam, who ascends the throne when he dies. Elisha becomes gravely ill and Jehoash of Israel comes to him. Elisha instructs him to shoot an arrow eastward through the window and tells him that he has shot the arrow of the Lord's deliverance, and of Israel's deliverance from Syria. He instructs Jehoash to hit the floor with his sheaf of arrows. The king obeys, striking the floor three times. Elisha is angry with him for not having struck it five or six times, because now instead of consuming Syria he will only overcome it three times. Elisha dies and the Moabites, shortly thereafter, invade the land. The Moabites throw a dead man into Elisha's tomb and when the man's body touches Elisha's bones, he revives. As prophesied, Jehoash recovers the cities of Israel.

THE REIGNS OF AMAZIAH, JEROBOAM, AZARIAH ZECHARIAH, SHALLUM, MENAHEM PEKAHIAH, PEKAH, JOTHAM, AND AHAZ, 14-16.

Amaziah is the son of Jehoash, the king of Judah. He reigns twenty-nine years, and is a good king, but like his father he does not destroy the pagan altars or drive the pagans from Judah. He kills the servants who murdered his father. He slays ten thousand people in Edom, and then challenges Jehoash, the king of Israel, to a battle. Jehoash warns him that he will lose, but he persists; when they meet it is as Jehoash said it would be. The spoils of Jehoash's victory are the treasures in the Temple and in Amaziah's house. When Jehoash dies, he is succeeded by his son Jeroboam. Amaziah is the victim of a conspiracy and is followed on the throne of Judah by his son Azariah. Jeroboam reigns for forty-one years. He is an evil king but he delivers Israel, which does not deserve to be delivered, through the grace of the Lord. He dies and Zechariah reigns in his stead. Azariah (also called Uzziah) reigns in Jerusalem for fifty-two years. He is a good king but he, too, does not remove the pagan altars or stop the pagan worship. Azariah is a leper. He is succeeded by his son Jotham. Zechariah is an evil king and he is slain by Shallum the son of Jabesh. Shallum reigns for a month and then is killed by Menahem who succeeds him as king. Menahem is a wicked king. During his reign Pul, the king of Assyria, invades Israel and Menahem taxes his people heavily to give Pul money so that he will leave Israel alone. Menahem is succeeded by his son Pekahiah. Pekahiah is also an evil king and he is conspired against and murdered by the son of one of his captains. This man, Pekah, ascends the throne upon his death. Hoshea does to Pekah as Pekah did to Pekahiah and succeeds him. While Pekah was ruling in Israel, Jotham began to rule in Judah. Jotham is a good king and when he dies his son Ahaz ascends the throne. Ahaz behaves like a heathen and indulges in heathen practices. Both Pekah and Rezin, king of Syria, war with Judah but they cannot overcome Ahaz. Ahaz asks the king of Assyria for aid and sends him as a gift all the treasures in the house of the Lord. The Assyrian king helps him and Ahaz goes to Damascus to meet him. He sees there an altar which he likes and has his priest make a copy of it and has it installed in the Temple for his use. When Ahaz dies he is succeeded by Hezekiah.

THE FALL OF SAMARIA AND THE CAPTIVITY OF ISRAEL; THE REIGN OF HEZEKIAH; THE INVASION OF SENNACHERIB; JUDAH DELIVERED FROM SENNACHERIB, 17-19.

Hoshea is a wicked king who pays tribute to the king of Assyria. When he fails to make one of his payments, he is imprisoned. Then the king of Assyria forces the Hebrews to go into exile. The editor says that Shalmaneser, the Assyrian king, is able to do this because God is angry at the sinful children of Israel. Shalmaneser populates Samaria with pagans. God is angry with these people because they do not fear Him and He sends lions to slay some of them. Shalmaneser then sends one of the exiled priests to teach the people to fear the Lord; however, they continue to practice all forms of the religions of the countries from which they came. Hezekiah reigns twenty-nine years in Jerusalem. He is an excellent king and routs the pagans and breaks their altars. The Lord is with him, and he wins a battle with the Assyrians and overcomes the Philistines. In the fourth year of Hezekiah's reign Israel goes into exile. In the fourteenth year of Hezekiah, Sennacherib, the Assyrian king, captures "all the fenced cities of Judah." Hezekiah is forced to pay him tribute. Representatives of Sennacherib come and accuse Hezekiah of plotting with Egypt against Assyria. They tell the people that the Lord will not rescue them, and that if they make peace with Sennacherib he will take them away to a land like their own land, "a land of corn and wine." The people, however, keep silent because they trust in Hezekiah and it is his will that they say nothing. The king is deeply troubled and he sends his servants to the prophet Isaiah to ask him for advice. Isaiah tells them that everything will be alright. God will make the Assyrian king and his forces return to their own land where He will make Sennacherib "fall by the sword." The Assyrian king again taunts Hezekiah and blasphemes against God. Hezekiah prays to the Lord that He save them from the Assyrians and show the Assyrians His might. Isaiah comes to Hezekiah to tell him that God has heard his prayer and will answer it—the city will be defended by Him. That night an angel kills 185,000 of the Assyrian soldiers, and shortly thereafter Sennacherib returns home. One day while he is worshiping he is killed by two of his sons, and a third, Esarhaddon, rules in his stead.

HEZEKIAH'S SICKNESS AND DEATH; THE REIGNS OF MANASSEH, AMON, AND JOSIAH; THE DISCOVERY OF THE BOOK OF LAWS; JOSIAH'S REFORMS, 20-23:20. Hezekiah is very ill and Isaiah comes to tell him he is to die. Hezekiah then prays to the Lord and begs Him to grant him his life, reminding Him of how true to the ways of the Lord he had been. The Lord hears him and tells him that He will heal him and add fifteen years to his life. The sign of this is that Isaiah makes the sun move back ten degrees in its course. The son of the king of Babylon hears that Hezekiah is sick and comes to visit him. Hezekiah shows him and his companions all his treasures. When they leave Isaiah comes to Hezekiah and asks him what he has shown his visitors. When he tells him the prophet says that the Lord has said that one day all these things shall belong to the Babylonians, and that Hezekiah's sons will be captured and made eunuchs in the palace of the king of Babylon. When Hezekiah

dies, his son Manasseh reigns. Manasseh rules for fifty-five years and is an extremely wicked king. He resurrects many pagan rituals and actually practices them himself. The Lord, in great anger, tells the prophets that He is forsaking Judah and will make her suffer enormously for her perfidy. When Manasseh dies his son, Amon, ascends the throne. He is as wicked as his father and he is slain by his servants. In turn, the people slay those who killed him and make his son Josiah king. Josiah reigns for thirty-one years in Jerusalem; he is a very good king. He tells his servants to go to the priest Hilkiah to find out how much silver the people have deposited in the Temple, and then to have the Temple repaired. Hilkiah finds in the Temple the Book of the Law. The king reads it and tears his clothes in supplication to the Lord. He sends his servants to the prophetess Huldah to ask about the book and about the fact that the Hebrew fathers did not live by its word. Huldah tells the servants that God says that He will forsake the people for their evil ways. He will not, however, forsake the king of Judah because he is pure of heart and he has humbled himself before the Lord. Josiah reads the Book of the Law to all the people and all join in a covenant to obey and worship God. Josiah institutes sweeping and thoroughgoing reforms—all pagan practices, symbols, and rituals are done away with, and all the pagan priests slain.

THE PASSOVER KEPT; THE LORD'S PERSISTENT ANGER AGAINST JUDAH; THE DEATH OF JOSIAH; THE REIGN OF JEHOAHAZ; JEHOIACHIN AND THE NOBLES TAKEN CAPTIVE TO BABYLON; THE REIGN OF ZEDEKIAH, 23:21-24:20. The Passover is observed in a very wonderful way. There has never before been a king as good as Josiah. (In general, scholars believe that the first version of the Book of Kings ended here.) Neither before nor after him was there any as examplary as he was. Despite Josiah's goodness the Lord persists in his determination to rout Judah as he had routed Israel. When Josiah dies he is succeeded by his son Jehoahaz. Jehoahaz reigns only three months when he is dethroned by the Pharaoh and taken to Egypt where he dies. The Pharaoh makes Jehoahaz's son, Eliakim, ruler in his father's stead, and he extracts great tribute from him. He changes Elaikim's name to Jehoiakim. Jehoiakim taxes the people heavily to meet the Pharaoh's demands. Jehoiakim rules for eleven years and he is a bad king. During his reign the country is attacked, in keeping with the word of the Lord, by many nations. Jehoiakim dies and his son Jehoiachin ascends the throne. Jehoiachin is an evil ruler. He is attacked by the Babylonians and captured along with his family. Nebuchadnezzar, the king of Babylon, and his men plunder the Temple and desecrate the holy objects therein, and then transport all the people of Jerusalem to Babylon. Nebuchadnezzar appoints Jehoiachin's uncle Mattaniah, whose name he changes to Zedekiah, king in Jehoiachin's stead. Zedekiah reigns eleven years and is a wicked king. He rebels against Babylon.

THE FALL OF JERUSALEM; THE CAPTIVITY OF JUDAH; THE REMNANT FLEE TO EGYPT; JEHOIACHIN RELEASED AND HONORED IN BABYLON, 25. Nebuchadnezzar once again attacks Jerusalem. In time there is a famine within the city and the walls of the city are breached. Zedekiah runs away but he is soon captured and taken to Babylon, having seen his children killed in front of his eyes and then having been blinded. The Babylonians then come and destroy the Temple and the city. Only the poor are permitted to remain; the others are taken to Babylon. Nebuchadnezzar appoints a man named Gedaliah to rule those left in Judah. Gedaliah is murdered. As a result, many people are afraid and flee to Egypt. Thirty-seven years after Jehoiachin was captured, he is released by the Babylonian king Evilmerodach. The king treats him well and accords him his proper royal status.

FIRST AND SECOND CHRONICLES

First and Second Chronicles, probably written between 350 and 250 B.C., are largely recapitulations of the historical material to be found in the books of Samuel and Kings. In fact, the author of Chronicles, who also wrote the Books of Ezra and Nehemiah, used Samuel and Kings as sources for his work. (He also used other sources which he himself mentions, for example, *The Book of the Kings of Israel and Judah* (II Chron. 27:7, 35:27, 36:8.) There is, however, some doubt among scholars as to whether these other works ever existed. But whether or not the works mentioned by the Chronicler are the actual sources he consulted, there is little doubt that he did consult some

works other than Samuel and Kings.) The Chronicler was a highly selective writer and it should not be thought that the Books of Chronicles are identical with Samuel and Kings. The Chronicler's outlook was primarily religious and he therefore stresses those events which have a particular religious significance and he gives a religious coloring to historical ones. For example, the most obvious difference between the treatment of certain events in Samuel and Kings and their treatment in Chronicles is the Chronicler's handling of the material concerning David and the building of the Temple. It will be recalled that in the account given in Samuel and Kings, it is to Solomon that the duty and pleasure of constructing the Temple fall; it was David's wish to build it but the privilege was denied to him. In Chronicles, however, the story is presented differently. While it is still Solomon who does the actual building, it is David who does everything else. He allots money for it and has already assembled building materials when he passes on to Solomon the final task. Because (as can more easily be seen in Ezra and Nehemiah) the Chronicler was writing for a people who had returned from exile united more than ever by their religion, he was very intent on maintaining this return to the older, more demanding religious ways. Toward this end he tried to make it seem as though there had been no break in Levitical activities. It is for this reason that the preparations for the building of the Temple are allotted to David; the Chronicler does not want to admit the existence of a gap of time as large as that between David and Solomon (a generation) in the carrying out of major religious functions. He wants to emphasize the constancy or religious ritual and practice throughout the history of Israel. It is also toward this end that the entire Book of Judges is omitted from Chronicles and the northern kings are completely ignored. Because the period spoken of in Judges was one of great unrest, and consequently of religious unheaval, and because the northern kings were generally evil in their ways, and thus untrue to Yahweh, the Chronicler chooses to ignore them. He is thus able to make it seem as though the life — that is, the religious life — of Israel had progressed continuously and smoothly from the time of the founding of the Hebrew nation.

SUMMARY OF I CHRONICLES

GENEALOGIES AND LISTS, 1-9. Lists are given of the descendants of Adam, Shem, Ishmael, Esau, Israel, Judah, David, Solomon, each of the twelve tribes, those who returned from Babylon, and the genealogy of Saul.

DEATH OF SAUL AND THE ADVENT OF DAVID, 10-16. The historical narrative picks up with the death of Saul and his sons at the battle of Mount Gilboa. Their deaths are seen as retribution for their sins. David is anointed king, and he captures Zion (Jerusalem). Next there is a list of David's warriors. The Ark is to be brought to Jerusalem. Uzza touches the Ark and dies. Hiram, king of Tyre, recognizes David. David's children are born at Jerusalem. David defeats the Philistines, and the Ark is finally carried to Jerusalem. There is a record of the Levites who provided the music at the installation of the Ark in the tent David has made for it. David sings a psalm of thanksgiving. There is a list of the Levites appointed for the Ark.

GOD'S COVENANT WITH DAVID, 17-21. God tells Nathan the prophet to bid David construct a house for the Lord. God promises to watch over David and his people. David extends his kingdom, triumphing over the Edomites, the Syrians, the Moabites, and the Ammonites. He captures Rabbah. David orders a census taken of the people, which displeases God (see comment on this in summary of II Samuel). A plague breaks out, which is stopped only when David builds an altar to the Lord.

THE PREPARATIONS FOR THE TEMPLE, 22-27. Before his death, David makes careful preparations for the construction of the Temple. He entrusts the task to Solomon. The Temple is to be as beautiful and splendid as man can make it. The divisions and duties of the Levites are given, along with lists of the porters, overseers, musicians, and officers of the kingdom.

SOLOMON SUCCEEDS DAVID, 28-29.

David gathers all the leaders of Israel and tells them that the Lord has chosen Solomon to rule over Israel and to build the Temple. He tells them to obey the word of God, and he gives Solomon the plans for the Temple. The people offer to serve in the building of the Temple. They offer sacrifices of thanksgiving to the Lord. The Lord makes Solomon great. David dies, and Solomon rules in his place.

(The Chronicler's portrayal of David is a very biased one. As a clergyman, his primary interest is in those actions and qualities of David which make that great king appear as a highly religious man of God. A comparison of the David depicted in Samuel-Kings with the David in Chronicles will provide a fascinating revelation of how the Chronicler used his materials.)

SUMMARY OF II CHRONICLES

SOLOMON'S PRAYER, 1-5.

Solomon offers up a great sacrifice to God. God tells him he may have anything he wishes. Solomon asks for wisdom. God is pleased at Solomon's wish and grants it; He gives him riches and power besides. Solomon trades in horses and chariots. Solomon makes an agreement with Huram (also called Hiram), king of Tyre, for timber for the Temple. He begins the construction of the Temple, and there follows a detailed account of the interior and furnishings of the building. Solomon brings the Ark into the Temple amid great and splendid ceremony.

THE DEDICATION OF THE TEMPLE, 6-7.

The Temple is dedicated. Solomon offers up a prayer that the Lord will always be willing to hear and grant the prayers of Israel. He offers a magnificent sacrifice, which is accepted by the Lord. God comes to Solomon at night and says that He will dwell in the Temple forever, and that He will always listen to prayer made there if the people follow His commandments. If, however, they disobey, He will then leave the Temple, and misfortune will come upon the people.

SOLOMON'S FURTHER ACTIVITIES, 8-9.

Solomon extends his empire and receives tribute from many of the surrounding peoples. The Queen of Sheba comes to Jerusalem. She asks him many difficult questions, but he answers them all. She and Huram of Tyre give Solomon many rich gifts. After a reign of forty years Solomon dies, and Rehoboam becomes king.

ISRAEL'S REVOLT, 10-12.

Rehoboam disregards the wise counsel of his fathers' ministers and oppresses the people. Under the leadership of Jeroboam, Rehoboam's brother, Israel (as opposed to Judah) rebels. Rehoboam, leading the armies of Judah and Benjamin, is about to attack his brother when God tells him to stop. Rehoboam builds up Judah. The Levites come to Jerusalem. Rehoboam forsakes the word of God and is punished—Judah is invaded by Shishak, king of Egypt. Shemaiah the prophet comes to Rehoboam and his princes with a message from the Lord. He tells them they are being punished for their wickedness, and they repent. When the Lord sees them humbled, He decides not to destroy them. Nevertheless, Shishak loots the Temple of the treasures that Solomon had installed there. Rehoboam remains king of Judah and he rules for seventeen years. Rehoboam and Jeroboam fight continually. Rehoboam dies.

THE REIGN OF ABIJAH, 13.

Abijah (also called Abijann in I Kings 15), the son of Rehoboam, becomes king. He, too, wars with Jeroboam. Abijah wins a great victory over Jeroboam.

THE REIGN OF ASA, 14-16.

Abijah dies and Asa, his son, succeeds him. Asa is a good king: he suppresses idol worship and causes Judah to return to the ways of its fathers in religion. Judah is peaceful and prosperous. Asa triumphs over the Ethiopians. Azariah the prophet tells Asa to continue to be strong and forthright in his purification of the religion of the people. God will help him if he battles against the idols. He is encouraged by this prophecy and destroys the idols. Asa's reign is peaceful until Baasha, king of Israel, threatens Judah. Then Asa makes an alliance with Benhadad, king of Syria, and thereby frightens Baasha into becoming peaceful. Hanani the prophet rebukes Asa for relying on Benhadad instead of on the Lord. Asa imprisons Hanani and oppresses some of the people. He dies after a reign of forty-one years.

THE REIGN OF JEHOSHAPHAT, 17-20.

Jehoshaphat, the son of Asa, assumes the throne. He strengthens his defenses against Israel and prospers. He sends learned men to teach the word of God throughout Judah. He receives tribute from the surrounding nations. Jehoshaphat makes an alliance with Ahab, king of Israel. Ahab asks him to join forces so that they might fight together against an enemy of Ahab's, and Jehoshaphat asks a prophet of the Lord what he should do. The prophet, Micaiah, tells him that he and Ahab will be defeated, but no one believes the prophecy. They fight against the Syrians and the prophecy is fulfilled: the Syrians triumph and Ahab is killed. Jehoshaphat returns to Jerusalem, where he is rebuked for his conduct by the prophet Jehu. The king appoints judges for the people. The Moabites and the Ammonites make war upon Judah, and Jehoshaphat prays to the Lord for help. The Lord answers his prayers and crushes the Moabites and the Ammonites. Jehoshaphat dies after a generally prosperous reign of twenty-five years.

THE REIGN OF JEHORAM, 21.

Jehoram, the son of Jehoshaphat, becomes king. He kills his brothers and all others who could be potential rivals. His reign is wicked but the Lord does not destroy Judah because of the covenant He had made with David. The Edomites revolt against Judah and they are defeated. Elijah the prophet warns Jehoram that because of his wickedness he and his people will suffer from a great plague. The Philistines and Arabians revolt and invade Judah. They loot the king's palace and kill all his sons but one — the youngest. Jehoram soon dies of a painful disease after a reign of eight years.

THE REIGN OF AHAZIAH, 22-23.

Ahaziah, the sole surviving son of Jehoram, is made king. He receives bad advice from his counselors and especially from his mother, Athaliah —namely, to ally himself with Jehoram, king of Israel, against Syria. He does so and is defeated. Jehu kills Ahaziah. When Athaliah learns that her son is dead, she kills all the rest of the royal house of Judah, but the young boy Joash is hidden from her. She takes the throne. After seven years of her reign, the priest Jehoiada leads a revolt. He overthrows Athaliah, kills her, and crowns Joash, the rightful king.

THE REIGN OF JOASH, 24.

Joash becomes king at the age of seven and reigns for forty years. Then he decides to repair the Temple. He makes a public collection, to which the entire nation contributes, and the work is done. Jehoiada dies, and the people turn away from God. Jehoiada's son Zechariah tries to call them back to the true way, but Joash kills him. For this wickedness the Lord permits the Syrians to defeat Judah. Joash is killed by his servants, and his son Amaziah comes to the throne.

THE REIGN OF AMAZIAH, 25. Amaziah hires an army of soldiers from Israel but is warned by a prophet not to use them because Israel is not favored by the Lord. He therefore sends home the Israelites, who are very dissatisfied and attacks Seir (Edom) himself. He defeats Seir, but meanwhile the Israelite army had not gone home but instead had attacked the cities of Judah. Amaziah brings back with him the gods of the Edomites and worships them. God is angry with him, and a prophet tells him he will surely be destroyed. Amaziah now determines to avenge himself on Israel and clashes with them. Israel wins, and Amaziah is killed.

THE REIGN OF UZZIAH, 26. Uzziah (Amaziah's son) obeys the Lord and strengthens Judah. He defeats the Philistines and several other peoples. In his strength he goes too far: he attempts to burn incense in the Temple, which task was reserved for the priests only. The priests oppose him and he is stricken with leprosy, from which he suffers to the day of his death.

THE REIGN OF JOTHAM, 27. Uzziah's son, Jotham, becomes king. His reign is generally good; he builds cities and strengthens the nation. He dies and Ahaz takes the throne.

THE REIGN OF AHAZ, 28. Ahaz worships idols and is punished by God. The Syrians defeat Judah and take away many of its people, and Israel wins an even greater victory over Judah. However, the captives taken by Israel are returned. Ahaz is beset by enemies on every side, but he never thinks to call on the Lord for aid. Instead he turns to idols, for which he is severely punished. He dies, and his son Hezekiah comes to the throne.

THE REIGN OF HEZEKIAH, 29-32. Hezekiah begins his reign by cleansing the Temple and restoring the Temple worship, which had become corrupted by the practices of the preceding kings. Sacrifices are offered, and there is general rejoicing. Hezekiah sends letters to all Israel and Judah asking them to come to Jerusalem to celebrate the Passover. The invitation is scorned by many; nevertheless, a great assembly of people gathers in Jerusalem. Among them are many who have not sanctified themselves as the law prescribes. Hezekiah prays to the Lord that their offerings will be accepted too, because they have shown their good intentions in coming to observe Passover according to the law. God answers the king's prayers. The people receive the priestly blessing and then go out and destroy all the idols. Hezekiah makes sure that the people donate enough for the priests and Levites to live on. Then Sennacherib, king of Assyria, invades Judah. Hezekiah strengthens Jerusalem and prepares for war. Sennacherib sends men to Jerusalem to talk against Hezekiah and his plan of trusting in the Lord. They attempt to lower the people's confidence in him, but Sennacherib's plans are frustrated. The Lord answers Hezekiah's prayers and crushes the Assyrians—Judah is saved. The rest of Hezekiah's reign is prosperous. He dies and Manasseh, his son, rules in his place.

THE REIGNS OF MANASSEH AND AMON, 33. Manasseh is an evil king. He undoes all the good work that his father had done: he brings back the idols and even sets them up in the Temple; he employs witchcraft and magic, etc. As a punishment, Manasseh is taken prisoner by the Assyrians and carried away to Assyria. There he humbles himself before the Lord. The Lord pardons him and returns him to Judah. There he returns to righteousness, restoring the worship in the Temple and throwing out the idols. Manasseh dies and his son Amon becomes king. Amon turns to idols and is killed by his servants, who revolt against him. Amon is succeeded by his son Josiah.

THE REIGN OF JOSIAH, 34-35.

Although young, Josiah reforms the worship of Judah. He cleanses the Temple, smashes the idols, and returns his people to the ways of God. In the process of repairing the Temple, a book of the law (what we now call the Book of Deuteronomy) is found. When it is read to the king, he expresses great sorrow because it is clear that the people have departed from the true observance of the word of God. Huldah the prophetess announces that Lord is very angry with the people of Judah because of their evil actions. The Lord, however, is not angry with Josiah because he at least is trying to restore purity in the religion of the nation. Then Josiah causes the newly found book to be read to the entire people. He makes a covenant with the Lord to obey His commandments, and the people of Jerusalem subscribe to it as well. Josiah keeps the Passover at the appointed time, and he distributes Passover offering to all the people.

Josiah is killed in action against the Egyptians. He is followed on the throne by his son Jehoahaz.

THE REIGNS OF JEHOAHAZ, JEHOIAKIM, JEHOIACHIN, AND ZEDEKIAH, 36.

Jehoahaz reigns only three months when he is deposed by the king of Egypt, who places Jehoahaz's brother Eliakim on the throne. Eliakim reigns under the name of Jehoiakim. Jehoiakim is a wicked king and is vanquished by Nebuchadnezzar, king of Babylonia, who carries him off in chains to Babylon. He is succeeded by his son Jehoiachin, who reigns only three months when he too is taken away to Babylonia. Nebuchadnezzar makes Zedekiah, the brother of Jehoiachin, king of Judah. He rebels against the Babylonians, but he does not turn to the Lord for aid and he does much that is evil. The Lord sends prophets to him to warn him of impending disaster, but Zedekiah does not listen to them. Then the Babylonians return, capture Jerusalem and burn it, loot the Temple, and carry away the survivors to Babylon. The Book of Chronicles closes with a repetition of the first four chapters of the book of Ezra. (This is a device used by the Chronicler and other biblical writers to give a feeling of continuity to their work.)

EZRA AND NEHEMIAH

The Books of Ezra and Nehemiah are concerned mainly with events that occurred after the Babylonian Exile. While we can determine how the writer of Chronicles used his sources, by comparing his work to the Books of Samuel and Kings, we have no corresponding documents to reveal his use of sources in Ezra-Nehemiah. It is probable that the writer of the Books of Chronicles (of which Ezra and Nehemiah were once parts) had documents and traditions concerning the two men, and used them not so much to write history

as to complete his task of showing how the Temple and its officers stemmed from an ancient tradition, which survived down to the time of the Chronicler himself. (As a result, we know very little of Ezra and Nehemiah as men.) One may well say that these two books exist as explanations of two important events: how the wall around Jerusalem came to be built (Nehemiah) and how the religious tradition was revived in Jerusalem (Ezra). There are several historical problems arising from the study of these books. For instance, the date given in Ezra 7 is the seventh year of the reign of Artaxerxes. Unfortunately, there were two kings named Artaxerxes, and so the year in question could be either 458 B.C. or 398 B.C. Then too, there is the puzzling and unexplained repetition of the list in Ezra 2 and Neh. 7. These questions have not and perhaps cannot ever be resolved.

SUMMARY OF THE BOOK OF EZRA

THE PROCLAMATION OF CYRUS, 1-4. The Lord stirs the spirit of Cyrus, the king of Persia, to have a temple built for Him in Jerusalem. Cyrus proclaims that all of the children of Israel may return to Jerusalem to engage in the holy work. Then the Hebrews gather themselves together, with all their property, and prepare to return. There follows a list of those who made the trip back to the land of their father. The children of Israel come to Jerusalem and immediately set about rebuilding the Temple. The enemies of the Israelites falsely inform the king of Persia (now Artaxerxes) that the Israelites are planning a rebellion and that the rebuilding of Jerusalem should therefore be stopped. Artaxerxes orders that the work be halted.

THE TEMPLE REBUILT, 5-6. The Persian governor of the province comes to the Jews and asks them by what authority they are rebuilding the Temple. They tell him that it is by proclamation of King Cyrus. The governor writes to the king (now Darius) and Darius confirms Cyrus's proclamation. The work can now go on. Soon the Temple is completed and dedicated.

EZRA COMES TO JERUSALEM, 7-10. Ezra the scribe comes to Jerusalem in the reign of Artaxerxes with full power to reform the religious practices of the Jews and to set up a new government based on religious rules. Chapter 8 contains a list of those who came back to Israel with Ezra. Ezra is horrified when he discovers how many of the Israelites have taken non-Jewish wives, and he prays to God that the nation may be spared the punishment of this terrible disobedience of God's word. Ezra and the priests and other leaders resolve to cast the foreign wives out. Chapter 10 closes with a list of those who had taken such foreign wives.

SUMMARY OF THE BOOK OF NEHEMIAH

NEHEMIAH'S PRAYER FOR JERUSALEM, 1-5. Nehemiah learns of the plight of the Jews in Jerusalem. He is the cup-bearer to Artaxerxes, and the king asks him why he is sad. Nehemiah says it is because the land of his ancestors is desolate. The king grants him permission to go to Jerusalem and restore the holy places there, and especially the walls of the city. There follows a list of the sections of the wall that were erected and the names of the workers involved. The workers have to carry arms because they are continually being attacked by their enemies, the Arabians (i.e., the Samaritans) and the Ammonites. The people cry out to Nehemiah because of their great debts and the excessive interest they must pay. He puts an end to usury. He is noble and unselfish, for he takes no salary for all the work he does as director of the rebuilding of the walls.

THE PLOTS OF THE ADVER-SARIES, 6-10. The Arabians and the Ammonites again try to trick Nehemiah, but he outwits them. Finally the wall is finished. Nehemiah appoints rulers for Jerusalem. Next comes a long lsit of those who returned from Babylon, basically the same list as in Ezra 2. Ezra reads the Law of Moses and publicly explains its meaning to the people. They are at first frightened, but Ezra encourages and comforts them. The nation celebrates the Feast of Tabernacles (Succoth). A day of solemn fasting is appointed, and the people gather together to confess their sins. A short history of the Jewish people is given and a prayer is made to the Al-

mighty. The nation makes a covenant with the Lord to keep His law, and chapter 10 lists the names of those who signed it.

RESIDENTS OF THE CITIES, 11-13. Chapters 11 and 12 set forth the list of those who resided in Jerusalem and in the other settlements and also of the priests and the Levites. The ceremonies surrounding the dedication of the wall are described. Nehemiah leaves Jerusalem and then returns there. When he comes back he finds conditions are very bad, and he sets about correcting them. He repurifies the Temple, enforces the Sabbath laws, and once again forbids mixed marriages.

ESTHER

The Book of Esther is remarkable in many ways. It is the only book in the Bible that does not mention the name of God. The story it tells is one that seems to commend revenge, which the Pentateuch forbids. Moreover, Esther becomes the concubine of the king before she is made queen, and of course she marries a non-Jew. All these qualities have caused many people through the centuries to think that the book should not be part of the Bible. This idea arises from the misconception that the Old Testament is a book only about religion; in fact, there are many different kinds of works in the Bible (see General Introduction). Esther is a short story, told with the greatest skill, about the salvation of the Jewish people from the hands of a wicked oppressor. The story was written very

late, perhaps about 150 B.C. It takes place in Persia, but inspection of Persian records (of which we have very many) offers no historical confirmation of the events recounted in the book. Therefore Esther should probably not be thought of as history but rather as a story bound up with the celebration of Purim. As the Book of Esther indicates, Purim was a holiday celebrated by the Jews of Persia. Its observance gradually spread westward, and the Book of Esther was important in that westward movement. Every year, on Purim, the entire Book of Esther is read aloud in the synagogue. Purim (Hebrew for "lots," because Haman chose the day for the destruction of the Jewish people by lot) is a joyous holiday, with a near-carnival atmosphere.

SUMMARY OF THE BOOK OF ESTHER

QUEEN VASHTI DEFIES KING AHASUERUS, 1-2. Ahasuerus, king of the vast Persian empire, holds a feast for all his nobles. After seven days of merry-making he commands his queen, Vashti, to appear and

show her beauty to the assembled nobility. She refuses to come. The king's wise men advise him not to let this disobedience go unpunished because, otherwise, wives will disobey their husbands throughout the kingdom. They counsel him to choose another queen. He agrees, and a giant competition is held all over the empire to find the new queen. One of the girls in this contest is Esther, a young Jewish maiden who has been brought up by her cousin Mordecai. Upon the advice of Mordecai, she tells no one that she is Jewish. Esther is loved by Ahasuerus, and he decides that she shall be his queen. At this time Mordecai overhears a plot against the king. He tells Esther, who tells the king. The plotters are caught, and the event is recorded in the official records.

HAMAN'S PLOT, 3-4. Haman is made prime minister of the realm. Everyone bows to him except Mordecai. When Haman learns that Mordecai is a Jew, he decides to destroy not only Mordecai but the entire Jewish people. Haman tells the king that there is a people who keep themselves apart from everyone else and who do not observe the laws. He asks permission to destroy this people, which Ahasuerus grants. Haman then writes to the governors of all the provinces that the Jews are to be killed on the thirteenth day of the month of Adar. This letter is published, so that the entire empire knows what is to occur. When Mordecai hears the news, he, like the rest of the Jews, mourns and fasts. Mordecai tells Esther about Haman's plan, and he tells her that she will not escape death even though she is the queen. She tells Mordecai to gather all the Jews in the capital city, Shushan, and have them fast for three days; meanwhile she will speak to the king.

ESTHER'S BANQUET, 5-7. Esther invites the king and Haman to a banquet. Haman is proud that he alone has been invited to the banquet, but he is still angry at the disrespect shown him by Mordecai. Haman's wife suggests to him that a gallows be erected, and that Haman ask the king to order that Mordecai be hanged. The gallows is put up.

That night the king cannot sleep. He commands that the official chronicles be read aloud. When he hears once more of the plot that Mordecai frustrated, he asks what reward was given to him. He is told that he received nothing. The king asks who is in the court. Haman is there, for he has come to ask that Mordecai be hanged. The king asks him what he thinks should be done for the man whom the king favors. Haman, thinking the king is referring to himself, says that he should be handsomely and publicly rewarded. The king agrees and tells Haman that the man in question is Mordecai. He orders Haman to honor Mordecai as he proposed. Haman obeys, and then goes home and tells his wife what has happened. She says that she thinks that the tide of events has changed, and that Mordecai will overcome Haman. He goes to the banquet. At the banquet Esther appeals to the king for her life and the lives of all her people. The king asks who has threatened her. She accuses Haman, and the king is furious. He orders that Haman be hanged on the gallows that was prepared for Mordecai, and the sentence is carried out.

THE JEWS ARE AUTHORIZED TO RESIST, 8-10. Then Mordecai is brought to the king, who makes him his prime minister. The king authorizes Mordecai to write to the Jews in all the provinces saying that they have the right to resist those who will try to kill them on the thirteenth of Adar. This letter is published all over the empire, and the Jews are made very happy. When the day comes, the Jews, aided by the royal armies, destroy their enemies. Mordecai writes to the Jews all over the Empire that they should celebrate each year on the fourteenth and fifteenth days of Adar their deliverance from destruction. The holiday is to be called Purim, the feast of lots, after the lots that Haman had cast to destroy them. The holiday is confirmed by royal decree, and Mordecai becomes great in the service of the king.

WISDOM LITERATURE

Three of the books of the Old Testament—Proverbs, Job, and Ecclesiastes—are examples of that type of ancient literature called "wisdom literature." Wisdom literature was produced not by prophets (who wrote prophecy) or by priests (who wrote law) but by wise men or sages (see Jer. 18:18, where these three classes of men are given equal rank). This kind of writing was international in scope; in fact, it seems to have flourished most extensively in Egypt (the Egyptian influence is directly visible in Prov. 22:17-23:14, which closely parallel in form and content and earlier Egyptian wisdom book). We have wisdom books as well from Babylonia, and apparently even the small nation of Edom was known for its sages (see Obad. 8 and Jer. 49:7). Ancient Israel, because of its central geographic position, came in contact with this wisdom tradition early. It will be recalled that Solomon exchanged wisdom with the Queen of Sheba and King Hiram of Tyre (I Kings 10:1).

Wisdom literature is the result of sober and deep reflection by wise men on the perennial problems of human existence. Because these problems are the same everywhere, one of the distinguishing characteristics of this literature is its detachment from any particular time or place. (In fact, there are no allusions to specific persons, places, or events in Israelite history at all, if we exclude the brief mention of Solomon in Ecclesiastes.) Thus, what we have seen to be primary throughout the Bible until now — the overriding awareness of being the chosen people, utterly unique among all the nations of the world—is strikingly absent here. The wisdom books focus on the individual, not the national grouping. As a result of this detachment, we find in these books a singular dearth of

exhortations to worship and virtually a complete lack of references to religious institutions or practices. This is all the more remarkable because the wisdom books were composed in the post-exilic period, when life in Palestine was characterized by a great revival of religious feeling and activity. This rise in the importance of religion, symbolized by the reconstruction of the Temple, may have come about because the dispersion of the Jews undermined their feelings of nationalism; in exile they had been kept together not so much by a common far-off birthplace as by a common faith which governed their every action. It is apparent, therefore, that despite the religious fervor surrounding them, the wisdom writers, in their effort to deal with more universal and timeless things, felt free to range beyond specifically religious issues. (It is noteworthy that although God is mentioned in the wisdom books, nothing whatever is made of any special relationship between Him and His people.)

Solomon has traditionally been thought of as the source of the wisdom of Israel. He was supposed to have been the author of the Books of Proverbs, Ecclesiastes, the Song of Songs (one of the main reasons the latter two of these were included in the canon at all was that they were said to have been written by Solomon), and the Wisdom of Solomon and other apocryphal books. We cannot know how much, if any, of this material was actually composed by him. But whether or not any of this literature can really claim Solomon as its author, there is good reason to think that it owes its existence in large measure to the cultural climate which prevailed during his reign. Despite the fact that wisdom literature flowered after the exile, it is probable that it owes its beginnings as a form to Solomon's era. His reign was marked by a singular freedom from insularity and provinciality. Under his leadership, the country developed a most cosmopolitan culture and grew and prospered in many ways. It is therefore easy to understand why the Israelites came to attribute to Solomon so many of the sage utterances of the wisdom books.

THE BOOK OF JOB

(For background, see introductory material on wisdom literature above.)

FORM OF THE WORK. The Book of Job consists of a prologue (chaps. 1-2) and an epilogue (42:7-17), both in prose, which frame the body of the text (3—42:6), in verse. It is generally thought that the prose portions of the work were written at a later time and by a different hand than the rest of the book. It will be noted that there are no references within the body of the book to the events recounted in the prologue.

Although some writers have said that the Book of Job is really a drama (thus showing Greek influence), this theory must be rejected. There is no development, either of character or situation, leading to a climax, in Job; in fact, the book is a dialogue, a form which was often employed in ancient works (although Job is the only example of it in the *O.T.*). This dialogue has a cyclical structure. There are three cycles of discussion, in each of which Job and his three friends speak at length. There is no dramatic exchange; no speaker interrupts any other. The book is meditative, not theatrical.

In each of the cycles, the typical pattern is as follows: each of the friends speaks to Job and is answered by him. (The text of the third cycle is disordered because of editorial changes and therefore does not conform to this pattern.)

THEMES. The Book of Job is concerned with the problems of suffering and justice—why do the evil prosper and the good decline? A consideration of these great, perennial questions leads to a larger one—what is the nature of the relation of man to God? Job's friends put forth the orthodox view that the relation is knowable and definite. If man obeys God's word, then God will reward him with material wealth; if he disobeys, then God will punish him. However, Job knows in his innermost being that his punishment has been inflicted unjustly because he has not sinned. His friends see only the surface of things, and decide that he must have sinned or else he would not be suffering as he is. Job seeks a confrontation with God; he must know the reason for his suffering, even though he might die in the attempt. He gets what he asks for—the Lord responds to his questionings. But the Lord's answers are really no answers at all; they serve to make further discussion impossible. God says that man can never understand the reasons for Divine actions, and the result of the Book of Job is to re-establish the relation of God to man on a new basis. God is unknowable to man; He is impossibly remote and alien. The friends are rebuked for their narrow ideas, and Job is awed into humble self-abasement.

SUMMARY OF THE BOOK OF JOB

PROLOGUE, 1-2. The prologue introduces Job and gives us a brief summary of his life. First, note that Job is not a Hebrew but an inhabitant of the land of Uz—he is one of the "children of the East." The story is told about an Uzite probably to avoid having Job's heretical statements placed in the mouth of a Hebrew. In any event, Job is "perfect and upright"; he does no evil and is rewarded by the Lord with great wealth. The scene then shifts to Heaven. The angels congregate around the throne of the Lord, and among them is "Satan." ("Satan" is here *not* the Devil; the word "satan" in Hebrew means "adversary" and is used throughout with the definite article—"*the* Satan," "the adversary." The appearance of a Satan shows that Job was written at a late date, after the Hebrews had been exposed (during the Babylonian Exile) to Persian religion, which contains the idea of a God of goodness and a God of evil.) The Lord asks Satan whether there is anyone on earth who compares with Job for moral uprightness. Satan replies that Job's perfection is not to be marveled at because, after all, God rewards him with great material prosperity. (The implication is, of course, that the relation between God and man is contractual in nature—that is, if man keeps his side of the agreement, i.e., obeys God's commandments and does not sin, then God in turn is bound to reward man.) Satan says that Job will not be so upright if God takes away all that He has given. Then, says Satan, Job will curse God to His face. God takes up Satan's challenge; He permits Satan to do what he will with Job's possessions, so long as Job is spared physically. Then, in a series of rapid strokes, Job's wealth is wiped out. He loses his cattle and his children

(the author of Job links them together as forms of wealth). Job accepts these calamities as God's judgment and makes no complaint: "Naked came I out of my mother's womb, and naked shall I return thither: the Lord gave and the Lord hath taken away; blessed be the name of the Lord." Again the scene shifts to Heaven. God asks Satan how he explains Job's pious behavior now. Satan replies that Job's afflictions have thus far been only superficial because they have not touched his physical being: "all that a man hath will he give for his life." But, says Satan, let God only smite Job in his body, and then he will curse the Lord to His face. The Lord agrees to this challenge, and gives Job into Satan's hand, with the sole condition that Job's life be spared. Then Satan causes Job to be covered from head to toe with a painful disease (usually translated as "boils," but the word is not clear). At this point, Job's wife tells him to "curse God and die," but he rebukes his wife and remains steadfast in his piety. Now Job's three friends—Eliphaz, Bildad, and Zophar—arrive to comfort him. They see him from far off and do not recognize him at first, so greatly has he changed from his prosperous days. Out of compassion for him, they sit on the ground with him for seven days, and no one says a word.

THE FIRST CYCLE: JOB'S LAMENT, 3. Job finally breaks the silence by cursing the day he was born. He asks why he did not die at birth but instead was permitted to live, only to be afflicted so sorely. He implies (3:23) that God is smiting him by design.

ELIPHAZ REBUKES JOB, 4-5. Eliphaz answers Job with the argument that all the friends will repeat in various guises throughout the book. "Remember, I pray thee who ever perished, being innocent? Or where were the righteous cut off?" That is, Job's friends reason backwards: since good men prosper and wicked men are punished, then if Job is punished, he must have sinned. And, therefore, since Job must have sinned, he should "despise not the chastening of Almighty," (5:17b) because the Lord is doing it only for Job's good.

JOB'S REPLY, 6-7. Job repeats his desire to be delivered from his suffering by death. He turns to his friends and says that they are mistaken in their ideas. He maintains that his suffering has been undeserved. He now addresses himself to God. He says that since he cannot live much longer, he will not keep silent but instead will continue to insist upon his innocence. He asks God why He has afflicted him so bitterly, and without cause.

BILDAD'S ANSWER, 8. Bildad reaffirms what Eliphaz has said. If Job is suffering, then he must have done something to deserve it: "Behold, God will not cast away a perfect man, neither will He help the evildoers."

JOB'S REPLY, 9-10. Job states for the first time his desire to obtain an accounting from God. He says that his complaints are hopeless because God is not a man and therefore cannot be confronted. However, if somehow God would consent to have His acts judged, and if He would consent to treat Job as an equal, then Job would press his demands for an accounting (9:34-35). If, Job continues, he could get an accounting from God, he would ask Him the reasons He has decided to destroy him even though "thou knowest that I am not wicked" (10:7a).

ZOPHAR'S COMMENT, 11. Zophar is angered by what he considers Job's presumption and wishes that the Lord would only speak and recount the full list of Job's sins. He asks Job how he can dare to place himself on an even footing with God, for Job is a mere man while God is almighty.

JOB'S RESPONSE, 12-14. Job first affirms God's power and wisdom. God does, knows, and controls everything; of this he, as well as his friends, is aware. Nevertheless, Job knows himself, and he knows that he has *not* sinned. His faith in the existence and power of God is intact (it never wavers throughout the book), "but I will maintain mine own ways before him." If only God will suspend His wrath against him, Job is willing to put his case to the Lord (13:21-24). Job now muses on the brevity of life (14:1-2).

THE SECOND CYCLE: ELIPHAZ REPRIMANDS JOB, 15. Again Eliphaz rebukes Job for presumption (15:7-9). He reiterates the orthodox view that God rewards the good and punishes the wicked in this life.

JOB ANSWERS, 16-17. Job says that his friends offer him little comfort (16:2b). He feels besieged from all sides: his friends belabor him for his nonexistent sins, and the Lord visits him with painful affliction. Again he wishes he might plead his case directly with God.

BILDAD'S REPLY, 18. Bildad describes the fate of the wicked.

JOB'S RESPONSE TO BILDAD, 19. Just as the friends are growing weary of Job's words, so is he growing tired of theirs. He asks them how long they are going to continue to belabor him. He reasserts his innocence: "I cry aloud, but there is no judgment" (7b). He asks his friends to pity him because God has set His hand against him. The famous passage beginning at verse 25 ("For I know that my Redeemer liveth") is difficult to understand, and the assumption that Job is referring to a messiah is unfounded.

ZOPHAR'S REPLY, 20. Zophar repeats, in different words, what Bildad has given in chapter 18—a description of the fate of the wicked.

JOB'S ANSWER, 21. Job now explicitly challenges his friends' orthodox view that the good prosper and the wicked suffer. He denies that this is in fact the case; on the contrary, observation shows that the reverse is more likely to occur. "Wherefore do the wicked live, become old, yea, are mighty in power?"

THE THIRD CYCLE: ELIPHAZ ACCUSES JOB OF GREAT WICKEDNESS, 22. Eliphaz says that Job in his presumption is very wicked. He begs Job to humble himself and return to the Lord. He reasserts that if Job does so, he will then be rewarded with silver and gold.

JOB'S REPLY, 23-24. Job wishes only that he knew where he might find God so that he could argue his case. He would demand an accounting, but he cannot locate the Almighty. He says that the wicked grow and prosper, and God is seemingly indifferent. He concludes: "And if it not be so now, who will make me a liar, and make my speech nothing worth?"

BILDAD'S RESPONSE, 25. Bildad denies that man can justify himself in the sight of God.

JOB'S REPLY, 26-31. Note here the disarray of the third cycle of speeches. The pattern of a statement by one of the friends, followed by a reply by Job, falls apart here. Scholars have tried to mend matters by assigning sections of these five chapters to various of the friends, but no rearrangement is entirely satisfactory. It is clear that an editor or editors has worked over the original, without much care as to the result. In chapter 26, Job again affirms his faith in the omnipotence of God. Chapter 27 is often assigned to Zophar (who has no speech in this cycle as it now stands) because it seems to be more appropriate to one of the friends than

to Job. It is a restatement of the fate of the wicked (compare chaps. 18 and 20). Chapter 28 is a beautiful hymn to wisdom which is completely out of place here; it has been inserted by the editor. In chapter 29 Job seems to pick up the thread. He recalls his former prosperity and worldly eminence. But now, he says, he is loathsome in all eyes. He again asserts that he has been treated unjustly by God. He insists that he is willing to be judged and, if found wanting, to take the dire consequences.

ELIHU ANSWERS JOB, 32-37. These chapters in which Elihu speaks mark another editorial insertion. Elihu has not appeared until now, and there has been no indication of his existence as a character. His speeches come after Job's words finish (see the end of chapter 31) and before those of the Lord begin. Moreover, it is plain from the style in Hebrew that his speeches were not written by the same author who composed the body of the book. Elihu has been brought in because in the original poem the friends have not answered Job adequately: this much is clear from 32:5. Elihu reinforces the orthodox answer to the exceedingly unorthodox Job, and he is no more successful than they are.

In chapter 32 he is introduced, and his silence up to this point is explained. He is the youngest of those present, and thus has deferred to his elders until he sees that they cannot answer Job. He says that Job is mistaken in thinking that the Lord is unresponsive to Job's pleas. He does answer, but Job does not understand. The Lord communicates with man not only through visions but through the infliction of suffering as well (33:19). The purpose of this suffering is to lead the good man to recognize his error and return to the Lord, whereupon the Lord redeems the sinner. Next Elihu replies to Job's assertion that God has undermined righteousness here on earth because

He permits evildoers to flourish. God, because of His perfect nature, cannot be wrong: therefore it is Job who must be wrong. He says that men who suffer may cry out to God for relief and not be answered; this only shows that they were not worthy of God's favor. In chapters 36 and 37 Elihu reaffirms that God favors men to the extent that their conduct pleases Him. Moreover, the Lord uses punishment as spiritual discipline, and He is mindful of the sinner's reaction when he is punished. The sinner should not complain but instead be thankful that the Lord has been gracious enough to punish him and thus give him a chance, through repentance, to return to Divine favor.

THE LORD REPLIES TO JOB, 38-40:2. Then the Lord answers Job from out of the whirlwind (answering thus from the air, He retains His place above that of man on earth). The Lord's response is really no answer to Job's questions at all. Rather, His speeches deny Job's right to an explanation. Job will merit such an explanation only when he is on the same level with the Lord, i.e., never. The Lord begins by demanding where Job was when He created the universe. Has Job "commanded the morning?" Has Job "entered into the springs of the sea?" Has Job perceived the breadth of the earth?" Can Job do any one of the many things that are possible only to God? Chapter 39 is a further series of questions to Job, these dealing with the animal kingdom. Is the unicorn willing to serve Job? Does the hawk fly by Job's wisdom?

JOB'S RESPONSE, 40:3-5. Job is utterly silenced and awed by the voice of the Lord. He knows he has gone too far, and he says that hereafter he will be silent.

THE LORD'S FURTHER WORDS TO JOB, 40:6-41:34. The Lord continues with more questions to Job. Can he draw out leviathan (a sea monster) with a hook?, etc. He concludes majestically: "Whatsoever is under the whole heaven is mine" (41:11b).

JOB'S REPENTANCE, 42:1-6. Job humbles himself completely before the Lord. He understands that he has spoken of things which he did not comprehend. He had known of the Lord through the words of others; now "mine eye seeth Thee." He repents of his actions in "dust and ashes."

EPILOGUE, 42:7-17. The Lord now rebukes Job's three friends because they "have not spoken of Me the thing that is right, as My servant Job hath." That is, they have erred in giving an incorrect description of God. They are told to offer sacrifices in order to be restored to God's favor. The epilogue concludes with Job regaining twice his former wealth, which marks, by implication, a return to the contractual idea of the relation between God and man—Job receives riches as a reward for his piety and suffering. For this reason, the epilogue (like the prologue) is disappointing and greatly diminishes the impact of the rest of the book. The point of God's questions to Job was that God's ways are *not* man's ways, and that they are *not* comprehensible to man; that until man comes to an understanding of those ways (which time will never come), he cannot succeed in fathoming the order of the world. Thus he cannot enter into a contract with God because he can only know what he is offering to Him and he can never know what he will (not to mention ought to) receive in turn. A man cannot possibly anticipate God's responses to his supplications, or understand those responses when and if they come. It is this that Job comes to understand, and the importance of this realization is seriously undercut when he is compensated *for his suffering*.

THE BOOK OF PSALMS

The Book of Psalms is a collection of one hundred and fifty lyric poems, divided into five sections. The text presents problems. Tradition has it that the Psalms are the work of King David, but this is unlikely. There are, for example, many poems that are labeled as the work of Moses, Solomon, and others (although these labels themselves are not reliable). There is duplication within the collection—psalm 108 reappears as 57: 7-11 and 60:5-12; psalm 70 is identical to 40:13-17; psalm 14 is the double of psalm 53 (in addition, the psalm that appears in I Chron. 16: 8-36 is made up of psalms 105:1-15, 96:1-13, and 106:1, 47-48. Then, too, the divine name in psalms 42 to 83 is Elohim and not Yahweh. These peculiarities of the text make it virtually impossible that the Psalms as we have them are the work of one man, but it does not rule out the possibility that David composed some of them, perhaps the nucleus of the book, and others were added later.

The Psalms are a poetic anthology, with great variations in content and tone. Some poems express the most exalted religious sentiments and seem to have been composed for use in the services in the Temple; others are quite secular in feeling and show no especial connection with ritual or devotion. The best psalms, it may be safely said, mark the lyric high-point of the Old Testament; but there are many undistinguished poems in the collection as well. The psalms have often been printed (in English) as a separate volume (called the Psalter), and have long been widely read as devotional poetry. It is probable that the twenty-third psalm "The Lord is my shepherd") is the best-known piece of the Old Testament.

Nearly all the poems are preceded by inscriptions. Some of these relate to the reputed author—e.g., "A psalm of Asaph" or "A psalm for the sons of Korah"—but, as has been remarked, these are unreliable. It has also been theorized that "Asaph," "Korah," "David," etc., are not the names of the authors at all, but rather the names of various musical groups or guilds which provided music at the Temple. These inscriptions also supply musical directions of a technical nature that are not clearly understood. Several psalms (e.g., 58) are called *"michtams"* (meaning unknown); others are *"maschils,"* which may mean "meditation"; *"selah,"* which occurs often, is unknown.

The scholar who has done the most important work on the Psalms is Hermann Gunkel. His main contribution was his analysis of the poems into various types. He distinguished five main categories. The first is the "hymn," a work originally composed to be sung either by a chorus or a soloist within the setting of the Temple service. Gradually, such poems became detached from a specifically devotional context and were composed as a vehicle for the writer's feelings. Examples of this type are Pss. 7, 19, 29, 65, 68, 96, 98, 100, 103-5, 111, 113-5, 117, 135, 136, and 145-50. The second type is that of the "communal lament." These psalms deal with some disaster which has befallen the community—e.g., war, famine. Apparently the Hebrews would gather on such occasions at the Temple and beseech Yahweh to save them from whatever the threat might be. Examples are Pss. 44, 58, 64, 79, 80, 83, 106, and 125. The third class are the so-called "royal psalms." These all are concerned with a king who seems to have been an Israelite ruler of the pre-exilic period. (Examples: 2, 18, 20, 21, 45, 72, 101, 110, and 132.) The fourth type is the "individual lament," which is similar to the first type with the important difference that these are not communal but individual in character. This kind of psalm is very numerous: 3, 5-7, 13, 17, 22, 25-28, 31, 35, 38-9, 42-3, 51, 54, 57, 59, 61, 63-4, 69-71, 86, 88, 102, 109, 120, 130, 140-3. This group is typified by intense emotion, the supplicant describing how he is sorely beset by enemies. The fifth of the main classifications is that of "individual songs of thanksgiving." This is a smaller group than any already listed, being represented by Pss. 18, 30, 32, 34, 41, 46, 92, 116, 118, and 138. It should be noted that there are psalms elsewhere than in the Psalter, and of these the following fall into this class: the Psalm of Hezekiah (Isa. 38:10-20) and the Prayer of Jonah (Jonah 2:3-10). These categories are not iron-clad; some psalms fall into several groups (and Gunkel has subclasses as well).

THE BOOK OF PROVERBS

(For background, see introductory material on Wisdom Literature above.) The Book of Proverbs is not, as the name implies, simply a collection of proverbs; it is, rather, a group of collections. It has eight component parts, as follows: (1) "The proverbs of Solomon," 1-9; (2) "The proverbs of Solomon," 10:1-22:16; (3) "The words of the wise," 22:17-24:22; (4) "These things also belong to the [sayings of] the wise," 24:23-34; (5) "These are also proverbs of Solomon, which the men of Hezekiah, king of Judah, copied out," 25-29; (6) "The words of Agur the son of Jakeh," 30; (7) "The words of king Lemuel," 31:1-9; (8) an alphabetic poem on the qualities of the good housewife, 31:10-31. The first five of these are associated with the person of Solomon, while the remaining four seem to have non-Israelite origins. Scholars think that the Book of Proverbs represents the result of the coming together of a native Israelite school of wisdom and the teaching of foreign sages. Thus it is generally accepted that the Egyptian wisdom book of Amenemope provided the original of 22:17-23:11, although the borrowing was done with considerable freedom on the part of the Hebrew translator. It is difficult to assign dates to the various collections of proverbs, but it is thought (there is disagreement on this point) that the first collection (1-9) is the oldest, and groups two through five are also pre-exilic.

Every culture has its proverbs—short, pointed statements summing up attitudes or observations. There are many such proverbs here, but there are also longer passages which deal with a single topic and are really short moral essays. Since the Book of Proverbs has no narrative line, a complete synopsis would not be possible in the space here available; instead only a sample (the first nine chapters) will be analyzed.

The book starts with a short, didactic preface, which explains the worth and use of proverbs. Next there is a warning against yielding to the temptation of committing a crime (1:7-19). Then we are introduced to the figure of the personification of wisdom (who reappears frequently). She denounces those who turn away from her (1:20-33). Chapter 2 is concerned with wisdom in its aspect of affording a path to righteousness, and chapter 3 explains the spiritual advantages that wisdom bestows. (Already in these early chapters there is established the opposition between the wise and the wicked which runs throughout the book. For the writers of Proverbs, there are only these two kinds of men; there is no gray area in between, and there is no attention paid to the fact that all men are wise in some of their actions and unwise in others.) Here, wisdom's advantages are described in spiritual terms, but generally this is not the case. The wise man is not only more righteous than the wicked, but he is also more prosperous. The generally secular tone of Proverbs has often been remarked. A father's good advice fills 4:1 to 5:6, and the remainder of chapter 5 is devoted to praise for married life. In chapter 6 the reader is admonished against going bond for someone, against being lazy, and against committting various other sins. The next chapter exhorts against adultery and gives a realistic picture of a harlot alluring a man. In chapter 8 the personification of Wisdom returns, and we are given an idea of the benefits it can bring (e.g., she says both that "wisdom is better than rubies" and "riches and honor are with me"). The last chapter in this first collection of proverbs returns to the contrast between wisdom and foolishness; here they are both personified.

Clearly these chapters are not really unified at all. Instead, they are loosely connected. by the common theme of wisdom, discussed in various ways. It is in the next collection (10: 1-22:16) that we get recognizable

proverbs. Professor Sandmel notes the following characteristics of these proverbs: "brevity, parallelism, the regularity of the form, the cheerfulness of the tone, and lastly but importantly, the secular rather than the religious character." In addition to secular advice there is a tendency to declare that faith is necessary for the good life. The writer of Deuteronomy had applied the idea of rewards and punishments to the history of Israel, and had tried to demonstrate that obedience to the word of the Lord brings prosperity while disobedience causes disaster. In Proverbs the sages are applying the idea of rewards and punishments to the life of the individual. (The idea of life as a contract between man and God, with each having certain obligations to fulfill toward the other, will come in for further scrutiny, leading to refutation, in Job.) In Proverbs the older idea that wisdom brings success is in the process of being replaced by the newer idea that wisdom is the greatest good a man may obtain in life (thus, "The fear of the Lord is the beginning of wisdom: and the knowledge of the holy is understanding"—Prov. 9:10). (However, this notion of the great worth of wisdom is not the last word— compare the estimate of wisdom in Ecclesiastes, which comes to very different conclusions.)

ECCLESIASTES

(For background material, see section on Wisdom Literature above.) Ecclesiastes is, in the main, a rather rambling and disjointed series of cynical and/or skeptical meditations about human life. The first eleven of its twelve chapters present the views of its world-weary author, and it is generally thought that the piety of the last chapter was introduced to make the book more acceptable to the orthodox. (Editorial insertions also appear elsewhere in the book.)

The book stands in sharp and instructive contrast to the Book of Proverbs, its companion piece in the wisdom literature of the Old Testament. Proverbs presents the doctrine that wisdom, the gift of God, is both necessary and sufficient for guiding man to the good life. Ecclesiastes repeatedly denies the value of wisdom.

The book is in prose, but often so highly condensed and allusive that it resembles poetry; certainly, many of its sharply phrased statements have passed into the reservoir of proverbial utterance in English. It is somewhat difficult to read because the author skips from one topic to another without making much of an attempt to develop his statements.

Nevertheless, very soon certain themes emerge as characteristic—the futility ("vanity") of human activity, the lack of justice in the world, the relatively low estimate of wisdom, the idea of God as completely unknowable! The book is definitely a post-Exilic composition.

SUMMARY OF ECCLESIASTES

"VANITY OF VANITIES, ALL IS VANITY," 1:1-11. The book starts with an identification of the speaker. He is Koheleth (perhaps a name), the Preacher, the son of David (i.e., Solomon, and king of Jerusalem. The Preacher then announces the theme of his meditations: "Vanity of vanities; all is vanity." ("Vanity" here means "futility.") No matter where one looks a man's acaivity is pointless. Seen against the backdrop of the great, abiding phenomena of nature, which occur and recur in perpetual, cyclical movement, the life of man is indeed "vanity." There is nothing that is truly new; everything that men think of as new is only something old that the present generation is rediscovering for itself.

THE EXPERIENCE OF THE PREACHER, 1:12-2:26. The Preacher says that he tried to understand the meaning of life through the pursuit of wisdom. He has seen everything, and his conclusion is that life is vanity. The result of all his wisdom is that he finally comes to understand that "in much wisdom is much grief: and he that increaseth knowledge increaseth sorrow." Realizing that wisdom is not the key, he turns to pleasure. He indulges in all manner of gratifications, and that too is all vanity. He realizes that wisdom is better than foolishness, but, unfortunately, both the wise man and the fool have the same end—death. And thus, wisdom is again seen to be vanity. He thinks that no matter what sort of man he is, all his works will

pass into the hands of those who come after him—and who can tell whether his heirs will be wise or foolish?

A TIME FOR EVERYTHING, 3:1-15. In the first eight verses of this section the Preacher says that there is a fit season for every kind of activity. In 3:11 he strikes a note that will recur in the book: "no man can find out the work that God maketh from the beginning to the end." That is, for the writer of Ecclesiastes God is impossibly far away, and His ways are unfathomable.

THE INJUSTICE OF LIFE, 3:16-4:16. The Preacher observes that injustice is widespread. He compares men to animals in that both go to the same end. Death is the great leveler—no one knows whether it be true that the souls of men ascend after death, while those of animals descend into the earth. Since this is the case, the best thing for a man to do is to "rejoice in his own works" (i.e., in whatever life brings to hand). The Preacher returns to his contemplation of injustice. He then turns to the emptiness that is the consequence of being isolated in the world: "two are better than one."

THE FOLLY OF RASH VOWS, 5:1-7. Be not hasty to make vows, the Preacher advises, but when you do make a vow to God, be sure to fulfill it.

THE VANITY OF LIFE, 5:8-6:12. While a poor laboring man gains pleasure from the honest completion of his work, the rich gain gratification from the fact that they are envied by those who lack their possessions. But wealth always works to its owner's detriment because it warps his character—it makes him greedy and unable to gain joy from his wealth. Thus the man who gains pleasure from his work is better off than the rich man. In addition, the rich suffer from another ailment—their possessions go to spoiled and thoughtless children. What really ails man is his wandering imagination, which leads him to the pursuit of vanity. Chapter 6 ends with a typically skeptical statement: "For who knoweth what is good for man in this life . . . who can tell a man what shall be after him under the sun?"

WISDOM AND FOLLY COMPARED, 7:1-8:10.

Chapter 7 starts with a series of proverbs illustrating the difference between wisdom and folly, and praising the former. The Preacher then observes that the wicked prosper and the good perish. He counsels men not to be too righteous or too wicked. He then turns to the relative worth of men and women. While he has found one man out of a thousand to be worthy, he has found no woman who is not a snare and a delusion. Chapter 8 begins with more proverbs in praise of wisdom.

THE INEQUALITIES OF LIFE, 8:10-9:18.

The Preacher observes that life often has strange twists: sometimes the righteous are dealt with as if they were wicked, and vice versa. When he saw that to be the case, he turned to pleasure: "Then I commended mirth, because a man hath no better thing under the sun than to eat, and to drink, and to be merry." When he sought wisdom, he learned that all the wisdom in the world is insufficient to fathom the works of God (8:16-17). Again he recurs to the thought that all men, no matter what their character, come to the same death; for the Preacher, death is the great evil. "For to him that is joined to all the living there

is hope: for a living dog is better than a dead lion." The reason this is true is that the living know at least that they shall die, but the dead know nothing at all. He continues with advice for living the good life. "Go thy way, eat thy bread with joy, and drink thy wine with a merry heart . . . Live joyfully with thy wife whom thou lovest all the days of thy life." He continues with the well-known advice: "Whatsoever thy hand findeth to do, do it with thy might; for there is no work, nor device, nor knowledge, nor wisdom, in the grave, whither thou goest." He reflects that there is no justice in this life: "the race is not to the swift, nor the battle to the strong." Even wisdom, which might seem to offer more lasting rewards than anything else in life, is fragile indeed.

THE EXCELLENCE OF WISDOM, 10:1-11:8.

He presents further illustrations of the differences between wisdom and folly, and of the excellence of wisdom. After this, the Preacher turns to the virtues of charity. "Cast thy bread upon the waters: for thou shall find it after many days." The implication is that one should be charitable if only because one never knows what reversal one may oneself suffer, and thus one never knows the time when one may need charity from others.

ADVICE TO THE YOUNG, 11:9-12:14.

The Preacher tells the young man to rejoice in his youth, but always to be mindful that he will be judged by God for the consequences of his often thoughtless acts. He begins the last chapter of his skeptical book on a note of piety (generally believed to have been inserted by a later editor): "Remember now thy Creator in the days of thy youth." The young person should be mindful of the Lord because all too soon, as the Preacher indicates in a series of hauntingly beautiful images (12:2-6), the time will come when he will have reached the end of his life. At this point, we again have an attempt by the editor (12:9-14) to attribute a religious tone to Ecclesiastes. It seems clear, however, that "the conclusion of the whole matter" was *not* "Fear God, and keep His commandments for this is the whole duty of man." Perhaps it was for the pious editor, but not for the writer of Ecclesiastes.

THE SONG OF SONGS

Because the **Song of Songs** is not a religious work but rather (in all probability) an extraordinarily beautiful collection of love poems, there has been a certain amount of controversy over its inclusion in the Bible, as well as many attempts to see in it some meaning beyond that conveyed on a literal level. Some Jewish theologians have interpreted it to be an allegory of the love of God for the children of Israel; Christian scholars have viewed it as an allegory of Christ's love for the Church. It is unlikely that the work was ever intended to convey either of these meanings. Its inclusion in the Old Testament is probably due to one or both of the following reasons: to the ancient Hebrews physical love was not only good but one of the most wonderful things God had given to man, and therefore it is not at all inconceivable that they would have put its praise into their most precious book. However, it is more likely that the reason it was included is that tradition ascribes the composition of the book to King Solomon. The *Song of Songs* is not one poem but many, and scholars are not sure that these are related in any way. This presents certain problems to the reader, for the poems are not separated in any clear fashion and it is often difficult to understand what is going on. The only unifying element which can be definitely discerned is that a major portion of the poems deal with a bride and groom and the events taking place before and after their marriage. The other poems, which are not clearly related to these ceremonies, seem to be simple love poems spoken to each other by a man and a woman (however, the speakers may still be the bride and bridegroom). We do not know the exact date of the composition of *Song of Songs,* but we do know that in the form in which we have it, it cannot possibly be any earlier than 300 B.C. (the Song of Songs is also known as the Song of Solomon and Canticles).

THE BRIDE AND THE DAUGHTERS OF JERUSALEM, 1:1-1:8. The bride speaks to her attendants of her love for her husband-to-be. She says his love is better than wine and then goes on to describe herself. She explains that although her skin has been darkened by the sun shining upon her as she works in the vineyards, she is still attractive to look upon. When she says ". . . mine own vineyard I have kept not," she means that she has neglected herself and let her beauty deteriorate. We are to understand, however, that she is being modest, for her appearance is extravagantly praised by her attendants and her groom. She yearns after her love, apparently a shepherd in the field with his flocks, and is told to follow the footprints of the sheep until she finds him.

THE BRIDE AND BRIDEGROOM AND THE BRIDE'S REVERIE, 1: 9-3:5. The bride and groom speak of the love they bear each other. The groom addresses his bride in lines 1:9-1:11, 1:15, 1:17, and 2:2. All the other lines through 2:6 are spoken by the bride to her beloved; in 2:7 she seems again to address herself to her attendants. These passages and many others in the *Song of Songs* need no explanation, for they are exquisite declarations of love, which all can understand easily. The next passage is also spoken, or thought, by the bride.

She imagines that it is spring and her lover, like "a young hart" full of joy at the rebirth of the flowers and the singing of the little birds, comes to take her away. (The famous passage about "the little foxes" was added by a commentator and bemoans the fact that beauty can fade, i.e., that "the little foxes [can] spoil our vineyards.") In the next section the bride falls into a reverie. She recalls how one night when in bed, she reached out for her lover and did not find him there. Unable to be without him, she rose and searched the city until she found him near some watchmen and, holding him all the while, brought him to her mother.

THE WEDDING PROCESSION; THE BRIDEGROOM PRAISES THE BRIDE; THE BRIDE PRAISES THE BRIDEGROOM, 3: 6-5:16.

The bridegroom arrives and is compared to Solomon in the grandeur and opulence of his train. (It has been suggested since we have understood the groom to be a shepherd that the comparison is not to be taken literally but is a description of the way even the poorest of men feel on their wedding day.) We are told that he comes surrounded by sixty heroes of Israel and rides in a litter made of wood from Lebanon colored purple and gold. The next poem may be spoken by the groom to the bride, or else may be simply a poem from a man to his beloved. It begins with a stirringly beautiful description of the body of the loved one, generally comparing the various parts of her body to things in nature. He praises her love, saying how much he values it, and then goes on to compare her to an enclosed garden in which grow various plants and spices. His love responds by asking him to enter his garden and "eat his pleasant fruits," that is, she invites him to love. It is possible that what follows here is intended as a parallel to 3:1-4, for here the bride also wakes to find that her lover is not with her. The "daughters of Jerusalem" ask her what is so special about her beloved to cause her to yearn after him so much. She answers with a poem (again this may simply be a love poem unrelated to the rest of the work). Her lover is described tenderly and the parts of his body are compared to various beautiful things, for example, his cheeks to a "bed of spices," his legs to "pilars of marble."

THE MUTUAL DELIGHT OF THE BRIDE AND BRIDEGROOM, 6-8.

The main portion of chapter 6 is an impassioned poem from the groom to the bride who at its end is addressed as "Shulamite." What this means is not known. (It may be the bride's name.) The following poem is also about the bride (this too, like the one preceding, may be unrelated to the general theme of the poems, i.e., the nuptials). It is a particularly sensuous poem, more open even than the one in chapter 4. The love imagery is very beautiful and very graphic. At the end of the poem the bride asks her lover to come with her to the vineyards so that they may make love surrounded by nature's bounty. Chapter 8 speaks mainly about the enduring qualities of love, which is said to be "strong as death."

PROPHECY AND THE PROPHETS

INTRODUCTION. Our word prophet comes from the Greek word *prophetas,* which means literally one who speaks for another, especially for a god. This Greek word is a fair equivalent for the Hebrew word *nabi,* which denotes a spokesman—one who speaks for God. While prophets did sometimes make predictions (some of which came true while some did not), this was not their only or even their main function, which was to declare the will of Yahweh to the people. Their concern was not for the distant future but for the present and the immediate future. Other Old Testament terms for them indicate their character: keepers, watchmen, men of God, servants of God, and messengers of God. Their function was to assert moral and religious truths at times of national and spiritual crises. They performed this function with such honesty, acuteness, and power that much of what they say still has value for us today.

The great prophets of the eighth, seventh, and sixth centuries—Amos, Hosea, Isaiah, Micah, Jeremiah, Ezekiel—are sometimes called the reform prophets or the classical prophets. They represent the full flowering of Hebrew prophetic genius. They are the end result of a long period of development of which something should be known if the achievements of the classical prophets are to be understood.

DIVINERS, SEERS, AND PROPHETS. Primitive methods of divination were practiced at early stages of Israel's religious development and survived for a long time among the superstitious. Reading the future from dreams, from the entrails of sacrifices, from games of chance, and from unusual happenings in nature was long practiced by seers or diviners. Sometimes these seers, men who could see things which were lost or hidden from common eyes, would for a small sum of money answer questions. These questions could be quite trivial, as we see in I Sam. 9:1-10:16, where Saul and his servant appeal to Samuel to help them find some asses which have gone astray. Early prophets may have performed some or all of these functions; however, at some point a distinction seems to have been made between "seer" and "prophet," the former being noted for his ingenuity in interpreting signs and dreams, and the latter for his gift in "speaking for

Yahweh," perhaps in a state of delirium or ecstasy. Similarly, while both priests and propets were attached to shrines and temples, a distinction of function was made, so that while the priests taught the religious beliefs, took care of the ceremonies, and operated Urim and Thummim (the sacred lots which gave yes-or-no answers to questions), the prophets commented on current events and pronounced the will of Yahweh through their oracles.

ECSTATIC PROPHECY. Prophecy was frequently associated with possession by the spirit, a sort of frenzy or ecstasy in which the possessed one babbled unintelligibly, cried out as if mad, and performed weird dances and other strange acts. This possession can still be observed today in parts of the Near East and indeed in certain sects in our own country. It is the phenomenon of speaking in tongues, described in the New Testament (Acts 2) and discouraged by St. Paul (I Cor. 14:19). Frequently a whole group was seized by the spirit in this way. A good example of this may be seen in I Sam. where, as was often the case, the ecstasy was assisted by music, for the "sons of the prophets" as they were called, came down from the high place to the music of a harp, tambourine, flute, and lyre, and were joined by Saul, who also prophesied (i.e., spoke ecstatically). On another occasion (I Sam. 19) Saul again was seized by the spirit, spoke ecstatically, and afterward lay naked all day and all night. We must remember that these strange seizures and acts probably authenticated the prophet in the opinions of many onlookers. Several references in the Books of Samuel and Kings suggest that eventually there were large numbers of the "sons of the prophets," apparently living in communities, on occasion under royal patronage, otherwise supporting themselves by begging and by fees received for performing cures and wonders. When Amos says "I am no prophet, nor a prophet's son" (7:14, R. S. V.), he is in all probability dissociating himself from such groups.

"THE PROPHETIC SUCCESSION."

From time to time there were individual prophets who stood out from the crowd, as it were, and who offered genuine religious and ethical judgments. R. B. Y. Scott (in *The Relevance of the Prophets*) traces what he calls "the prophetic succession" right back to Moses, "a man who knew the presence and the moral will of God as an intense experience, who discerned his summons in current events and situations, and who declared that Yahweh demanded obedience and loyalty" (p. 63). His loyalty and obedience was expressed by adherence to the covenant relationship and to the Ten Commandments. Scott demonstrates that many of the classical prophets "believed their message was not new, but was a recall to the essential religion of the formative period of Moses" (p. 64). He distinguishes four stages in the development of the "succession" after the time of Moses. These stages form four convenient groups in which the history of the Old Testament prophecy may be studied.

(1) Individual prophets from the time of Samuel (about 1050) to (Micaiah about 850). With the exception of Samuel, who was an important leader (see above, p. 60), these men made only short appearances, but are important because they show that there really was a succession of responsible prophets side by side with the ecstatic prophets. Examples are Nathan, who reproached David for his slaying of Uzziah and his sin with Bathsheba; Gad, Shemaiah, and Ahijah who advised kings in various crises; and Micaiah, who bravely contradicted all the prophets who promised victory to Ahab. These men anticipated the classical prophets in making political and ethical judgments. Also, Nathan anticipated the reform prophets by his use of a prophetic "sign"—tearing his garment to represent the disruption of the tribes.

(2) Elijah and Elisha. Elijah appeared (I Kings 17) when recognition of the Phoenician Baal, Melkart, a fertility god, was undermining Israel's faith in Yahweh. By asserting that Yahweh withheld His rain, Elijah asserted his power over the fertility of the land. The outcome of his dramatic challenge to the 450 prophets of Baal justified his faith and convinced the people to return their loyalty to Yahweh (notice the ecstatic frenzy of the Baalite prophets, who perform a limping dance, mutilate themselves, and "prophesy" in vain: I Kings 18:27-9). When the king unlawfully got possession of Naboth's vineyard (Chap. 21), Elijah told him that he had done evil and would be punished. Both in asserting absolute loyalty to Yahweh and in demanding absolute justice, Elijah showed that he understood the spiritual and moral demands of the convenant. In this respect he pointed the way to the reform prophets of the next century. Elisha, who was the servant and follower of Elijah and a leader of one of the groups or guilds of prophets, seems not to have been as striking a figure as his master. The stories which survive about him are largely miracle stories, the product of folk-imagination. He is relatively unimportant in the succession.

(3) In the eighth century begins the great age of Hebrew prophesy. Since each figure will be discussed in relation to his book, they need be only briefly mentioned here. The chronological charts should be studied so that historical background is understood. Amos and Hosea preached in Israel about the middle of the eighth century, followed by Isaiah and Micah in Judah. A whole group of prophets may be associated with the years before the exile, the exile itself, and the years that follow: Jeremiah, Zephaniah, Nahum, Habakkuk, and Ezekiel. In some cases the dating is disputed.

(4) Last came the post-exilic, post-classical prophets of the Persian period. The anonymous poet who wrote Isaiah 40-55 must be associated with the period of Cyrus, and Haggai and Zechariah with the rebuilding of the Temple in Jerusalem, c. 520-515. Malachi, Obadiah, and Joel probably fall in the next century. (Jonah and Daniel are not really prophetic books at all; see the introductions to these books.) This late period is characterized by much imitation of early prophecy, often anonymously, and by the re-interpreting and editing of earlier prophets. There was some original work, besides that of the prophets just named, but much of this was inserted in earlier books, notably the beautiful Servant Songs which are included in the Book of Isaiah as we now have it. Toward the end of the period we can discern a shift to a new kind of writing—apocalyptic— such as we find in the Book of Daniel.

THE COMPOSITION OF THE PROPHETIC BOOKS. The prophetic books contain four main types of literary material: short, pithy oracles, often in splendid poetry; homiletic addresses, sometimes the work of editors; biographical narratives; and first-person autobiographical passages. These units are often put together rather haphazardly without a modern historian's concern for chronology or pattern. The present-day reader who dips into Isaiah or Hosea may be baffled by them at first unless he has some idea how these books developed into their present state.

The term "writing prophets" as applied to Amos and his successors is probably misleading. These prophets may have written down certain passages, and Jeremiah unquestionably dictated to Baruch when prevented from preaching publicly, but it seems certain that in many cases both prophecies and stories about the prophets were circulated orally. Prophets were speakers; they addressed themselves in speech to the people at large, often on special religious occasions or at times of crises, and when their messages seemed especially relevant. If, as many modern scholars now think probable, many of the prophets were associated with cultic shrines, other members of the cult may have played an important part in preserving the records of the prophecies and of historical events connected with them. Disciples or followers of the prophet who were especially impressed with the oracles may have committed them to memory and passed them on to their own followers in turn. While some passages may have been set down in writing, oral transmission probably predominated. We see in Isaiah 8;16 how that particular prophet committed his message to his followers.

In any case, it is clear that adaptations and alterations were sometimes made to make the prophecies relevant to new situations. Collections of oracles might be combined and so substantial additions might be made to the original material. The outstanding example of this is our present "Book of Isaiah," where on the scroll containing the work (already edited) of Isaiah of Jerusalem was copied, in chapter 40-55, the work of an anonymous sixth century prophet whom scholars call Second Isaiah. Still later, a miscellaneous collection of oracles which make up the last ten chapters was copied on to the same scroll. There is no prophetic book which has not been edited and enlarged to some degree in this way. This is true even of the post-exilic This is true even of the post-exilic chariah on, prophecy became imitative and literary and was in all likelihood written down instead of spoken.

We have said that the chief function of the prophet was to speak for Yahweh, to remind the covenant people of the covenant imperatives. Often they did not succeed in this, and in every generation new voices were needed for the task. Eventually the movement lost its freshness and fervor and trailed off into concern for ritual purity, legalism, and apocalyptic. Yet the lessons of the greatest prophets still remain today and, as a modern historian has claimed, "the existence of the Old Testament, of the Jewish people, of the Christian Church are posthumous monuments to their greatness." (Gottwald, *A Light to the Nations*, p. 281).

THE BOOK OF ISAIAH

COMPOSITION OF THE BOOK. The "Latter Prophets" of the Old Testament were copied on four large scrolls, roughly the same length— the books of Isaiah, Jeremiah, and Ezekiel, and the book of The Twelve. It is clear enough that the last of these is a collection or anthology of prophetic material. It is not quite so obvious at first sight that this is true in the case of the other three books, but such in fact is the case. Each contains a nucleus of original oracles and narratives by the prophet who gave the book its title, but each has been reinterpreted, re-edited, and ultimately greatly enlarged. We must realize that the circle of disciples and their followers who carried out this process were not trying to deceive the public, but rather to bring their admired teacher up to date and to make sure that his message would seem clear and relevant to the current audience. It is also important to emphasize that these additions are not necessarily inferior to the original nucleus. Some of the most glorious passages in the whole of the Old Testament are from an anonymous sixth-century prophet whose work happened to be copied on to the scroll which we call the Book of Isaiah.

This book as we have it contains sixty-six chapters. Most modern scholars agree that Chapters 40-66 are not by Isaiah of Jerusalem, but reflect conditions of about two centuries later. Chapters 40-55 are usually attributed to a sixth-century prophet whose name is not known, but whom scholars call "Second Isaiah" simply because his work is contained in the same scroll as the oracles of Isaiah. Chapters 56-66 are thought to be a disciple or disciples of Second Isaiah.

However, not all the oracles in Chapters 1-39 are original with Isaiah. Chapters 34 and 35, for example, accord more with the thinking of chapters 56-66 than with that of Isaiah of Jerusalem, and Chapters 24-27 contain material which is probably even later than Second Isaiah. When we turn to the large collection of oracles on foreign nations, Chapters 13-23, we see that some mention nations, such as the Chaldeans and Medes, which were not prominent in Near Eastern history until long after Isaiah was dead. Most of the important additions will be indicated in the summary. For the reasons given by scholars for thinking these passages are additions, consult a standard commentary.

INTRODUCTION TO CHAPTERS 1-39: ISAIAH OF JERUSALEM. Isaiah began his long ministry in 742, the year the great King Uzziah died, and was still active at the turn of the century when Sennacherib besieged Jerusalem. He seems to have had court connections and is sometimes thought, because of his elegant style, to have been an aristocrat. That he was a man of the city with great respect for kingship and for civic and religious institutions seems clear. His earlier oracles, in Chapters 1-5, condemn religious dishonesty and disobedience, social injustice, and greed. By the time the youthful King

Ahaz succeeded (735), the external political situation was a frightening one. Tiglath-Pileser III had made Assyria a powerful enemy of the little countries of the Near East. His invasion of Israel in 742 may account for the oracle of doom in Chapter 6. When Pekah of Israel and Rezin of Syria planned an attack on Judah, hoping to replace Ahaz with their own candidate, Isaiah advised him to stand firm, trust Yahweh. be tranquil, and avoid entangling alliances. But this Ahaz was not strong enough to do. Even when Isaiah assured him that Israel and Syria would be overthrown, Ahaz was still afraid. In his fear, he appealed to Assyria—successfully, for Tiglath-Pileser attacked and defeated the alliance. But the net result for Ahaz was that Judah became a vassal of Assyria and even took over some Assyrian religious practices. It was at this point that Isaiah apparently decide to withdraw from his public ministry, put his trust in the faithful remnant, and turn over his oracles for preservation by his disciples, looking toward a future day when perhaps his message would be understood.

It is not quite certain whether or not Isaiah really remained silent for the rest of Ahaz' reign (735-715). Some scholars think there are references to the fall of Samaria in 722-1. In any case he seems to have been active again after Ahaz died and was succeeded by Hezekiah. (One theory about the Messianic passages in Chapters 9 and 10 is that they were composed for Hezekiah's coronation.) Some of the oracles against foreign nations were composed at this time. Ashdod and other cities revolted against Sargon II about 714-711 B.C. The last period of Isaiah's preaching coincides with the time when the leaders of Judah were seeking an alliance with Egypt. Isaiah disapproved of this "covenant with death," as he had disapproved of overtures to Assyria. But by now Hezekiah was involved in a revolt against Sennacherib of Assyria. In 701 Sennacherib defeated most of the coalition against him. Hezekiah held out as city after city in Judah fell until he was shut up "like a caged bird" in his own city. Finally he had to submit, at a price, to save Jerusalem from destruction. In this crisis Isaiah's faith remained the same. Perhaps Assyria was the rod of God's anger to punish Judah for her misdoings. Perhaps Sennacherib in his turn would fall. Perhaps Jerusalem would survive. Whatever happened, king and people should wait in tranquility, for Yahweh was Lord of history. For the Introduction to Chapters 40-66, see below, p. 112.

SUMMARY OF THE BOOK OF ISAIAH

SUPERSCRIPTION, 1:1. This title covers the contents of the original book through the present Chapter 39, and tells us that Isaiah prophesied under Uzziah, Jotham, Ahaz, and Hezekiah.

SHORT ORACLES ON JUDAH AND JERUSALEM, 1 — 2:5. In a brief introductory poem, Yahweh calls on heaven and earth to witness that His children are rebels who do not really know Him.

Next (verses 4-9), the prophet reproaches the sinful nations that have despised the Holy One of Israel and whose land and cities lie desolate with only a small remnant left.

In his next oracle (10-17) the prophet emphasizes the point that without obedience to the moral code, the outward acts of religion are hateful to Yahweh. Sacrifices, burnt offerings, vain oblations, new moon festivals, even prayer itself weary

Him when not accompanied by well-doing. "Wash ye, make you clean; put away the evil of your doings from before mine eyes; cease to do evil, learn to do well; seek judgement, relieve the oppressed, judge the fatherless, plead for the widow." Be obedient and you shall prosper; rebel, and you will fall to the sword. The prophet (24-26) laments that Jerusalem, the faithful city, has become a harlot. Yahweh will smelt away her dross and she will be faithful once more.

This group of oracles closes with the beautiful anonymous poem which also occurs in Micah (4:1-4, where there is an additional verse). The nations shall beat their swords into plowshares and their spears into pruning hooks and war shall be no more.

THE DAY OF THE LORD AND THE FALL OF RULERS, 2:6-3:15.
(The text is bad.) Idolaters are condemned. Foolish and proud man shall be humbled and terrified. Food and water will be short in Jerusalem (this may predict the Assyrian siege) and people will attack each other. Jerusalem shall be in ruins, and Yahweh will judge Jerusalem and her leaders, for their greed has ground the faces of the poor.

THE DAUGHTERS OF ZION, 3:16-4:1.
The vain and haughty ladies of Jerusalem, with their outstretched necks and wanton eyes, walk mincingly with tinkling feet. For their pride Yahweh will take away their anklets, bracelets and other jewelry, sashes, perfume boxes, rings, and garments. "Instead of sweet smell there shall be stink; and instead of a girdle a rent; and instead of well-set hair baldness; and instead of a stomacher a girding of sackcloth; and burning instead of beauty." The women will long to be protected by such few men as survive. (An eschatological passage follows.)

YAHWEH'S VINEYARD, 5:1-7.
Introducing his parable in the man-ner of a ballad-singer, Isaiah sings his friend's song of his vineyard. His friend cleared the land, planted choice vines, and prepared a wine press; but the land yielded only wild grapes. In his disappointment, the owner of the vineyard says he will take away its hedge and wall and make it a wasteland. In the last verse the friend is identified with Yahweh and the vineyard with Judah. Notice the puns in the second part of the verse:

and he looked for justice (mishpat),
  but behold, bloodshed (mishpah);
for righteousness (sedhakah),
  but behold, a cry (se'akah)!
(R. S. V.)

WOES AGAINST THE UNRIGHTEOUS, 5:8-30.
In a series of strongly worded reproaches, Isaiah inveighs against greed, pride, hard-heartedness, and religious apathy. First he attacks those who acquire property at the expense of others: "Woe unto them that join house to house, that lay field to field." Then he assaults those who drink all day to the lyre, harp, and flute, but do not see what the Lord is doing; those who in their dishonesty cling to their sins; those who are wise in their own eyes; and those who take bribes. (The rest of the chapter seems to belong after 10:4.)

THE FALL OF ISAIAH, 6:1-13.
The opening words suggest that Isaiah's account of his vision is retrospective; perhaps he dictated it or wrote it down after his failure in 734 to persuade Ahaz to trust Yahweh made the prophet decide to stop preaching for a time, collect his various oracles, and add this and subsequent passages to explain and authenticate his work.

The passage is one of matchless beauty and power. The vision evidently comes to Isaiah as he stands in the Temple, perhaps in his capacity as one of its prophets. Suddenly he is intensely aware that God is present. Isaiah does not try to describe Him, but conveys a Presence of majesty and holiness. God is on His throne and His train fills the Temple. The six-winged seraphims fly above Him (R. S. V.) and sing "one . . . to another" (i.e., antiphonally). The smoke of the Temple incense seems like the cloud of God's glory, and His power shakes the threshold. Suddenly Isaiah realizes that he and the community of which he is a part are unclean. But a seraph cleanses his lips with a burning coal, and when Yahweh asks, "Whom shall I send, and who will go for us?" the prophet replies, "Here am I; send me." Then comes the warning that the mission will be a discouraging one. The people will be dull-witted, unperceiving, unhearing, unresponsive—"until cities be wasted without inhabitant, and the houses without man, and the land be utterly desolate."

THE CONFEDERACY OF SYRIA AND THE TWO SIGNS, 7:1-8.

Rezin, king of Syria, and Pekah, king of Israel, threaten Judah. Fearing a siege, King Ahaz goes to inspect the city's water supply, and there Isaiah, together with his son Shear-jashub ("a remnant shall return"), confronts him. The message of Yahweh is "Take heed, and be quiet; fear not, neither be faint-hearted for the two tails of these smoking firebrands," that is, Rezin and Pekah. Their plans will fail. "If ye will not believe, surely we shall not be established." But Ahaz evades the issue and will not ask for a sign. Nevertheless, Isaiah announces the sign: a maiden shall bear a child, who shall be called Immanuel ("God with us"), but before the child is old enough to tell good from evil, the land whose kings are now such a source of terror to Ahaz will be deserted.

Isaiah next prophesies that Yahweh, as Lord of history, will bring an invasion. The land will suffer and the people will be very poor.

At Yahweh's behest, Isaiah gives his next child another symbolic name, Maher-shalal-hash-baz (speed-spoil, haste-prey"). Before the child can say "father" or "mother," the riches of Israel and Syria will be taken away. Moreover, temporizing with Assyria will be dangerous, for like a flood she will cover the land of Judah. Yahweh is the only true sanctuary. (Ahaz did not become the man of faith Isaiah hoped for. He turned to Assyria, paid homage to Tiglath-Pileser, and set up an Assyrian altar in Jerusalem. It seems to have been at this point that Isaiah decided to give up prophesying publicly and to write down his oracles until they should be attested.) "Bind up the testimony," directs the prophet, "seal the law among my disciples. And I will wait upon the Lord . . . and I will look for Him." (Two brief fragmentary oracles follow.)

THE MESSIANIC KING, 9:1-12:6.

Two passages describing the coming Messiah are interrupted by a collection of oracles. It is disputed whether or not the Messianic passage in Chapter 9:1-6 is by Isaiah and whether or not it describes a real or ideal king. Traditionally it has been applied by Christians to Jesus of Nazareth, called the Messiah or the Anointed One, and this association has been reinforced by Handel's *Messiah* and by the reading of this passage in churches on Christmas Day. While Jesus certainly taught justice and righteousness and some phrases seem to fit Him well, it has been objected that He never aspired to be a political ruler such as seems to be intended here. A recent explanation is that the oracle was written for the enthronement of a king. There seems to be no very cogent reason for denying that it is by Isaiah or by a disciple of his. "The people that walked in darkness have seen a great light." The nation rejoices because the rule of the oppressor is broken, the soldiers' boots and the bloody garments of war are no more, and a marvellous king has come. "His name will be called Wonderful Counsellor, Mighty God, Everlasting Father, Prince of Peace."

The oracles in 9:8—10:34 seem to be mostly connected with the Assyrian invasion. Judah should take warning from the disasters which have overtaken Israel. Assyria is God's rod against fatherless nations, but is not aware of it. The remnant of Israel will be destroyed as in a forest fire. A remnant will return, "even the remnant of Israel, unto the mighty God." Zion should be brave, for Yahweh's anger will not last forever and the inhabitants are still His people. God, like a woodsman, will "lop the bough with terror . . . and the haughty ones shall be humbled."

The description of the Messianic kingdom (11:1-16) should be studied with 9:1-7. From the house of Jesse (i.e., the Davidic family) shall come a new shoot, a new monarch, "And the Spirit of the Lord shall rest upon him, the spirit of wisdom and understanding, the spirit of counsel and might, the spirit of Knowledge and of the fear of the Lord." He will judge with discernment, with wisdom and authority and with a sense of justice. His reign shall be peace. "The wolf also shall dwell with the lamb, and the leopard shall lie down with the kid; and the calf and the young lion and the fatling together; and a little child shall lead them." No dangerous creature shall hurt another, "for the earth shall be full of the knowledge of the Lord, as the waters cover the sea." (Verses 10-16 were almost certainly added later.) God will bring back the remnant from the far corners of the earth.

Two short thanksgiving psalms (12:1-6) have been inserted here to round off this section.

ORACLES AGAINST FOREIGN NATIONS, 13:1-23:18.

A number of these are probably by Isaiah, but some are not. The doom of Babylon is from a later period when Babylon is in danger from the Medes. Most of Chapter 14 consists of a dramatically effective taunt on the overthrow of a tyrant. The chapter concludes with two short oracles of doom by Isaiah, one (verses 14-27) affirming God's lordship over history and predicting the downfall of Assyria, and the other (28-32) dated in the year of Ahaz' death (715), warning the Philistines that they are in danger from Assyria (the smoke from the north of verse 31). A long doom against Moab, of uncertain date, follows in Chapters 15 and 16. With Chapter 17:1-6, we are back with Isaiah again, probably in 734, when Judah was in danger from Israel and Syria. The prophet declares that Damascus will become a desolate heap of ruins and that "the glory of Jacob shall be made thin." The rest of the chapter deals with pagan worship of the Asherim (poles or idols representing the goddess Asherah) and of Adonis, a dying and rising fertility god, concluding with a brief analogy between swift storms and swiftly changing events. The splendid doom on Egypt which follows (18:1-7) may well be from Isaiah's own hand. Several other oracles of uncertain date, mostly in Egypt, take us through Chapter 20. After Sargon's underling took Ashdod, God told Isaiah to walk naked and barefoot like a prisoner of war, as a sign that the Assyrians would lead the Egyptians captive. Pronouncements of doom on Babylon (probably c. 540 B.C.), Dedan, and Kedar (Arabian tribes), a reproach against thoughtless carousing when an invasion threatens, a curse on a royal official, and a doom on Tyre and Sidon conclude this collection of oracles.

A GROUP OF ESCHATOLOGICAL PIECES, 24:1-27:13.

This collection of eschatological prophecies, interspersed with psalms and prayers, comes from the post-exilic period. Certain apocalyptic motifs occur, such as the feast for all nations, the overthrow of the dragon, the punishment of the rebel "host of heaven," the resurrection, and the judgment, but many apocalyptic features, for example, bizarre symbolisms, elaborate calculations with dates and numbers, and the trick of attributing the writing to earlier authors, are lacking.

The first poem describes withering, desolation, and mourning of the earth as a result of the breaking of the covenant, appended to which is a short song of rejoicing. After a fragment on the fear of the day of the Lord, the violent shaking of the earth, like a drunkard, and the imprisoning of hosts of heaven and kings of earth, the confounding of sun and moon, and the final triumph of the Lord are described. A thanksgiving for the fall of a fortified city is followed by a prophecy that the Lord will hold a feast of wine and fat things for all peoples; "he will swallow up death for ever, and the Lord God will wipe away tears from all faces" (cp. Rev. 21:4 and the final lines of Milton's *Lycidas*). A short doom on Moab which compares that country to a man floundering in a dung pit precedes two linked psalms, one of which celebrates a triumph over a lofty city, while the other is a psalm in which the author expresses his yearning for Yahweh and his faith in His power, even to the resurrection of the dead. The ancient myth of the struggle with "that crooked serpent" Leviathan, "the dragon that is in the sea," is the subject of a short piece which describes how Yahweh will slay him with a "great and strong sword." Isaiah's parable which speaks of Judah as Yahweh's vineyard provides an idea for a short poem in which Yahweh declares His willingness to defend His vineyard from thorns and briars. In the future "Israel shall blossom and bud, and fill the face of the world with fruit." After a confused fragment about Israel's guilt and suffering, this whole eschatological collection ends with the image of the Lord as the great Thresher of the harvest. "And in that day the Lord shall beat off from the channel of the river unto the stream of Egypt, and ye shall be gathered one by one, O ye children of Israel. And it shall come to pass in that day that the great trumpet shall be blown and they shall come which were ready to perish in the land of Assyria, and the outcasts in the land of Egypt, and shall worship the Lord in the holy mount of Jerusalem."

ISAIAH'S ORACLES AGAINST ISRAEL AND JUDAH, 28:1-32:20.

Most of the material in this section is genuinely by Isaiah and the greater part of it is usually thought to have been written in the closing years of his career, when he tried to persuade Hezekiah not to join the anti-Assyrian revolt. However, the first oracle is probably earlier, since it seems to be before the siege of 724-721. Some verses describing the quickly fading beauty of Samaria are now applied to Jerusalem. Isaiah says that the rulers of Judah, even priests and prophets, "stagger with strong drink" (R. S. V.) and "err in vision"—i.e., perhaps give bad political advice. They reply that he is talking to them as if they were children, but are told that in an alien tongue they will be reproved for not reposing in Yahweh (there are obscurities in the passage) and that they may "go, and fall backward, and be broken, and snared, and taken." Once again the prophet address the scoffers who have, he says, made a pact with false gods, and hence a covenant with death. But justice and righteousness will "sweep away the refuge of lies," and the covenant will be annulled.

The attractive parable of the farmer (28:23-29) makes the point that Yahweh has a purpose and is wise and orderly in carrying it out. As the farmer sows each crop in the most appropriate manner and threshes or treats dill, cumin, and grain by whatever method works best for each particular seed, so Yahweh may be trusted to care wisely for His people.

"Woe to Ariel" (i.e., Jerusalem, 29: 1-8) perhaps belongs to 701 when Jerusalem was in fear of the Assyrians under Sennacherib. The city will be besieged and will be like a man lying in the dust and speaking only in a whisper. Yahweh will come with his terrible storm, but suddenly the nations who threaten Mount Zion will disappear as a dream passes.

In a short passage, 29:9-12, Isaiah reverts to the provision made at the time of his call (Chap. 6) that his hearers would hear but not understand, see but not perceive. "Stupefy yourselves . . . blind yourselves . . . be drunk but not with wine," he cries, "for the Lord has poured out upon you a spirit of deep sleep," so that the prophet's message is like "a sealed book." Following this are two brief poems (verses 13-17). In the first Isaiah pokes fun at worshippers who unthinkingly mouth the correct words and reminds them that the Lord can and will do marvellous things. In the second, he reproaches schemers—perhaps those who were putting out feelers for an Egyptian alliance—who hide their schemes from Yahweh and His prophet. The chapter closes with two eschatological passages.

Most of the next group of oracles are concerned with the Egyptian alliance. In the first (30:1-7), Isaiah, speaking for Yahweh, rebukes the rebellious children who carry out their own plan, not His. "Therefore shall the strength of Pharaoh be your shame, and trust in the shadow of Egypt your confusion." God tells Isaiah to write his oracles in a book that they may be a witness to the future.) We are reminded of a previous occasion, during the attack from Israel and Syria, when Isaiah turned over his prophecies to be preserved by his disciples; see Chap. 8.) If only, pursues Yahweh, the people would trust the Holy One of Israel; "In returning and rest shall ye be saved; in quietness and in confidence shall be your strength: and ye would not." Here an editor, at verse 18, has inserted a plea to the people who are suffering to wait patiently, for they will be shown the way. The concluding prophecy of the chapter

is that "through the voice of the Lord shall the Assyrian be beaten down." "Woe to them that go down to Egypt for help" is the theme of the next oracle (31:1-3). The schemers are reminded that "the Egyptians are men, not God." A confused passage follows, the gist of which seems to be that Yahweh will protect and deliver Jerusalem—evidently in 701.

A splendid picture of ideal kingship (32:1-8) may or may not be by Isaiah. The righteous king will be "as the shadow of a great rock in a weary land." Eyes and ears will be alert, and folly, knavery, and nobility will be seen for what they are. Next (verses 9-14) the speaker, perhaps now Isaiah himself, rebukes women, not the fashionable women this time (as in Chap. 3), but unthinking, over-confident girls who dance at the harvest festival, not realizing that the harvest will fail and the city be deserted. An eschatological passage which anticipates the pouring out of the "Spirit . . . from on high" has been linked to the oracle on women.

A LITURGY, 33:1-24. Chapters 33 through 35 differ from Isaiah proper in subject matter and style. The liturgy in this chapter is perhaps recited by the prophet-author during the services of worship. The opening "Woe to you destroyer . . . you treacherous one" is directed against an unnamed enemy, perhaps during the Maccabean struggle. A prayer for salvation is followed by a promise that God will be the deliverer. Further lamentations about the state of the land—"the highways lie waste, covenants are broken, the land mourns"—are answered by the repetition of promise. The heathen nations "shall be as the burnings of life," even the wicked of Israel will be destroyed, the Lord is the King who will save, and Zion will be "a quiet habitation."

TWO ESCHATOLOGICAL PSALMS 34:1-35:10. The first is a

vivid and carefully planned poem on the theme of God's vengeance. The nations and the whole of the earth are called to witness God's wrath against the heathen and specifically against Edom. "The sword of the Lord is filled with blood," and there is great slaughter of lambs, goats, oxen, and bulls. Edom will "become burning pitch" and the land will be taken over by birds of prey, thorns, nettles, thistles, and supernatural creatures. This is the Lord's command and is written in His book.

In complete contrast with this terrible picture is the glorious and moving psalm describing the new Eden which God in His heaven will create and the joyful return of the exiles. "The wilderness and the solitary place shall be glad for them; and the desert shall rejoice, and blossom as the rose. It shall blossom abundantly, and rejoice even with joy and singing." The prophet is told to comfort and encourage the weak and fearful, for God is coming to save them. The feeblest and most helpless of the exiles will be renewed. "Then the eyes of the blind shall be opened, and the ears of the deaf shall be unstopped. Then shall the lame man leap up as an hart, and the tongue of the dumb sing; for in the wilderness shall waters break out, and streams in the desert." Where the desert was there will be pools and springs, reeds and rushes. A special highroad will be prepared for the pilgrims returning to Zion, and it shall be called "the way of holiness," safe for all wayfarers and leading to the holy city. "And the ransomed of the Lord shall return, and come to Zion with songs and everlasting joy upon their heads; they shall obtain joy and gladness, and sorrow and sighing shall flee away."

THE INVASION OF SENNACHE-RIB, 36. King Sennacherib of Assyria captures all the fortified cities of Judah. The Assyrian armies come to Jerusalem, where their commander talks with several high Jewish officials. He tells them to tell Hezekiah that his plan to depend on Egypt for military assistance is doomed to fail, and he offers the Jews a chance to be reconciled with Assyria. If they refuse to pay tribute, then they face disaster at the hands of the Assyrian armies.

JUDAH DELIVERED, 37. When Hezekiah hears the Assyrian message he is overcome with despair, and he sends to Isaiah for counsel. Isaiah says that the king should not lose heart, because the Lord will defend Israel. The Assyrians renew their threats against Jerusalem, saying that it is foolish to trust in Yahweh. Other nations have trusted in their gods and they have been defeated; the same will happen if the Jews do not come to terms. Hezekiah prays to the Lord to smite Sennacherib. Isaiah again relays the Lord's word, saying that indeed He will defend His people. Then "the angel of the Lord" kills 185,000 of the Assyrian soldiers (perhaps an epidemic broke out in the Assyrian camp), and the remaining forces retreat to their own land.

HEZEKIAH'S SICKNESS, 38. Hezekiah falls deathly ill, and Isaiah tells him that he is about to die. The king prays, asking the Lord to remember that he has been faithful to Him. His prayers are granted, and he is given an additional fifteen years to live. The sign that his prayers have been heard is that the sun is reversed in its course by ten degrees.

HEZEKIAH RECEIVES ENVOYS FROM BABYLON, 39. The son of the king of Babylon sends envoys to Hezekiah to express his joy that the king has recovered from his illness. Hezekiah shows the envoys all the treasures of his palace and of the Temple. Isaiah asks him the identity of his visitors and what he has shown them. When Hezekiah tells him, the prophet replies that the result of his action will be that all the royal treasures, along with the royal family, will pass to Babylon.

INTRODUCTION TO SECOND ISAIAH. "Second Isaiah" is the name given by many scholars to the anonymous author of Chapters 40-66 of the Book of Isaiah. Other scholars, however, believe that these chapters are the work of several hands, and that it is only Chapters 40-55 (with the exception of certain passages) that can definitely be assigned to Second Isaiah, with the other chapters sometimes thought to be the work of his disciples, sometimes collectively called "Third Isaiah."

Second Isaiah was more than a prophet—he was a very great poet who was able to put his joyous visions of Israel and her future into poetry which some consider to be the greatest in the entire Old Testament. His message was very different from that of First Isaiah, and for good reason. In the 200 years or so that separate the two prophets, circumstances had changed radically for the Hebrews. Whereas First Isaiah wrote before the Babylonian Captivity, when the Israelites still lived in Judah under their own king, Second Isaiah wrote during the Exile, after Israel's punishment had been dealt out to her. Consequently, unlike First Isaiah, he had no need to warn the people of the penalties they pay if they transgress. The nation had already expiated its sins, and Second Isaiah comes not to chastise but to comfort and encourage. God is to turn to the Hebrews in the spirit of forgiveness, and once again gather His people to Him and restore them to their homeland. The note of hope which runs throughout Second Isaiah can be better understood against the background of the political events of the time. Chief among these was the imminent accession of the Persians, and of their great king, Cyrus, to supremacy in the Near East (culminating in the fall

of Babylon in 539 B.C.). The Hebrews hailed Cyrus as sent by God to deliver them, as he was indeed to do (see Ezra and Nehemiah). Cyrus was an extremely benevolent king, whose goodness was all the more extraordinary when compared to the evil perpetuated by most conquerors of the time. And although his humaneness had not yet been demonstrated on a large scale, the quality of the man was evident; as he rose, so did the hope of the Israelites. (Some scholars feel that Second Isaiah wrote immediately after the Persian capture of Babylon, rather than during Cyrus's rise to power.) Perhaps the most well-known part of Second Isaiah is what has come to be called the "Servant" poems. Their fame is due not only to their exceptional beauty but also to the fact that Christianity has seen in them an Old Testament prophecy of the coming of Christ. The traditional Jewish interpretation sees the Servant as the Hebrew nation, Israel. Scholars do not agree on whether these poems are the work of Second Isaiah or a later addition to the book.

THE LORD'S COMFORTING WORDS TO ZION, 40. The first words of Chapter 40 sound the keynote of Second Isaiah: "Comfort ye, comfort ye my people, saith your God." He speaks to the people, wretched in their exile, and tells them that God will relent in His harshness toward them. A new day is dawning, one in which the Lord will once again favor His people. Most of Chapter 40 is a hymn of praise to the greatness of the Lord. There is nothing that can compare to His greatness and majesty.

GOD'S ASSURANCE TO ISRAEL, 41:1-20. God, speaking in His own voice, reassures the people that He is with them: ". . . thou, Israel, art my servant . . . I have chosen thee, and not cast thee away. Fear thou not; for I am with thee; . . . for I am thy God: I will strengthen thee . . ."

THE LORD'S CHALLENGE TO FALSE GODS, 41:21-29.

The Lord challenges the false gods of the surrounding nations to show their divinity or else be scorned. The obvious implication is that they cannot meet such a challenge, and the chapter concludes with the statement that the other gods are "all vanity; their works are nothing: their molten images are wind and confusion."

THE LORD'S SERVANT, 42:1-9.

Here is introduced for the first time the ambiguous figure of the Lord's (suffering) Servant. The chapters in which he occurs have been used by Christians as evidence that Christ (who is identified with the Servant) is the fulfillment of Old Testament prophecy. Nevertheless, it is not at all clear who or what the Servant is or is supposed to be. Sometimes he seems to be a man (perhaps the prophet?), sometimes the nation of Israel. Some scholars believe that the passages concerning the Servant are parts of a longer work about him which somehow have been included in Isaiah. Here, he seems to be a prophet ("I have put my Spirit upon him: he shall bring judgment to the Gentiles").

PRAISE FOR THE LORD'S MIGHTY DELIVERANCE, 42:10-25.

Now the prophet tells the people to praise the Lord for the mighty manner in which He will deliver them from their bondage. The tone changes as Israel is rebuked for having been deaf and blind to the Lord's voice.

THE LORD THE ONLY REDEEMER, 43, 44.

Now, however, all that is changed. The Lord has heard the pleas of His people, and He will answer them: "O Israel, fear not: for I have redeemed thee." The Lord reiterates to the people that He is the only Redeemer, the only source of salvation. Even though Israel has wandered from the true path, the Lord freely wipes out the nation's sins and once more takes His people to him. He is the One, the Only, the All-powerful. Chapter 44 closes with still another statement that the Lord is omnipotent and that Israel owes everything to Him.

THE COMMISSION TO CYRUS, 45:1-7.

The Lord announces that He has given dominion over the world to Cyrus, the emperor of Persia. (This is one of the two mentions of Cyrus, part of the evidence that Second Isaiah lived considerably after (First) Isaiah of Jerusalem, for whom the threat was the Assyrians, and for whom the Persians do not even exist.)

THE LORD THE CREATOR; THE LORD AND BABYLON, 45:8-47:15.

The remainder of Chapter 45 is a hymn of praise to the majesty of the Lord, and especially of Him as creator of the entire world. He is the center of righteousness; there is none besides Him. Babylon has looked to its own gods instead of to Yahweh, and consequently Yahweh has judged her. No more will she be supreme among nations in power. Her time has come, and she is to be toppled from her eminence (by the Persians, under Cyrus).

ISRAEL'S UNFAITHFULNESS REBUKED, 48.

Israel has been obstinate and has persistently strayed from the path of the word of God; therefore she has been punished severely. Had she not sinned, her place would have been "as a river, and [her] righteousness as a sea." Nevertheless, for all their mistakes, the Lord has redeemed His people, and they may now look forward to returning to their homeland (20-22).

ISRAEL THE LORD'S SERVANT: THE RESTORATION OF ZION PROMISED, 49.

Israel, the Lord's servant, shall once again arise and be the object of respect in the eyes of the nations. For the Lord has returned to His people, and will restore them to their now devastated homeland.

THE LORD HELPS THOSE WHO TRUST IN HIM, 50.

Trust in the Lord will be rewarded: "Who is among you that feareth the Lord, that obeyeth the voice of his servant . . . let him trust in the name of the Lord, and stay upon his God."

WORDS OF COMFORT TO ZION, 51:1—52:12.

The prophet calls to those among his people who are seekers after righteousness to hearken to him. They must lift up their eyes to the heavens. It is time to awake, to gather strength, for the Lord has redeemed His people. No longer will Israel be forced to drink from the cup of affliction. Her tribulations have come to an end, and now her redemption is at hand. For now the Lord will deliver Zion from her enslavement: "Shake thyself from the dust; arise and sit down, O Jerusalem: loose thyself from the bands of thy neck, O captive daughter of Zion." It is time to "break forth into joy . . . For the Lord hath comforted His people, He hath redeemed Jerusalem."

THE SUFFERING OF THE LORD'S SERVANT, 52:13—53:12.

This passage is another of the "Servant" poems. It sets out, in very affecting language, the trials of the Lord's servant. The servant "is despised and rejected of men; a man of sorrows, and acquainted with grief." He is said to "have borne our griefs, and carried our transgressions." The servant was "oppressed," but he does not complain; he is a lamb brought to the slaughter. Jesus and the writers of the gospels knew the Book of Isaiah well, and especially this chapter; the language describing the servant has been used time and again to describe Christ. Of course, Second Isaiah knew nothing of Christ and was probably describing the sufferings of his people. The servant is nowhere said to be the Messiah but Christ is both the servant and the Saviour.

THE LORD'S EVERLASTING LOVE FOR ISRAEL, 54.

Here is another statement that Israel is to be restored to its homeland. The people's relation to God is likened to that between a wife and her husband. The people is a widow that the Lord has come to marry and raise up. His love is constant and will never change or depart.

MERCY FOR ALL, 55.

The Lord is merciful, and His mercy is infinite. The Lord is near at hand; seek Him, and He will slake your thirst with the waters of His mercy.

REWARDS FOR THOSE WHO KEEP GOD'S COVENANT, 56.

The Lord says that those who keep His covenant will be rewarded with His blessing, and in the immediate future: "my salvation is near to come, and my righteousness to be revealed." This is another reference to the restoration of the homeland to the exiled nation.

CONDEMNATION OF ISRAEL'S IDOLATRY, 57.

The righteous man shall be saved—but what of the evildoer? What will his fate be? The Lord says that He rejects such a man, he who "hast lied, and hast not remembered me." God is always ready to pardon, but those who remain mired in their evil will be punished: "There is no peace, saith my God, to the wicked."

OBSERVANCE OF FASTS AND THE SABBATH, 58.

The people complain that they have fasted as a token of their repentance and yet the Lord does not hear their pleas. The Lord replies that their fasting was a sham because it was not done sincerely. In fact, says the Lord, "ye fast for strife and debate, and to smite with the fist of wickedness." This is not what fasting is supposed to be, and therefore it is to no avail. If, however, the people wish to have their fasting mean something to the Lord, then they should "draw out [their] soul to the hungry, and satisfy the afflicted soul"; that is, they should acompany their fasting with some concrete good action to show that their hearts are in what they are doing. Then the Lord will accept the fasting and reward those who fast. Similarly it is with the Sabbath; to find favor with the Lord, one must honor the Lord on the Sabbath and not devote the day to the pursuit of one's own desires and pleasures.

A CONFESSION OF THE NATIONAL WICKEDNESS, 59.

Isaiah looks about him and describes the evil that is widespread in the land. There is no justice to be had; everyone is engaged in the pursuit of evil ("iniquity"). In such a state, living lives completely opposed to the word of God, we can expect no help from Him. The Lord is displeased that things are as they are. Isaiah reminds the people that the Lord will provide a champion of justice and righteousness.

THE FUTURE GLORY OF ZION, 60.

Once again the prophet returns to his theme of the coming restoration of the people and their return to Zion. The Lord shall "make of thee [the people] an eternal excellency, a joy of many generations." Israel shall come into a life of peace and prosperity (18). The Lord shall resume His place as the source of light for the nation, and the nation will be exalted. And all this coming soon: "A little one shall become a thousand, and a small one a strong nation: I the Lord will hasten it in his time."

GOOD TIDINGS OF SALVATION, 61-62.

The Lord has told Isaiah to "preach good tidings unto the meek; he hath sent me to bind up the brokenhearted, to proclaim liberty to the captives . . . to comfort all that mourn." Once again the prophet tells the people to be happy because the great day is here. The Lord is about to right the balance and return Israel to the position it should occupy among the nations. Zion shall no longer be forsaken. Jerusalem will once again be the shining place it

once was. The Lord has proclaimed: "Say ye to the daughter of Zion, behold, thy salvation cometh."

THE LORD'S VENGEANCE, 63:1-6.

The prophet has a vision of the vengeance of the Lord in the form of a man whose clothes are stained red. The prophet asks the man how his clothing came to be this color, and God's vengeance replies that the redness is from the treading the winepress of the Lord's wrath: "I will tread them [the enemies of Israel] in mine anger, and trample them in my fury; and their blood shall be sprinkled upon my garments, and I will stain all my rainment. For the day of vengeance is in mine heart, and the year of my redeemed is come."

THE LORD'S KINDNESS TO ISRAEL, 63:7-14.

Isaiah speaks of the love and kindness God displayed toward Israel. But then Israel strayed from His way and fought against Him; naturally, this rebellion caused Him to punish His people. But then he remembered Moses and the days of old; His heart softened towards them, and He redeemed them once more.

PRAYER FOR MERCY AND HELP, 63:15—64:12.

The prophet prays that the Lord restore the nation to its homeland (its "inheritance"). He beseeches the Lord to descend to earth and show Himself, in His full power and majesty, to His enemies. The people realize that they are only sinners, and they abase themselves before the greatness of God. Isaiah begs the Lord not to be angry too much longer, and to remember the devastation of Zion and Jerusalem. He finishes by asking "Wilt thou refrain thyself for those things [Zion and Jerusalem], O Lord? wilt thou hold thy peace, and afflict us very sore?"

PUNISHMENT OF THE REBELLIOUS, 65:1-16.

Isaiah describes what Israel looks like to the Lord. He sees men disobeying His commandments on every hand and He is greatly angered. He is tempted to destroy it but reconsiders because there does exist a small group who are truly His servants. These people will he elevate, and these people will he install in Palestine. But that great multitude who deny the Lord, they shall be annihilated.

NEW HEAVEN AND NEW EARTH, 65:17-25. The Lord says that He is creating a new heaven and a new earth, ones which will make those now existing seem pale by comparison. (That is, the new order that the Lord will establish in Zion will be as different from the present life in exile as night from day.) In this new world there will be no sickness or evil or injustice. This utopian

vision concludes: "The wolf and the lamb shall feed together, and the lion shall eat straw like the bullock . . . They shall not hurt nor destroy in all my holy mountains, saith the Lord."

THE LORD'S JUDGMENTS AND ZION'S FUTURE HOPE, 66. The Lord promises that those who have trusted in Him and followed His way will be vindicated, and that those who have departed from His way will be punished. To the righteous He holds out joy; they are to return to Zion. They are to inhabit the new earth, under the new heaven. The Book of Isaiah closes on a vision of Zion restored, in which the righteous will live and from which the wicked will be cast to their destruction.

THE BOOK OF JEREMIAH

INTRODUCTION. Jeremiah lived in times of uncertainty and violence. He was born some time during the reign of Josiah (640-609), whose religious reforms in 622 initiated a mood of national improvement and optimism. Unfortunately, Josiah was killed by Pharaoh Necho in 609, and his untimely death was only the first of a series of shocks for Judah. His successor, Jehoahaz (called Shallum in Jer. 22:11), was deposed by the Egyptians, who made another son, Jehoiakim, a puppet king in his brother's place. Jehoiakim undid much that his father had accomplished. Religious syncretism, social injustice, and political uncertainty marked his reign. For a while he remained faithful to the Egyptians, but after the victory of Nebuchadrezzar at the battle of Carchemish, he evidently decided he would do better with the rising Chaldeans (Babylonians). This led to invasions by the Chaldeans, Syrians, Moabites, and

Ammonites in c. 602, and later to the siege of Jerusalem. Jehoiakim died during the siege and was succeeded by his eighteen-year-old son, Jehoiachin (sometimes called Coniah). Jehoiachin capitulated to Nebuchadrezzar in 597 and with the queen mother, many of the nobles, priests, officials, and citizens was taken into captivity in Babylon. Nebuchadrezzar appointed Zedekiah, still another son of Josiah, to rule Judah. He seems to have been a well-intentioned but spineless king. He had several secret interviews with Jeremiah and probably favored his policy of non-alignment, but eventually was won over to the pro-Egyptian faction. When he refused to pay tribute to Babylon, the Babylonians attacked many Judean towns and besieged Jerusalem for over a year and a half, 589-7. Eventually the city fell, 587, and another group of captives was taken into exile. Gedaliah, a Jew of a good family and an excellent man, was made governor, but was assassinated about 582. Evidently fearful that the Babylonians would retaliate, a large group of Jews fled to Egypt, forcing Jeremiah to go with them.

In the midst of these events Jeremiah spent his prophetic career. Born into a priestly family in Anathoth, a little village north of Jerusalem, Jeremiah grew up steeped in the best traditions of Northern Israel (especially the work of Hosea) and in the life of the countryside. His call to prophesy came when he was a young man (see 1:4-16) and when (according to recent theories) the Babylonians were a rising force. They and not the Scythians (as used to be said) are most probably the foe from the north of which he often speaks. His early oracles (Chaps. 2-6 and possibly 8:4-9:1), the Temple sermon, and the calls to repentance, belong to the reign of Jehoiakim. The oracle against Egypt in Chapter 46 is probably connected with the battle of Carchemish, and Zedekiah's burning of Jeremiah's scroll (Chap. 26) and its subsequent re-writing by Jeremiah's scribe, Baruch, probably took place in the same year. Jeremiah's praise of the faithful Rechabites

(Chap. 35) and his imprisonment for foretelling the fall of Jerusalem (Chap. 20) may belong to the end of Jehoiakim's reign. Jeremiah's scriptures on the proud and selfish king may be read in 22:13-19.

The vision of the good and bad figs (Chap. 24), the incident of Hananiah and the yoke (Chaps. 27-8), and the letters to the exiles belong to the years after the first deportation (598). Many incidents are recounted of the siege years, 589-587. They include. roughly in this order, the warnings to Zedekiah (34:1-7, 37:1-10); the hypocritical freeing of the slaves (34); Jeremiah's arrest, supposedly for desertion (37:11-15); the secret interview with Zedekiah ("Is there any word from the Lord"; 37:16-21); the purchase of the field of Anathoth (32); the attempt of the princes to leave Jeremiah to die in the cistern (38:1-13); and a second secret talk with Zedekiah (38:14-28). After the fall of the city, Jeremiah was released from prison under Gedaliah's guardianship. It seems likely that he would have supported the governor in his efforts to rehabilitate the city. As recounted above, Jeremiah was forced to go to Egypt with a group of panic-stricken Jews after the assassination of Gedaliah, about 592.

SUMMARY OF THE BOOK OF JEREMIAH

SUPERSCRIPTION, 1:1-3. According to the editor, Jeremiah came from Anathoth and preached under Josiah, Jehoiakim, and Zedekiah, until Jerusalem was taken and the people exiled in 587. Actually, the book contains material written by Jeremiah several years after 587, besides editorial matter of a still later date.

THE CALL OF JEREMIAH, 1:4-19. Yahweh tells Jeremiah that He knew

him before he was even conceived and appointed him "a prophet to the nations." Jeremiah hesitates to accept such a responsibility—"Ah, Lord God! behold, I cannot speak: for I am a child"—but is told that he must go. However, he should not be afraid, for Yahweh will be with him. Yahweh touches Jeremiah's mouth to purify it, sets him over the nations, and explains that his task is in two parts —to destroy and tear down on one hand and to build and plant on the other. Two signs, the almond rod and the boiling pot in the north (portending danger from that direction)', accompany the call. Jeremiah must not be dismayed, for the Lord has made him a fortified city.

JEREMIAH'S EARLY MINISTRY, 2:1-6:30.

A series of oracles from Jeremiah's early ministry deals chiefly with Israel's faithlessness and failure to repent and with the punishments which may result, including the threat of danger from a frequently mentioned enemy, probably the Babylonians (i.e., here Chaldeans). Jeremiah considers Israel's history since she arrived in Canaan. In the desert she was faithful, but in Canaan she has chased after the worthless gods of Canaan. Priests, specialists in the laws, rulers, and prophets have all been unfaithful. The people have forsaken Yahweh, "the fountain of living waters and hewed out broken cisterns that they can hold no water." As a result they have suffered military reverses (Pharaoh Necho's victory over Josiah at Megiddo, 609, is probably meant). Jeremiah, like Isaiah and Hosea, registers his disapproval of alliances with either Egypt or Assyria. Israel in her sin is compared to a harlot and to a wild, degenerate vine which has unaccountably sprung from good seed, for she worships trees and stones, disregarding punishments sent to warn her, guilty of social injustice—"Also on your skirts is found the lifeblood of the guiltless poor" (R. S. V.) A long plea that Israel, the faithless wife, will repent and turn to Yahweh with a real change of heart (3:1- 4:4) is interrupted by some editorial material. A vivid description of the coming of the foe from the north closes with another call to repentance and an account of the prophet's own suffering, of the destruction and desolation which is to come. Jerusalem is spoken of as harlot who decks herself with paint and ornaments, but whose lovers turn against her and seek her life. In an ironic

passage, Jeremiah excuses the poor, who are foolish and ignorant; he will turn to the great, who surely know the Lord's ways. However, the rich are as faithless as the poor, and will be destroyed. There are more hints that punishment will come from the north. (A reference to the exile in 5:18-19 is probably editorial.) Diatribes against the people who do not realize that Yahweh is creator, against the wickedness of the rich, and against the shortcomings of priests and prophets close the chapter. Chapter 6 consists of miscellaneous threats and complaints. Jerusalem will be besieged. Gleaning the remnant of Israel for good grapes is a thankless task, for the people are corrupt and the leaders greedy and shallow, saying "Peace, peace; when there is no peace." The ancient paths which give rest to faithful souls are useless, for the people say, "We will not walk thereon," and Yahweh's watchmen (prophets) are denied, for the people say, "We will not hearken." The words on the prophets and the law of the Lord are neglected, and therefore offerings and sacrifices are meaningless. In this situation, the prophet is an "assayer and tester" (R. S. V.) of the people; but though he tries to refine the people as metal is refined in a furnace, his efforts are in vain.

THE TEMPLE SERMON, 7:1-8:3.

This section contains genuine teachings of Jeremiah, but as it stands is the work of the Deuteronomic editor. It contains Jeremiah's sermon in the Temple in which he denies that Temple rites and sacrifices give men security. Only a righteous life does that. Those who steal, murder, commit adultery, swear falsely, burn incense to Baal, and follow other gods make Yahweh's Temple into a den of robbers. The sins of the people—including making cakes for the queen of heaven (Ishtar)—are so great that the prophet is forbidden to intercede for them. The people have even built high places in the valley of Hinnom "to burn their sons and daughters in the fire"—a reference to child sacrifices, which are abhorrent to Yahweh. Disturbing corpses, thought to be blasphemous, is also mentioned as deserving of terrible punishment.

MISCELLANEOUS ORACLES, 8: 4-10:25.

A miscellany of oracles follows. Israel's "perpetual backsliding" is contrasted with the ways of migrating birds, who knew when to fly, while the poeple do not know the laws of God. They confuse the living law of the Lord with a law that can be written in a book. An invasion is regarded as punishment for sin. The prophet suffers deep grief over some unidentified calamity to the people. He is appalled, on another occasion, by their treachery and deceit. He laments the destruction of Jerusalem and Judah. He declares that the only reason for boasting consists not of wisdom or power or riches, but of the ethical nature of a God who exercises kindness, justice, and righteousness. A somewhat puzzling passage on the punishment both of the circumcised and the uncircumcised perhaps means that the rite itself is unimportant compared with the inner spiritual change of heart which is needed. A satirical piece on idols (10:1-10) is editorial. A dialogue between Jeremiah and Jerusalem speaks of the distress of the siege, the stupidity of the shepherds (i.e., rulers), and the desolation that is to overtake the cities of Judah. A prayer by the prophet, verses 23-4, concludes this section, for verse 25 is a late insertion.

THE COVENANT, SACRIFICES, AND A PLOT AGAINST JEREMIAH'S LIFE, 11:1-12:6.

In the strongest terms, Jeremiah is told to urge the people to obey the covenant, or they will be under a curse. It is not certain whether the reference is to the Sinai covenant or whether an oracle from Jeremiah has been reworked to provide support for the Deuteronomic Code. It does not really seem likely that Jeremiah would be in favor of the Code, with its emphasis on ritual and sacrifice. A short poem (verses 15-17) makes the point that sacrifice cannot ward off God's punishment. In an autobiographical passage, Jeremiah tells of a plot against him by his relatives at Anathoth. We do not know what the reasons for this plot were. The experience makes Jeremiah ask the question, "Wherefore doth the way of the wicked prosper?" which Yahweh answers, rather enigmatically, "If you have raced with men on foot, and they have wearied you, how will you compete with horses?" Evidently even worse experiences lie ahead for the prophet.

ISRAEL'S NEIGHBORS, 12:7-17.

Yahweh Himself laments Israel's destruction by her enemies. She is His heritage, His beloved, His vineyard. Her destroyers should be ashamed. The rest of the chapter (14-17) may be editorial.

PARABLES AND LAMENTS, 13:1-27.

Jeremiah is told to hide a loin cloth in the cleft of a rock and later to go and fetch it again. The loin cloth is spoiled and Yahweh points the moral: "Even so will I spoil the pride of Judah and the great pride of Jerusalem" (R. S. V.). The same pattern is followed in the parable of the jars. The jars are filled with wine; even so, kings, priests, prophets, and people of Jerusalem will be drunken. A short warning against pride may belong to 598, the year of the first deportation to Babylon. A dirge over the king and queen mother was doubtless for Jehoiachin and his mother Nehushta. Next, Jerusalem is addressed as a shepherdess who has left her flock. She will be shamed for the greatness of her sins. The prophet speaks ironically, "Can the Ethiopian change his skin, or the leopard his spots? then may ye also do good, that are accustomed to do evil." For her harlotry and abominations she will be shamed and scattered like chaff.

LAMENTS AND DIALOGUES, 14: 1-15:4. Some of the material here is editorial. The collection opens with a vivid description of the horrors of a drought. Noble and farmer alike suffer and even the wild asses pant for air. To a short confession of many backslidings, Yahweh replies that He will indeed remember the many iniquities He has observed. A prediction that false prophets will be the victims of famine and sword is followed by a short but touching lament in which Jeremiah weeps for "the virgin daughter of my people." The people make one more appeal to Yahweh: "we looked for peace, and there is no good; and for the time of healing, and behold trouble." Yahweh's reply (15:1-4), probably the work of the Deuteronomic editor, declares that even if Moses and Samuel spoke for the people, they deserve only "the sword to slay, and the dogs to tear, and the fowls of the heaven, and the beasts of the earth, to devour and destroy." A lament over Jerusalem, whose widows are more than the sands of the seas, whose mothers mourn their sons slain at noon day, is followed by the prophet's protest that he is suffering persecution and isolation because of his calling. He even questions God's good faith: "Wilt thou be altogether unto me as a liar, and as the waters that fail?" Yahweh's reply is stern. He must speak what is of value and not worthless things; then he will be as strong as a fortified wall and no one shall prevail against him, for Yahweh will be with him to save and deliver him.

A MISCELLANY, 16:1-18:17. These chapters contain a collection of threats, promises, prayers and other forms. Many of them are not by Jeremiah. A rather prosy explanation of Jeremiah's failure to marry because of his devotion to his prophetic vocation is followed by a very late prophecy of the return from the dispersion, by a threat of punishment for Israel's sin, and by a post-exilic prediction that all nations will turn to Yahweh. The poem which says that the sin of Judah is written both on the people's hearts and on the horns of the altars, i.e., in their rituals, is probably by Jeremiah. A short psalm contrasting "the man that trusteth in man" with "the man that trusteth in the Lord" remind us of Psalm 1, and is followed by two proverbs, one on the deceitfulness of the human heart and one on ill-gotten gains. In an unlikely setting, close to a statement on the greatness of the Temple and one on Sabbath observance, is a touching prayer by Jeremiah (17:14-18), "Heal me, O Lord, and I shall be healed; save me and I shall be saved." He has spoken the word of the Lord and been mocked for his pains. He wants his enemies put to shame: "Let them be confounded that persecute me, but let not me be confounded: let them be dismayed, but let not me be dismayed . . ." The parable of the potter (18:1-12) is effective. As Jeremiah watches the potter rework a spoiled vessel, he hears the word of the Lord, "O house of Israel, cannot I do with you as this potter? saith the Lord. Behold as the clay is in the potter's hand, so are ye in mine hand, O house of Israel." If He threatens a nation and it turns from its evil ways, He will repent of the evil that He intended. But the people say: "There is no hope: but we will walk after our own devices, and we will everyone do the imagination of his evil heart." A short poem on the unnaturalness of Israel's apostasy asks "Does the snow of Lebanon leave the crags of Sirion?" (R. S. V.) How can the virgin Israel make their land "desolate and a perpetual hissing"?

EVENTS IN JEREMIAH'S LIFE, 18:18-20:18. Probably this plot was the culmination of a long struggle between Jeremiah and a group of religious leaders. They plan to "smite him with the tongue," i.e., slander him. Jeremiah is very angry, especially as in the past he has begged God for mercy towards them. Now he asks God for terrible punishments to fall upon them, famine and sword for their children, childlessness and widowhood for their wives, death by pestilence and sword.

A somewhat confusing narrative follows. Jeremiah is told to take a potter's earthen flask and go to the Potsherd Gate with elders and priests. Then he is told to make a pronouncement about Tophet and the valley of Hinnom. Only later do we understand the meaning of the potter's flask. Yahweh will break the people of the city as the flask is broken. Apparently as a result of this incident, Pashur, the priest, probably an official responsible for keeping order in the Temple precinct, beats Jeremiah and puts him in the stocks. Jeremiah says that he should be called Terror, that Judah would fall to Babylon, and that he, Pashur, with all his house, would go into captivity. Then he turns to God with a bitter complaint: "O Lord, thou hast deceived me, and I was deceived: thou art stronger than I, and has prevailed: I am in derision daily, every one mocketh me." In spite of this mockery, he is compelled to speak the word of the Lord by "a burning fire shut up in my bones." Even while he hears his acquaintances whispering about him, watching for his fall, the prophet has not lost his faith in God, who is with him "as a dread warrior" (R. S. V.). "O Lord of hosts," he cries, "Who triest the righteous, who seest the heart and the mind, let me see Thy vengeance upon them, for to Thee I have committed my cause" (R. S. V.). He praises God and curses the day he was born.

JEREMIAH AND THE KINGS OF JUDAH, 21:1-23:8.

During the siege of Jerusalem (589-587) Zedekiah sends a deputation to ask Jeremiah if the Lord will make him withdraw. Jeremiah replies in the words of Yahweh that He will Himself fight against His people, "even in anger, and in fury, and in great wrath." Those who survive pestilence, sword, and famine will be carried away into Babylon. Next follow an oracle against the house of David and one against Jerusalem, and a Deuteronomic appeal to the "house of the king of Judah" to do justice and righteousness. "Weep ye not for the dead" (22:10-12) refers to Josiah, killed at Megiddo, and is addressed to his son, Shallum, i.e., Jehoahaz, who was exiled into Egypt and is probably "him that goeth away: for he shall return no more, nor see his native land." Next (verses 13-19) is a condemnation of Jehoiakim (609-598) for building a grand palace with spacious upper rooms and neglecting the poor and needy. As a result, no one will mourn for him and he will be "buried with the burial of an ass." After a lament over Jerusalem, whose sufferings in the siege are compared to those of a woman in labor, Jeremiah turns his attention to Jehoiachin (598/97), who succeeded his father during the siege, but was carried into captivity in Babylon three months later. The people ask "Is this man Coniah [a short form of the king's name] a despised broken idol? is he a vessel wherein is no pleasure? wherefore are they cast out, he and his seed, and be cast into a land which they know not?" Jeremiah's comment was "Write ye this man childless, a man that shall not prosper in his days: for no man of his seed shall prosper, sitting upon the throne of David, and ruling any more in Judah." Jehoiachin was not in fact childless, but the second half of the prophecy was accurate, for Zerubbabel, his grandson, though governor of Judah, never really reestablished the throne of David. Woes on false shepherds and promises of the return and of the restoration of the house of David close this section.

JEREMIAH AND THE PROPHETS, 23:9-40.

Jeremiah says he is like a drunken man at the spectacle of the adultery of the Lord. Both prophet and priest are ungodly. The prophets of Samaria prophesy by Baal, and the Jerusalem prophets are even worse, for they spread ungodliness all over the land by not honestly presenting the word of Yahweh. Their prophecies are only the reflection of their own dreams. The passage on the burden of the Lord (verses 33-40) is mostly editorial.

THE GOOD AND THE BAD FIGS, 24:1-10; 25:1-38. In a vision which recalls those of Amos, Jeremiah sees two baskets, one of freshly ripened figs and one of rotten figs too bad to eat. Yahweh interprets the vision. The good figs are those who are sent "into the land of the Chaldeans" (Babylon). "I will set mine eyes upon them for good, and I will bring them again to this land: and I will build them, and not pull them down; and I will plant them, and not pluck them up. And I will give them a heart to know me, that I am the Lord: and they shall be my people, and I will be their God: for they shall return unto me with their whole heart." But the bad figs are "the residue of Jerusalem, that remain in this land, and them that dwell in the land of Egypt." They will be "a reproach and a proverb, a taunt and a curse" and will be cut off by sword, famine, and pestilence.

WARNINGS TO JUDAH AND YAHEWEH'S WRATH, 25:1-38. Because of Judah's disobedience, the Deuteronomic editor prophesies her destruction. After seventy years (a vague round number) Babylon will be punished. The list of the nations who must drink the cup of Yahweh's wrath was probably intended to go with the oracles against foreign nations in Chapters 46-51. The chapter ends with a prophecy of the coming of Yahweh in judgment. It has affinities with later apocalyptic literature.

JEREMIAH IN CONFLICT WITH PRIESTS AND PROPHETS, 26:1-28:17. At the beginning of Jehoiakim's reign (609) Jeremiah delivered the temple sermon, of which an account has already been given in Chapter 7. The sermon caused an uproar. Indignant at Jeremiah's prediction that Jerusalem would be desolate, the priests and prophets attacked him and he was brought to trial, but the "princes" (i.e., court officials) and many of the people were on his side and denied that he deserved the death sentence. It is clear that the sermon placed Jeremiah in a dangerous position, but that he acted calmly and with dignity, insisting that he did not deserve it, as he was the spokesman of Yahweh.

The next two chapters, 27 and 28, skip to the reign of Zedekiah (597-587), at a time when a revolt against Babylon is being plotted. Putting on a yoke as a symbol of submission and addressing the kings involved in the conspiracy (Edom, Moab, Ammon, Tyre, and Sidon were involved), Jeremiah insists that Yahweh Himself has given these lands into the hands of Nebuchadrezzar, who is His agent. To Zedekiah he advises submission to the yoke of Babylon. He tells the priests and people not to listen to the prophets who say that the Babylonians will bring back the cult objects they took from the temple. Hananiah, apparently one of these optimistic prophets, says the cult objects will be returned in two years, and breaks the yoke from Jerusalem's shoulders as a sign that the yoke of Babylon will be cast off. But Jeremiah goes his own way and Hananiah dies that same year.

LETTERS TO THE EXILES, 29:1-32. Some time after this, Jeremiah composes an open letter to the elders of the exiles in Babylon: "Thus saith the Lord of hosts, the God of Israel, unto all that are carried away captives, whom I have caused to be carried away from Jerusalem unto Babylon; Build ye houses, and dwell in them; and plant gardens, and eat the fruit of them; Take ye wives, and beget sons and daughters; and take wives for your sons, and give your daughters to husbands, that they may bear sons and daughters; that ye may be increased there, and not diminished. And seek the peace of the city whither I have caused you to be carried away captives, and pray unto the Lord for it: for in the peace thereof ye shall have peace." In Yahweh's name, the people are assured that He has plans for them, that He will bring them back within seventy years (a vague round number). (A Deuteronomic passage promises to gather the exiles in from the nations.) The chapter concludes with a fragment of a separate letter about Shemaiah, who had apparently written to Jerusalem to ask Zephaniah why he had not put Jeremiah in the stocks for advising the people to settle down in Babylon. Jeremiah says Shemaiah will be punished.

THE BOOK OF COMFORT, 30:1-31:40. Most of these oracles of comfort come from a much later date than Jeremiah. The editor seems to have been influenced by Second Isaiah. Most of the oracles deal with the joyful restoration of Israel. However, the poem in 31:2-6 is widely thought to be Jeremiah's own. It confirms Yahweh's everlasting love for the people who "found grace in the wilderness" and promises that Israel will be restored and will again plant vineyards on the mountains of Samaria.

JEREMIAH AND THE FIELD AT ANATHOTH, 32:1-44. With this chapter we return to the period when Jerusalem is still under siege and Jeremiah in prison. He has an opportunity, as next of kin, to purchase some family land at Anathoth. Astonishingly, he takes the option, signing the deed in prison and having it properly witnessed and put away in an earthen pot for safekeeping. Thus he vividly dramatizes his faith that "houses and fields and vineyards" will again be occupied in the land. (The prayer in 16-25 is secondary.)

THE RESTORATION OF ISRAEL, 33:1-26. Except for verses 4-5, which seem to refer to the defenses against the Chaldeans, this chapter consists of late predictions regarding the return, the rebuilding of Jerusalem, and the restoration of the Davidic monarchy and the Levitical priesthood.

PROMISE TO ZEDEKIAH, 34:1-7. Through Jeremiah, Yahweh tells Zedekiah that He is giving the city over to the hand of the king of Babylon, that he, the king, will have to go to Babylon, but that he will die in peace. It seems as if a condition—perhaps that Zedekiah should submit—proposed by the prophet has been dropped out. In any case Zedekiah was in fact blinded and taken to Babylon.

THE SLAVE-OWNERS OF JERUSALEM, 34:8-22. During the siege, the slave-owners, partly because their slaves were now a burden, partly for what they claimed were religious reasons, vow to release their slaves. When the siege is lifted, they reclaim their slaves. Jeremiah censures them for this piece of hypocrisy.

THE RECHABITES, 35:1-19. The Rechabites were a primitive religious group who strove to maintain the "pure" standards of the nomad life, free from the corruptions of Canaan. They lived in tents, did not farm, and refused to drink wine because it was connected with the agricultural life of Canaan. They had been forced to withdraw inside the walls of Jerusalem because of the siege. Jeremiah seems to admire them, regarding their refusal to drink wine as a manifestation of obedience to their code. He holds them up as an example to the disobedient people of Jerusalem.

THE BURNING OF THE SCROLL, 36:1-32. In 605, Nebuchadrezzar defeated the Egyptians and the Assyrians of Carchemish. This put Judah, whose King Jehoiakim had been the choice of the Egyptians, in a serious position. Jeremiah chooses this crucial time, when Judah was in danger of "the foe from the north," to publish his oracles. He dictates them to his secretary, Baruch, since for some reason which we are not given, he has been forbidden to enter the Temple area. At his master's direction, Baruch reads the scroll before the prophets. When the princes (court officials) hear of this, they in turn demand a reading. What they hear alarms them so much that they decide that the king ought to know about it, althought at the same time they advise Baruch and Jeremiah to hide. The king does not take the scroll as seriously as the officials do. As the reader proceeds, grimly the king cuts piece after piece from the scroll and burns it in the brazier, in spite of the protests of the elders, until the entire scroll is burned up.

Jeremiah then once more dictates the contents of the scroll to Baruch, saying as he does so that the king of Babylon will certainly destroy the land and that Jehoiakim's body will be exposed to the elements. (This prophecy does not seem to have come to pass.)

THE SIEGE OF JERUSALEM, 37: 1-40:6. After Jehoiakim died and Jehoiachin was taken to Babylon, Zedekiah (597-587) was appointed King of Judah by the Babylonians. Jeremiah is still free to preach at this time, but neither Zedekiah nor the people pay attention to him. Zedekiah and the Pharaoh Hophra conspire to rebel against Nebuchadrezzar. This move disturbs Jeremiah, who consistently regards the Babylonian (Chaldean) conquest of Judah as the will of Yahweh. When the prophet tries to leave Jerusalem, at a time when the siege is temporarily lifted, he is arrested as a deserter and imprisoned. The king reveals his anxious state of mind by interviewing Jeremiah secretly and asking him "Is there any word from the Lord?" He may have hoped for good news, but Jeremiah's reply is stern: "Thou shalt be delivered into the hand of the king of Babylon." During the final days of the siege, Jeremiah's enemies complain to the king that he is undermining the morale of the soldiers and obtain

the royal permission to put him to death. They cast him into an empty cistern, where he sinks in the mud. Fortunately an Ethiopian eunuch takes pity on his plight and persuades the king to let him rescue the prophet, who is pulled up with ropes. The king interviews him once more, but Jeremiah's stand is unchanged: surrender to Babylon and be spared; continue to fight and neither king nor city shall escape.

Finally, a breach is made in the wall of the besieged city. Zedekiah flees, but is caught and forced to watch his sons killed. Then he is blinded and he and the people are taken to Babylon. Jeremiah is released from the court of the guard and entrusted to the care of Gedaliah. (Much of the rest of this chapter is secondary and so are the first six verses of Chapter 40.)

GEDALIAH, 40:7-41:18. The authentic narrative resumes at this point. Gedaliah is appointed governor and persuades many of the Jews to serve the Chaldeans. Many fugitives return to Judah to gather the crops and live under Gedaliah's governorship. Unfortunately, Gedaliah, though a promising leader, is too good-natured for his own safety. When Johanan comes to warn him that one Ishmael is planning to kill him, Gedaliah refuses to take action. Ishmael assassinates him, kills a large number of innocent pilgrims, and captures the people of Mizpah. These people are luckily rescued by Johanan.

ESCAPE TO EGYPT, 42:1-43:7. The rescued citizens of Mizpah and Johanan and his companions consult Jeremiah as to whether they are wise in trying to flee to Egypt. They promise to act according to the word of Yahweh, but when the prophet tells them that Yahweh wishes them to remain in Judah, they accuse him of lying, of following Baruch's advice instead of God's, and of wanting to deliver them into the hands of the Chaldeans. They flee to Egypt, taking with them Jeremiah, Baruch, and the people left in Gedaliah's charge.

JEREMIAH IN EGYPT, 43:8-44:30. After his arrival in Egypt, Jeremiah hides some large stones under the pavement at the entrance to Pharaoh's house, as a symbol that Nebuchadrezzar will come and set up his throne in that spot, bringing with him pestilence, captivity, and the sword. Jeremiah further censures the people (much of this is Deuteronomic), but the women insist that their attentions to the queen of heaven (Ishtar) are effective and will be continued.

AN ORACLE ON BARUCH, 45:1-5. Baruch seems to have suffered in Yahweh's service much as Jeremiah suffered, but like his master is told that he must be prepared for even more suffering: "Behold, that which I have built will I break down, and that which I have planted I will pluck up, even this whole land. And seekest thou great things for thyself? seek them not . . ."

ORACLES AGAINST FOREIGN NATIONS, 46:1-51:64. Some of these oracles have been added or edited later. Parts of the oracle against Egypt may be original and are perhaps related to the battle of Carchemish. The oracle on Nebuchadrezzar is secondary. An oracle against the Philistines, the historical background of which is uncertain, is followed by an enormously long oracle against Moab, which may be genuine in part, if indeed the Moabites joined the Babylonians in attacking Egypt. A prophecy of war against the Ammonites says that will be dispossessed and that Rabbah will become a desolate mound. The oracle against Edom reflects the hatred of the Israelites for their kinsmen because they took advantage of the siege and fall of Jerusalem to occupy land in Judah. The same situation is reflected in the Book of Obadiah. It does not seem very probable that Jeremiah was concerned about this particular situation. The oracle against Damascus is probably a late addition. The oracle against the Arab tribes Kedar and Hazor may find its origin in historical events of Jeremiah's time, but the exact circumstances are not known. The substantial group of oracles (50:1-51:64) directed against Babylon seem not to be from Jeremiah, since they are mainly about Babylon's fall and the return of the exiles and since they fail to recommend submission to Babylon, a chief feature of Jeremiah's policy.

THE CAPTIVITY AND THE RELEASE OF JEHOIACHIN, 52:1-34. This chapter reproduces II Kings 24:18-25:30, omitting the narratives about Gedaliah covered in Chapters 40-43. No doubt this historical narrative was added to show that Jerusalem fell, as Jeremiah said it would, and to continue the story of the city and the exiles down to the release of Jehoiachin from prison.

THE BOOK OF LAMENTATIONS

INTRODUCTION
The word Lamentations means "dirges." We have seen dirges before in the Bible, notably David's lament for Saul and Jonathan (II Sam. 3:33-4) and Amos's for the virgin Israel (Amos 5:1-2). Lamentations consists of five dirges. The first four are alphabetical acrostics, that is, the twenty-two stanzas begin with the successive letters of the Hebrew alphabet. The fifth contains the right number of stanzas, but is not an acrostic; perhaps the author never completed his work. The alphabetical order may have been intended as an aid to memorizing the poems. The reader can get a good idea of the original

poetry from the R. S. V., where the translator has preserved the Hebrew line division and the break (called a caesura) in the middle of the line.

The book was traditionally ascribed to Jeremiah, but the artificial style is quite unlike his. Moreover, Jeremiah would have repudiated some of the ideas of the author, who admired royalty, advocated an Egyptian alliance, and was concerned with the ritual aspects of religion. Probably the poems were written by a contemporary or contemporaries of Jeremiah (soon after the fall of Jerusalem in 586 B.C.), though some critics would place them later. The dirges are still sung today in synagogues on the ninth day of Ab.

SUMMARY OF THE BOOK OF LAMENTATIONS

The first dirge (Chap. 1) describes the grief and suffering of Jerusalem:

How lonely sits the city
    that was full of people
How like a widow she has become,
    she that was great among the
        nations!   (R. S. V.)

Remembering all the precious things she has lost, the city weeps bitterly, weeps for the maidens, youths, and children taken captive, weeps for her princes, weeps for hunger, and weeps for the exile of Judah: "Is it nothing to you, all ye that pass by? behold, and see if there be any sorrow like unto my sorrow . . ." The poet acknowledges that the city's sin is a cause of her suffering. "Jerusalem hath grievously sinned; therefore is she removed," and "the Lord is righteous; for I have rebelled against His commandment." He holds the city's miseries up before the Lord, praying that His enemies in turn may suffer.

The second dirge (Chap. 2) brings out more clearly the fact that Yahweh's "fierce anger" is the cause of the city's ruin. He has done what He has long threatened. He has destroyed not only the palaces and strongholds of Jerusalem, but also His own sacred places, altar, and sanctuary. "The law is no more," and the prophets receive only fake visions. Children faint from hunger in the streets and even in their mothers' arms.

Should women eat their offspring,
    the children of their tender care?
Should priest and prophet be slain
    in the sanctuary of the Lord?
            (R. S. V.)

In the third poem (Chap. 3) the poet speaks as an individual who has experienced the sufferings of the siege. Yahweh has walled him about with suffering, has torn him as a bear tears its prey, has driven arrows into his heart. Yet he is resigned in his affliction, recognizing that sin and rebellion are the cause of suffering. He repents his wrong-doing, calls on Yahweh and weeps, and puts his ultimate trust in God's justice and mercy. "Though he cause grief, he will have compassion according to the abundance of his steadfast love" (R. S. V., 3:32). This is the central message of the book.

The fourth poem (Chap. 4), like the first and second, laments the fall of Jerusalem. It contrasts her past grandeur and holiness with her present state of misery and humiliation.

How the gold has grown dim,
    how the pure gold is changed!
The holy stones lie scattered
    at the head of every street.
The precious stones of Zion
    worth their weight in fine gold,
how they are reckoned as earthen
        pots,
    The work of a potter's hands.

The princes who were whiter than snow are black and shriveled, the women now eat their children. Better to have perished by the sword. The sins of priests and prophets, who shed the blood of the innocent, are punished, for God has scattered them. The inhabitants of Judah were deeply embittered because their neighbors, the Edomites, joined in the looting of the city, and the poet closes with a threat that their iniquity, too, will be punished. The final dirge is a prayer on behalf of the whole nation. They remind Yahweh that they are now orphans and slaves.

The land is conquered, the people are starving, the women ravished, the princes overpowered, the elders insulted, the youths enslaved. "The joy of our heart is ceased; our dance is turned into mourning. For their sins Yahweh has forgotten them." Yet He is king forever, and the final prayer is "Renew our days as of old."

THE BOOK OF EZEKIEL

INTRODUCTION

The exile is a great milestone in the history of the Jewish people. Behind it lies the ancient religion of the Hebrews, while after it appear what we can begin to call Judaism. Ezekiel, the contemporary and disciple of Jeremiah, is therefore an important figure, because he helped to shape what Judaism was to be. Unfortunately, the book which bears his name bristles with difficulties. The text is corrupt and the style turgid, repetitious, and obscure. Critics disagree on important points such as the date of the book and the location of Ezekiel's ministry, whether it took place in Palestine, Babylon, or both. While most scholars agree that the book has undergone fairly substantial editing, probably in the fifth century, the extent of this editing is in dispute. Some scholars think that the editing has been so thorough that the characteristic style of the book, which can be recognized even in translation, is the editor's rather than the author's.

The strange psychological make-up of the prophet adds to the difficulties. To a greater extent than any other classical prophet, he was subject to trances, ecstasies, periods of muteness, and perhaps paralysis. He employed strange symbols, allegories, and eccentric signs to a much greater extent than his predecessors, and some of his visions are much more weird and complex. His claims to have been transported from Babylon to Jerusalem "in the spirit" to see the pagan rites being celebrated in the Temple (Chaps. 8-11) have led some historians to suppose that he actually did return there and others to credit him with second sight. Yet despite his eccentricity or perhaps because of it, Ezekiel's strange personality has a certain fascination for those who are willing to work through the difficulties of the book.

According to the traditional account, Ezekiel was deported to Babylon by Nebuchadrezzar with the first group of exiles in 597. Five years after that, in 593 or 592, he received his call in the strange vision of the throne-chariot (Chap. 1), and thereafter prophesied in Babylon for over twenty years. Archaeological studies seem to support this, for details in the book display a close knowledge of Babylon in the early sixth century. Perhaps the problems of his knowledge of Jerusalem can be solved by assuming that the exiles frequently had news of their homeland or (less probably) by assuming a return visit to the sacred city.

Ezekiel's task in preaching to the exiles was not an easy one. Many thoughtful Jews must have questioned whether the ancient relationship with Yahweh still held when their country was taken away from them and when the Temple was destroyed. "How shall we sing the Lord's song in a strange land?" asked a poet. Ezekiel's attempts to clarify the position of the exiles seem to be compounded of judgment and promise. He sees the exile and the fall of Jerusalem as the divinely ordained punishment for past sins. But the vision of the valley of dry bones (Chap. 37) shows that he hoped for the miracle of a new beginning for Israel. The bones gained flesh, the wind blew upon them, and "they stood upon their feet, an exceeding great army." So Israel would become one living nation again and be restored to her homeland. If Chapters 40-48 contain a kernel of Ezekiel's own thinking, he pictures the restored community as an ecclesiastical one, centering on the Temple and its ritual. This would agree with his emphasis elsewhere on the importance of cultic purity, and his distress at the pagan rites in the Temple itself. It must be remembered that Ezekiel was a priest as well as a prophet and therefore emphasized the priestly outlook much more than earlier prophets did. He also emphasized the holiness of God more than His compassion or justice, and even implied that the very act of restoration was an act of self-vindication, carried out so that Israel and the nations might know that Yahweh was Lord.

In conclusion we may say that Ezekiel, though perhaps less attractive than his great predecessors, has an importance equal to theirs in the history of religion. His book reflects the thought of a great period of transition. His belief in the restoration of a purified Israel under a Davidic king had important consequences and his emphasis on individualism has been important both in later Judaism and in Christianity. The book in its present form falls into four parts: (1) visions and oracles before the fall of Jerusalem, (2) oracles against pagan nations, (3) oracles and visions on the restoration, (4) the vision of the restored Temple and community.

SUMMARY OF THE BOOK OF EZEKIEL

SUPERSCRIPTION, 1:1-3. Ezekiel writes that his call came to him in the fifth year of the exile (i.e., 593 or 592) by the river Chebar (a canal which passed through Nippur, a city south of Babylon). It is not known what he meant by "the thirtieth year." The editorial comment in verses 2 and 3 tells us that the prophet was the son of Buzi, the priest.

THE CALL OF EZEKIEL, 1:4-3:27. The first part of Ezekiel, Chapters 1 through 24, deals with events which took place before the fall of Jerusalem in 587. Ezekiel's call is the most elaborate and the strangest of all recorded of the prophets. It seems that the violence of an electrical storm mingled with the prophet's own imaginings to produce an extraordinary vision of Yahweh in glory. The imagery of the vision combines motifs from Hebrew and Babylonian religious symbols. The throne-chariot of Yahweh is borne by four living creatures, each with four faces (a man, a lion, an ox, and an eagle), and four wings. The creatures move harmoniously, animated by the spirit, gleaming like fire. Beside each of the creatures is a wheel, with a wheel within it, so that the chariot can move in any direction. The wheels are like topaz, and the rims are full of eyes. The whole chariot symbolizes the all-seeing power, purpose, and majesty of the deity. Above the throne is "the likeness of a firmament," shining like sapphire. The sound of the creatures' wings sounds like the roaring of mighty waters. Above the firmament is the throne and on it "the semblance of a man" (A. T.), who shines like bronze and about whom seems to be something like a rainbow. (Notice how throughout his description of the vision, Ezekiel is careful to say only what it resembles. He wishes to avoid saying that the deity actually appeared in these shapes, yet he wishes to convey the presence of God in mystery and majesty.) Before this vision the prophet prostrates himself. A voice addressing him as "son of man" (i.e., human being, "mortal man" as in A. T.) tells him to stand to receive his commission. Fearless in the midst of thistles and scorpions, he is to speak to the rebellious house of Israel. As a sign of his calling he is given a scroll covered with lamentations to eat, a scroll which tastes like honey in his mouth. To the sound of wings, the spirit lifts him up, and he dwells "overhelmed" (R. S. V.) for seven days at Tel-abib by the river Chebar. At the end of the seven days he is told that he is the watchman for the house of Israel; that is, if he does not warn men against wickedness, he will be responsible for their sins. Once again he sees the glory of the Lord on a plain and is told that, bound and mute, he will be unable to prophesy until the Lord opens his mouth.

THE FATE OF JERUSALEM AND JUDAH, 4:1-7:27.

At the divine command, Ezekiel performs a series of acts which dramatize the coming fate of city and people. He draws a sketch or plan of Jerusalem under siege. He lies for 390 days on his left side and 40 days on his right, apparently to indicate how long Israel and Judah would be punished. He prepares emergency rations of coarse bread and water to signify the privations of the siege. He cuts his hair with a sword and divides it into three parts to show the different fates of the inhabitants and Yahweh's anger against them. He inveighs against the mountains of Israel and prophesies the horrors of the days of doom.

THE VISIONS OF THE TEMPLE AT JERUSALEM, 8:1-11:25.

The spirit takes him by a lock of hair and carries him to Jerusalem where, north of the altar gate, he beholds the "image of jealousy" (R. S. V. "abomination"; a pagan image, perhaps the Asherah, consort of Baal). Penetrating the wall, Ezekiel sees heathen rites performed before pictures of reptiles, beasts, and idols. By the north gate are women weeping for Tammuz (a dying and rising fertility god, somewhat like Osiris or Syrian Adonis), and in the inner court of the Temple are twenty-five men worshipping the sun. Horrified by these abominations, Ezekiel beholds the slaughter of the idolators and the departure from the Temple of the glory of Yahweh by the same throne-chariot in which He first appeared to the prophet. By the east gate he sees twenty-five men, some of whom he names. One of them, Pelatiah, dies, and Ezekiel asks, "will Thou make a full end of the remnant of Israel?" He is told (in what may be an editorial addition) that the exiles will return to Israel and will be given a new spirit. "I will take the stony heart out of their flesh, and will give them a heart of flesh." The glory of Yahweh leaves the city and Ezekiel tells the exiles what he has seen.

PROPHECIES OF DOOM AND EXILE, 12:1-14:23.

Once again at God's command, Ezekiel performs signs which symbolize the exile. He acts out the hasty packing of baggage and by night digs a hole through the wall, as though fleeing secretly. He drinks water and eats bread trembling, as though in fear. Yahweh promises him that the prophecies will be fulfilled. The prophet denounces prophets who offer their own notions as prophecy, instead of waiting on the word of Yahweh; he also denounces sorceresses, diviners, and idolators. Jerusalem will be punished with the sword, famine, wild beasts, and pestilence.

FOUR ALLEGORIES, 15:1-17:24.
Jerusalem is like a useless vine, good
for nothing but firewood. She is like
a faithless wife, who takes the gifts
of her husband to make heathen
images, offers her children as sacrifices, builds unlawful shrines, and
commits harlotries with Egypt and
Assyria. For all these sins she shall
be exposed in her nakedness; yet she
shall be ashamed and Yahweh may
yet resume His covenant with her.
As a great eagle plucks the top of
a cedar and takes up seed and scatters it on fertile fields near rivers,
so Nebuchadrezzar plucks up the king
of Judah (Zedekiah) and the people
of Judah and takes them to Babylon. To another eagle a well-rooted
vine turns for water as Zedekiah
turned to Hophra, Pharaoh of Egypt,
and for this it shall wither away.
Finally comes the allegory of the
cedar which is to be planted on a
lofty mountain of Israel. The cedar
is to be noble and fruitful, and birds
of all kinds shall nestle in it. All
the trees shall know that Yahweh
has power to bring down the high
tree, raise up the low, dry up the
green tree, and make the dry tree
perish. (This final allegory may be a
Messianic addition from a later
period.)

**INDIVIDUAL RESPONSIBILITY,
18:1-32.** This chapter enunciates one
of Ezekiel's most important doctrines.
He begins by quoting a popular proverb, "The fathers have eaten sour
grapes and the children's teeth are
set on edge." In the words of Yahweh he repudiates this principle of
collective guilt and responsibility.
"Behold, all souls are mine." Each
man will be held responsible for his
own acts. This is illustrated by three
hypothetical men. The righteous man
who has broken no religious laws
and who has been moral and upright in his dealings with neighbors,
debtors, and the poor "shall surely
live." However, his son may be a
robber, murderer, adulterer, oppressor, and idolater, and "he shall
surely die; his blood shall be upon

him." In turn his son, the righteous
man's grandson who re-enacts his
grandfather's religious and moral
piety, "shall surely live." Further-
more, the wicked man who turns
from his wickedness shall live, for
God has no pleasure in the death of
the wicked. On the other hand, the
righteous man who turns away from
righteousness and commits evil will
die in his sins. The chapter ends with
an assertion of the justice of Yahweh
and a plea for repentance. "Cast
away from you all your transgressions, whereby ye have transgressed;
and make you a new heart and a
new spirit: for why will ye die, O
house of Israel?"

**MISCELLANEOUS LAMENTS, OR-
ACLES, AND PROPHECIES, 19:1-
24:14.** In two dirges in which Israel
is compared to a lioness and to a
vine, the fates of Jehoahaz, Jehoiachin, and Zedekiah are lamented.
In an oracle which is addressed to
the elders of Israel in exile, he speaks
of the unfaithfulness of the people in
Egypt, in the wilderness, and in
Canaan itself. Eventually the people
will be purged, pardoned, and restored. After a short oracle against
the south (Judah?) follows a series
of fascinating prophecies of the
sword of Yahweh. The passages are
in verse and may have been sung and
accompanied by a sword-dance.
Yahweh's sword is whetted and
polished for slaughter; it is the rod
of His wrath, and will come down
once, twice, thrice, bringing terror
and destruction. The sword is also
the sword of the king of Babylon.
The hour of the prince of Israel
(Zedekiah) has come and the sword
of the Ammonites will be sheathed
and they will be destroyed.

Three oracles describe Jerusalem as
a city of blood, as silver which will
be smelted, and as an aggregation of
classes—princes, priests, prophets,
people—all guilty. Chapter 23 depicts
the adulterous wives of Yahweh and
part of Chapter 24 pictures Jerusalem under siege as a cauldron boil-

ing on a fire; "woe to the bloody city, to the pot whose scum is thereon. . . . I will ever make the pile for fire great."

THE DEATH OF EZEKIEL'S WIFE AND THE FALL OF JERUSALEM, 24:15-27.

This is almost the only fact we know about the prophet's personal life. Yahweh tells him he is to lose his wife, the delight of his eyes; yet he is not to mourn, perhaps as a sign to the exiles that they should not lament the unbearable news of the fall of Jerusalem, which will reach them shortly. This concludes the first part of the book: events and oracles up to the fall of Jerusalem.

ORACLES AGAINST PAGAN NATIONS, 25:1-32:32.

These form the second part of the Book of Ezekiel as it now stands. There are similar collections of oracles against foreign nations in Amos, Isaiah, and Jeremiah. While some are original with the prophet and some are actually earlier than 587, some have been added at later times. As post-exile ideas of the return developed, it was often believed that the surrounding nations, which had despised Israel and her God, would be punished and defeated and forced to recognize Yahweh. (See above on Second Isaiah.)

Israel's old enemies, Ammon, Moab, Edom, and the Philistines are attacked first. They will be punished, and says Yahweh, "They shall know that I am the Lord." Next a series of dirges and oracles tell of the coming destruction of Tyre and its descent into Sheol. There is also an oracle against Tyre's companion city, Sidon. The group of poems ends with the promise that these countries will be the object of Yahweh's vengeance and with the prophecy that the scattered peoples of the house of Israel will be gathered together and will live securely in their own land again. Next comes a series of seven oracles against Egypt and the pharaohs, some in the form of dirges. The great sea-

dragon (A. T. crocodile) which lies in the Egyptian waters is complacent, but Yahweh will draw it out with hooks and cast it into the desert, so that all Egypt will know that Yahweh is Lord of creation. Yahweh's sword will descend on Egypt and her strength shall fail her. She will become the slave of Nebuchadrezzar. Several short oracles along the same lines follow. In Chapter 31 Egypt is likened to a great cedar tree which reaches to the sky and draws its nourishment from the great deep. The birds build their nests in it and under its branches the animals bear their young. Even the trees of the Garden of Eden cannot surpass it. Yet it will be cut down by the Babylonians, doomed to go down into the underworld and lie with the pagans who have been slain by the sword. A dirge for Pharaoh, who will be destroyed by Yahweh, and one for the teeming multitudes of Egypt conclude this section.

THE PROPHET AS WATCHMAN AND THE FALL OF JERUSALEM, 33:1-33.

From this chapter through Chapter 39, the book is concerned with the restoration of Israel. It seems as if once Jerusalem had fallen, Ezekiel took heart and was able to plan for the future; however, it must be remembered that there may be large editorial passages here. The first chapters deal with the responsibilities of prophet and people.

Again addressing the prophet as "son of man," Yahweh orders Ezekiel to tell his fellow countrymen that he, the prophet, is their watchman. It is his duty to warn the people when danger is at hand; it is the people's duty to heed the warning. If the prophet does not blow the warning trumpet and one of the people is lost, his blood is the prophet's responsibility; but if wicked man does not heed the warning, the responsibility is his. "As I live, saith the Lord God, I have no pleasure in the death of the wicked; but that the wicked turn from his way and live; turn ye, turn ye from your evil ways; for why will yet die, O house of Israel?" Again Yahweh repeats the warning that the righteous man who finally sins will die for his sins, whereas the wicked man who turns from his sin will surely live and not die. "O ye house of Israel," Yahweh concludes, "I will judge you ever one after his ways."

When a fugitive brings the news that Jerusalem has fallen, Ezekiel is released from the muteness that came upon him the evening before. Once again he speaks for Yahweh, threatening punishment for the abominations the people left in Judah have committed. But the people are indifferent: Ezekiel is regarded merely as a singer of love-songs.

ISRAEL'S SHEPHERDS AND THEIR SHEEP: THE RESTORATION OF ISRAEL, 34:1-36:38. While the prophet is the watchman of his people, the leaders are their shepherds and are responsible for them. But they have often failed in their task: the sheep have been scattered and the shepherds have often looked out merely for themselves. Yahweh now promises to seek out His scattered sheep Himself, to gather them in from the various countries, to restore them to good pasture in the mountains of Israel, to be their shepherd and protect them, to send down showers of blessings on them and to see that they dwell in safety, to raise up a Davidic (Messianic?) king for them, and to make with them a covenant of peace. (Much of this passage is probably editorial.) After an oracle against Mount Seir, promising destruction to Israel's ancient enemies, the Edomites, there follows an address to the mountains of Israel: "But ye, O mountains of Israel, ye shall shoot forth your branches, and yield your fruit to my people of Israel; for they are at hand to come." The cities shall be inhabited again and man and beast shall multiply. Yahweh was angry with His people, because they defiled the land by their ways and profaned

His name in the midst of the heathen. But now to vindicate His own holiness, He will cleanse them and restore the land. "A new heart also will I give you, and a new spirit will I put within you: and I will take away the stony heart out of your flesh, and I will give you a heart of flesh. And I will put my Spirit within you, and cause you to walk in my statues, and ye shall keep my judgments, and do them. And ye shall dwell in the land that I gave to your fathers; and ye shall be my people, and I will be your God." Yahweh's people and His honor will be vindicated in the sight of all onlookers, "And they shall say, this land that was desolate is become like the garden of Eden."

THE VALLEY OF DRY BONES AND THE ALLEGORY OF THE STICKS, 37:1-28. The Lord set Ezekiel down in a valley which was full of dry bones and asked, "Son of man, can these bones live?" And the prophet answered, "O Lord God, thou knowest." And Yahweh ordered him to prophesy over the bones and to say "O ye dry bones, hear the word of the Lord." Then the prophet tells of the miracle that only Yahweh could bring about: "So I prophesied as I was commanded: and as I prophesied, there was a noise, and behold a shaking, and the bones came together, bone to his bone. And when I beheld, lo, the sinews and the flesh came up upon them, and the skin covered them above: but there was no breath in them. Then said he unto me, Prophesy unto the wind, prophesy, son of man, and say to the wind, Thus saith the Lord God; Come from the four winds, O breath, and breathe upon these slain, that they may live. So I prophesied as he commanded me, and the breath came into them, and they lived, and stood up upon their feet, an exceeding great army. Then he said unto me, Son of man, these bones are the whole house of Israel . . ."

The Lord promises to restore His people to their land (it is this and not a physical resurrection from the grave that is meant); and promises "[I] shall put my Spirit in you, and ye shall live, and I shall place you in your own land: then shall ye know that I the Lord have spoken it, and performed it. . . ." (The emphasis on Yahweh's self-vindication is characteristic of this book.)

In a brief allegory, the prophet is told to take two sticks and label them "for Judah and for the children of Israel his companions" and "for Joseph, the stick of Ephraim and for all the house of Israel his companions." The two were to become one stick, symbolizing the reunification of the southern and northern kingdoms.

GOG AND MAGOG, 38:1-39:29. These puzzling and almost inexplicable chapters (probably not by Ezekiel) contain many repetitions and inconsistencies. The author says that Yahweh is bringing Gog from the land of Magog. Yahweh's anger will be aroused at his coming and He will summon the forces of storm and rain against him. Gog and his forces will be destroyed on the mountains of Israel and their bodies given to the birds and animals as a sacrifice. The weapons will be burned as fuel and the bones of the dead buried. Yahweh's holiness will be vindicated. The author seems to regard these events as fulfilling the prophesies of Jeremiah and others. Perhaps he did not intend to picture an ordinary historical war, but some kind of cosmological conflict with Gog representing the forces of dark and evil. This curious narrative closes the third part of the book.

THE RESTORED TEMPLE, 40:1-44:31. The last nine chapters of the book describe the restored community: Jerusalem. Perhaps Ezekiel laid the foundations for these plans, but many passages here are later than his time: certainly the accounts of the Sacred Calendar in Chapters 45 and 46, and the directions for divisions of land and the rebuilding of Jerusalem in Chapter 48. In fact, a number of scholars think we have

nothing from Ezekiel himself after 43:12.

From Babylon the prophet is transported to Mount Zion, where a supernatural being carrying a measuring rod takes him on a tour of the visionary Temple and city. They inspect and sometimes measure the outer and inner courts, the place of sacrifice, the vestibule, nave, and chambers of the Temple, and the priests' chambers. Before the fall of Jerusalem, Ezekiel had seen in a vision the glory of Yahweh leave the Temple. Now he sees the glory once more fill the Temple and hears Yahweh speak, promising to dwell in the midst of a purified Israel forever. The Temple is to be a place set apart and holy. No foreigner or uncircumcised person is to enter it and only "the sons of Zadok," a priestly family, are to serve in it.

THE SACRED DISTRICT; VARIOUS REGULATIONS, 45:1-46:24. The sacred district surrounding the Temple where the priests and Levites are to live is next described, and regulations about weights and measures, the prince's offerings, the sacrifices, cooking arrangements, and other matters are set forth.

THE SACRED RIVER, 47:1-12. From below the threshold of the temple rises a sacred river which blows toward the Dead Sea, deepening as it goes and freshening the Sea's salt waters. It is a source of life, abundance, and healing. Fish live in it in abundance and on its bank grow trees which will bear fresh fruit every month. "The fruit thereof will be for meat and the leaf thereof for medicine." (There is an Eden-like quality about this imagined stream.)

THE ALLOTMENT OF LAND, 47:13-48:35. The boundaries of the new nation are described. Only the land west of the Jordan is included. The land is to be distributed evenly among the tribes. Not only natives but aliens are to have a share. The tribal territories are arranged north and south of the sacred area and the prince's lands which adjoin it. Dan, Asher, Naphtali, M a n a s s e h, Ephraim, Reuben, and Judah are to the north and Benjamin, Simeon, Issachar, Zebulun, and Gad to the south.

Finally, the measurements of Jerusalem are given and the gates, called after the twelve tribes, are named. In the renewed community Jerusalem has a special place, and in recognition of this she will be given a new name, Yahweh-Shammah, "the Lord is there."

THE BOOK OF DANIEL

INTRODUCTION

The Book of Daniel is not really a book of prophecy at all in the sense that Amos or Isaiah are books of prophecy. However, as it claimed to have been written by someone living in the Babylon early in the exile who foretold in it the history of the next five centuries, it was placed with the prophets in the Greek Bible and subsequently in the Latin and English translations. In the Hebrew Bible it stands, more appropriately, with the Writings. The book is in two parts, six chapters recounting heroic stories of Daniel and his three friends in the Babylonian court and six describing Daniel's bizarre visions which purport to predict fates of kings and kingdoms down to the villain of the book, Antiochus Epiphanes, who ruled Palestine in the second century B. C. However, it is clear from both internal and external evidence that the author's knowledge of the Babylonian and other early periods he describes is extremely hazy, while his knowledge of later periods is sound and detailed. It is certain, in fact, that the book was written during the Maccabean Revolt in the second century B. C., probably in the year 164, and that its message was intended for those stirring times. The historical background of the book is the struggle of one body of Jews to maintain their religious integrity against foreign influence and persecution. During the fourth and third centuries, a process of Hellenization had begun to transform parts of the Near East. The Jews of

the Diaspora were profoundly affected by this process and even the Jews of Palestine were influenced by it. Many Jews began to read Greek literature and philosophy, wear Greek clothes, interest themselves in democratic forms of government, build gymnasiums and banqueting halls after Greek models, and even develop a taste for Greek cooking, so far as the dietary laws permitted. Even Greek funeral customs were copied. The Torah itself may have first been translated into Greek at this time. Naturally there were some Jews who resented this Hellenizing process and tried to resist it. Among them were the Hasidim ("the pious"), who struggled to retain their traditions and who preached loyalty to the Torah (the Law) at all costs. The Book of Daniel in all probability issued from this circle of conservative and devoted Jews. The struggle between this group and the Hellenizers came to a head in the reign of the Seleucid monarch Antiochus IV, called Epiphanes. A power struggle over who should be the high priest in Jerusalem evidently convinced Antiochus that peace would best be served by a rigorous enforcement of Hellenism on the people and an equally rigorous attack on what in his eyes was an unimportant local sect. His troops were allowed to plunder and kill in Jerusalem and the city walls were pulled down. The Books of the Law were destroyed and possession of them was made a capital offense. The Temple was the next object of attack.

Treasure was taken away and the offering of sacrifice was forbidden. But the worst was to come. A symbol of the pagan god of heaven (equivalent to the Greek Zeus) was set up and a pig, abhorrent to the Jews, sacrificed to it. This was evidently "the abomination of desolation" mentioned in Daniel 11:31. All over the country Jews were ordered to make sacrifices on pagan altars and Antiochus' soldiers were sent to see that they did so.

Many people did sacrifice, but in 168 at the little Judaean village of Modein an elderly priest named Mattathias refused. He killed the officer sent to enforce the king's command and also killed a renegade Jew who made the sacrifice as ordered. Then Mattathias and his five sons took to the hills where, joined by other zealots, they started a guerilla campaign against Antiochus. Thus began the heroic Maccabean Revolt, so named after Mattathias' son Judas Maccabee (which may mean "hammer"), who took over when his father died. The success of this heroic band of men was astonishing. They managed to defeat the professional troops of Antiochus and to retake Jerusalem, all but the citadel. Three years from the date of the "abomination of desolation," in the month Kislev (our December 25) they cleansed the temple and rededicated it. The Feast of Lights or Hanukkah (rededication) celebrates this event.

It seems most probable that the Book of Daniel was written by one of the Hasidim at about this point—after the success of Jerusalem, but when people might be wondering whether victory would be permanent, or whether a time of further persecution, suffering, and testing might follow. The writer seems to have feared the latter, for his purpose is to encourage heroic resistance to persecution, zeal for the Law, and faith in God and His ultimate rule over history. As he wanted his book to be taken seriously by the people,

he issued it under the name of an ancient hero, perhaps the Daniel mentioned in Ezekiel and in the Ras Shamra tablets. This was not then considered a dishonest practice, as we should think it, but a legitimate means of getting a hearing for a pious message. The circumstances of the book's composition also explain the "apocalyptic" nature of the last six books. This term comes from a Greek word meaning "to uncover, to disclose." In actual fact, apocalyptic writings "disclose" their meaning only to a circle already informed, for the style is typically obscure and cryptic, purposely so, since the message is not intended to reach the enemy. Apocalyptic is also characterized by extraordinary visions, bizarre symbols, and supernatural revelations, and is capable of weird and extravagant interpretations so that even in our own day contemporary meanings have been read into the book and into the New Testament Apocalypse, the Book of Revelation. In spite of its bizarre quality, Daniel in its day served a noble cause and still has some historical interest because of its religious ideas. For one thing, the writer's conception of angels is more developed than anywhere else in the Bible, though it was to be developed still more by the Pharisees. Here the angel, Michael, has a name and a function in God's scheme of things. Even more striking is the writer's "eschatology," that is, he is concerned with the "end" of history. While he believes that God has a detailed masterplan for history, and that everything that happens is part of that plan, he believes that the history of the world, as we understand history, will soon come to an end, that the earthly kingdoms will pass away, and that their place will be taken by an eternal spiritual kingdom. This will happen, he thinks, very soon, shortly after the death of Antiochus Epiphanes. In connection with this eschatological belief, the author asserts a doctrine of the resurrection of the dead. Not all the dead, according to his thinking, will be resurrected (that belief belongs to a later period); only the most pure and the most wicked (see 12:2). The pure and the wise, including doubtless the Hasidim, will share in the spiritual kingdom, the consummation of God's victory. In that faith the victims of persecution should stand firm, wait, and hope.

Note: Part of Daniel, 2:4b to 7:28, is written in Aramaic, a language closely related to Hebrew and one which had for some time begun to supplant it in Palestine. It is not certain why these passages were so translated—possibly to make them more widely available.

SUMMARY OF THE BOOK OF DANIEL

DANIEL AND HIS THREE FRIENDS AT THE COURT OF NEBUCHADNEZZAR, 1:1-6:28.

Some of the Jewish exiles in Babylon are chosen to be trained for service in the court of Nebuchadnezzar. Among these are Daniel and his three friends, Hananiah, Mishael, and Azariah, better known by their Babylonian names Shadrach, Meshach, and Abednego. Faithful to the dietary rules of the Torah, they live on vegetables and water, but nevertheless are endowed by God with wisdom which exceeds that of the Babylonian sages and magicians. When Nebuchadnezzar has a dream which he cannot recall, it is not the Babylonian wise men, but Daniel, inspired by God, who is able to tell it and interpret it. The strange image with the golden head, breast, and arms of silver, belly of bronze, legs of iron, and feet partly of clay prefigures the kingdoms which will succeed Nebuchadnezzar. Impressed, the ruler prostrates himself and acknowledges Daniel's God. In the next test of virtue, the three friends refuse to worship the golden idol set up by Nebuchadrezzar, but survive unharmed the burning fiery furnace into which they are cast. Once more the king is impressed and promotes the three exiles. Next, Nebuchadnezzar dreams of a huge tree which is chopped down by an angel. Daniel explains that the king will lose his mind and be like an animal. Just so, a year later the king becomes insane and eats grass like an ox. When he

recovers, he once more acknowledges Daniel's God.

Belshazzar, Nebuchadnezzar's successor (he was not, as Chap. 5 says, his son), holds a great feast for a thousand of his nobles. They drink from the sacred vessels taken by Nebuchadrezzar from the Temple of Jerusalem. But as a mysterious hand writes "Mene, Mene, Tekel, and Parsin" (R. S. V.) on the walls, the king grows pale and sends for Daniel to explain the strange words. Daniel says that Belshazzar's kingdom will be given to the Medes and Persians. Daniel is clothed in fine purple and a chain of gold, but Belshazzar is killed that very night and Darius the Mede succeeds him. (This Darius is a figure of the story, not a real historial figure. The author is probably thinking of Darius I, who conquered Babylon twenty years later. Cyrus and Cambyses actually followed Belshazzar.) Darius gives Daniel high office, but jealous officials plot against him. Disregarding an edict against praying to anyone but the king, Daniel prays to God and is punished by being cast into the lions' den. Again he survives unharmed, and again the word goes out that the God of Daniel is to be reverenced. Daniel prospers during his reign and during the reign of Cyrus.

THE VISIONS OF DANIEL, 7:1-12:13.

In the first vision (Chap. 7) Daniel sees four strange beasts who, as he learns from the cryptic comments of an angelic interpreter, symbolize the four great kingdoms of recent history. The lion with eagle's wings represents Babylon, the bear with ribs in its mouth the Medes, the leopard with four heads and four wings Persia, and the ten-horned beast with iron teeth the Seleucid (Hellenistic) Empire. The little horn with eyes and a mouth which springs up in the fourth beast and destroys three other horns represents Antiochus Epiphanes. (Daniel does not say so, but contemporaries would recognize the description.) The "Ancient of Days," that is, God sitting in judgment, sentences the fourth kingdom to destruction and spares the others for a season. "With the clouds of heaven" comes "one like the Son of man," (literally like a mortal man) who represents "the saints of the Most High," the holy community of Israel who are to inherit the everlasting kingdom which is to come (the cryptic reference to time in verse 25 is meant to point to the time of Antiochus' persecution of the Jews 168-165 B.C.).

In the second vision, (Chap. 8) a ram with two horns (the empire of the Medes and Persians) is challenged by a goat (the Greeks) with a single large horn (Alexander the Great). When the large horn is broken, i.e., after Alexander's death, four horns appear, which stand for the four kingdoms of that era. From them springs a little horn, who sets himself against the host of heaven and its prince (i.e., God), profanes the Temple, interrupts the sacrifice, and casts down truth. Again, the writer's contemporaries would recognize that this was a description of Antiochus Epiphanes. The passage hints that the Temple will be restored in three years and two months (verse 14).

In the third vision, (Chap. 9) Daniel puzzles over the prophecy in Jeremiah that the desolation of Jerusalem would last seventy years. He works it out as "seventy weeks of years," i.e., 490 years, which are divided into three periods of seven weeks, sixty-two weeks, and one week. By the end of this period the Jews will have atoned for their sins and the desolation of Jerusalem will be over. Though attempts to figure this all out arithmetically do not work out exactly, probably what is meant is the 49 years from Zedekiah to the priest Joshua, 435 years from Joshua to the priest Onias III, and the period between his assassination and the Maccabean world and the coming of the eternal kingdom.

The final vision (Chaps. 10-12) takes place after Daniel has been fasting and mourning for 21 days. A man clothed in linen and girded with gold promises him a vision of the distant future. What is revealed is a cryptic but detailed history of events in Near Eastern history from the Persians to Antiochus Epiphanes. Most of the references can be worked out (see for example the *Interpreter's Bible*, VI, pp. 347-8), but are too numerous to summarize here. The history is carried down to the point where it tells how a "vile person" (Antiochus Epiphanes again) will crush "the prince of the covenant" (probably the high priest who was killed during the dispute which preceded the persecution), set up an abomination in the Temple, and magnify himself above God. However, the writer comes to grief when he tries to predict the future, for he prophesies that Antiochus will meet his doom between the Mediterranean and Jerusalem, with no one to help him, whereas Antiochus actually died (in 63 B.C.) in Persia. In the epilogue to the book it is said that the archangel Michael will come to deliver the Jews from their suffering, and "many of them that sleep in the dust of the earth shall awake, some to everlasting life and some to shame and everlasting contempt." The pure will become more pure and the wicked will remain in their wickedness. Daniel is told to go his way and rest until the end comes. "When the end of the days" comes he will arise to enjoy his share in the kingdom.

THE BOOK OF HOSEA

Hosea's preaching mission followed soon after that of Amos, and should be studied with it. The two are often contrasted. Amos is said to be the prophet of justice and Hosea of mercy. This is an oversimplification, as Amos feels deeply for Israel and is never detached or heartless, whereas Hosea, like Amos, is deeply concerned for the demands of righteousness. However, Hosea does emphasize the divine compassion of Yahweh and believes that He will ultimately save His people.

We know nothing about Hosea except what we can learn from his book. He preached in Israel in the last years of Jeroboam II and afterward. The political situation was very unstable, particularly after the death of Jeroboam, and Israel showed a tendency, deplored by Hosea, to drift into alliance with either Assyria or Egypt. The religious situation was disquieting. The mass of the people seem to have forgotten their covenant obligations and were attracted to the local Baalism of Canaan. The Baals were the gods of fertility cults which were characterized by the worship of images, the setting up of many shrines, and by great agricultural festivals which were the occasion of drunkenness and other excesses. At such festivals ritual marriages were often enacted, which were supposed to ensure fertility during the coming year. Cultic prostitution seems to have been common. It was this situation which Hosea tried to deal with.

The book consists of oracles, biography, and what appears to be an autobiographical passage. It is confusing to read, partly because Hosea's deeply emotional style is sometimes difficult to follow and partly because the manuscript was reedited, perhaps several times, to make it applicable to a somewhat later situation in Judah. The text is corrupt and the authorship of several passages is questioned.

SUMMARY OF THE BOOK OF HOSEA

TITLE, 1:1.
Hosea certainly began his mission before the end of the reign of Jeroboam, and continued it until the time of the Syro-Ephraimitic War of 735-734 B.C. There is no internal evidence that his ministry was longer than this and the name of the other kings may have been added later.

HOSEA'S MARRIAGE, 1:2-3:5.
Here is one of the most puzzling passages in the whole of prophetic literature, yet it is important to try to understand it, since it lies at the heart of Hosea's message.

In Chapter 1 we hear that Yahweh told Hosea to take a harlotrous wife and harlotrous children, because Israel herself had committed harlotry in forsaking her God. Accordingly Hosea took Gomer as his wife and she bore him (literally "to him") a son. At Yahweh's direction the child was called Jezreel, as a sign that as a condemnation of Jehu and Jezebel, Yahweh would demand the blood of Jezreel. (The fact that this prophecy was not fulfilled does not seem to have troubled Hosea's disciples or editors, who let the prophecy stand.) Gomer conceived again—this time the sentence is not framed so that one is absolutely sure whether the child is Hosea's own or not—and the infant (a girl) is named Lo-ruhamah, which means "Not pitied" or perhaps "Loveless." This name seems to imply that Yahweh's pity and patience are exhausted. The name of the third child, a boy, is Lo-ammi, "Not my people." This name seems to indicate that Yahweh has broken the convenant and rejected Israel. (The authenticity of 1:10-2:1 is disputed.) Next, while the children are told to plead for their mother (i.e., Israel) to put away her harlotry, lest she be destroyed, and to abandon her lovers who, she says, "Give me my bread and my water, my wool and my flax, mine oil and my drink," she thinks the Baals, the fertility gods of Canaan, give her these things, and does not recognize that these are the gifts of Yahweh. He will punish her for following the Baals and offering them sacrifices. Yet the prophet, who sees the analogy between his domestic situation and the relationship between Yahweh and Israel, says he will try to speak persuasively and tenderly to her, so that she will not confuse him with the Baals. She will no longer call him Baal, but husband and, says Yahweh, "I will betroth thee unto me in righteousness, and in judgment, and in loving-kindness, and in mercies. I will even betroth thee unto me in faithfulness: and thou shalt know the Lord . . . and I will say unto them which were not my people, thou art my people, and they shall say, thou art my God."

Chapter 3, written in the first person, seems to recount a somewhat similar experience. Yahweh says, "go again, love a woman who is beloved of a paramour and is a adultress even as the Lord loves the people of Israel" (R. S. V.). The prophet apparently obeys, for he says he has bought the woman and proposes to help her in a kind of probationary isolation, so that she will give up harlotry. Similarly, the children of Israel should be denied some of the externals of religion, until they learn to seek Yahweh and fear Him.

What do these narratives mean and what is the relationship between them? Are these real events? Do Chapters 1 and 3 refer to the same events or different ones? If the latter, in what order should we consider them? There are scores, perhaps hundreds, of answers to these questions. Many commentators, especially in medieval times, were troubled by the involvement of a prophet with a prostitute and tried to read the whole episode as an allegory. But there are many details which cannot be allegorized and the difficulty cannot really be solved this way. It is better to recognize that the story is in some sense literal. In this case, does all of Chapters 1 and 3 give different accounts of the same events? It would seem not, since the details are different. Or does Chapter 3 represent an earlier stage, Chapter 1 a later? Probably it is simplest to take the narratives in the order given, to suppose, as the Hebrew wording would suggest, that Gomer's "harlotry" was at first only potential, but became actual after the marriage, indeed perhaps only after the birth of the first child. (There are linguistic arguments against the suggestion that Gomer was a cult prostitute.) Hosea at some point reclaimed her, apparently hoping to rehabilitate her by his faithfulness and love.

What is clear is that through this personal experience of disappointment and disillusion, Hosea gained an insight into Yahweh's love for Israel and His disappointment in her apostasy. He was the first to use marriage as an image of the covenant relationship between Yahweh and His people. The loyalty and affection he felt for Gomer helped him to understand Yahweh's "steadfast love" (R. S. V.) for Israel. In Martin Buber's words, Yahweh said to him, "continue loving, thou art allowed to love her, thou must love her; even so do I love Israel." (*The Prophetic Faith*, New York: Macmillan, 1949, p. 113.)

ISRAEL'S UNFAITHFULNESS AND ITS CONSEQUENCES, 4:1-13:16.

The prophet speaks of Israel's apostasy and wickedness. There is no fidelity, no knowledge of God, and in consequence cursing, lying, murder, theft, and adultery flourish. Drunkenness prevents understanding, people seek counsel of wooden idols, harlotries multiply. "A people without insight must come to ruin" (A. T.). Both Israel and Judah will be punished. They think that Yahweh will heal and will revive them, but he tells them their shallow repentance is like a cloud or a mist which soon vanishes, "for I desired mercy and not sacrifices: and the knowledge of God is more than burnt offerings." (Note the frequent expression of this idea in Hosea: if the people really knew Yahweh—the word conveys a close, intimate relationship—they would love and serve Him.) The prophet is also troubled about Israel's flirtations with foreign powers. Ephraim (Israel), he says scornfully, is like a half-baked cake, like a silly dove, toying first with Egypt, then with Assyria. In Yahweh's name, he sneers at the sacred bull of Samaria: "the workman made it; therefore it is not God." Punishment will come upon the land, "for they have sown the wind, and they shall reap the whirlwind." They will go into exile, to Assyria or to Egypt, and nettles will possess the land. Because they have not listened to Yahweh, they will become wanderers among the nations, and will wish the hills and mountains would fall upon them. "Sow to yourselves in righteousness, reap in mercy; break up your fallow ground; for it is time to seek the Lord, till he come and rain righteousness upon you."

Yet (Chap. 11) Yahweh cannot help but recall the covenant relationship with His people. "When Israel was a child, then I loved him, and called my son out of Egypt." He remembers how He guided the infant nation: "I led them with cords of compassion, with the bands of love" (R. S. V.). "How can I give you up O Ephraim," He cries. "How can I hand you over, O Israel? . . . I will not carry out my fierce anger; nor will I again destroy Ephraim; for I am God and not man" (A. T.). Yet once more with a sudden change of mood He thinks of the faithlessness of Israel and Judah and urges them to return to Him. They have forgotten Him and the words of His prophets, and will therefore be destroyed. They have sacrificed to idols, kissed man-made calves; therefore they shall vanish like a cloud, like chaff above the threshing floor, or like smoke. They have forgotten all that God has done for them, they have taken unto themselves kings and princes. They have rebelled against God and will perish by the sword.

CALL TO RETURN AND PROMISE OF FORGIVENESS, 14:1-9.

Again there is a sudden change of mood (suggesting to some critics that this passage may be spurious), as Yahweh calls Israel to repentance. No longer will the people worship man-made idols. Yahweh promises "I will heal their backsliding, I will love them freely; for mine anger is turned away from him. I will be as the dew unto Israel: he shall grow as the lily, and cast forth his roots as Lebanon."

THE BOOK OF JOEL

INTRODUCTION

The Book of Joel describes the invasion of a plague of locusts which relentlessly strip the countryside and then turn their attention to the city. The devastation is described in vivid poetry. Observers of locust plagues in Palestine in 1915 and 1928 attest to the exactness of the descriptions, both of the swift advance of the locusts and of their terrible effects on the morale of the people. To the poet the scourge suggests that the Day of Yahweh is at hand, when the repentant faithful will be delivered and their enemies punished. The book is clearly post-exilic, but an exact date cannot be established. Somewhere between 450 and 350 B. C. is probable.

SUMMARY OF THE BOOK OF JOEL

TITLE, 1:1.

"The word of the Lord that came to Joel . . ."—a common superscription.

THE PLAGUE OF LOCUSTS AND THE DROUGHT, 1:2-2:29.

The prophet calls the whole community, including old men and drunks, to see the locusts: "What the cutting locust left, the swarming locust has eaten. What the swarming locust has left, the hopping locust has eaten, and what the hopping locust left, the destroying locust has eaten" (R. S. V.). With their powerful teeth, the locusts have nibbled the vine and fig trees, stripping off the bark and leaving the branches white. Because the grain and wine and oil have failed, there can be no sacrifices. Pomegranate, palm, and apple are withered. The prophet begs the priests to call a solemn assembly to pray for deliverance from the locusts and from the drought which is making the seeds shrivel in the clods and devouring the fields, so that even the beasts are suffering. He urges the priests to blow the trumpet in Zion, for now the locusts are attacking the city; the day of the Lord is coming, a day of darkness and gloom. The locusts leave behind them only a wilderness. They attack with the speed and order of an army. Since "the day of the Lord is great and very terrible," the speaker urges repentance: "Rend your heart and not your garments." Once more the prophet begs the priests to proclaim an assembly and fast to which all, even the nursing babe and the bride, should come to implore Yahweh's help, or the heathen will say, "Where is their God?" Yahweh's response is gracious. He promises grain, wine, and oil, the removal of the "northerner" (the locusts), rain, fruitfulness, and the return of "the years that the locust have eaten." There will also be a spiritual gift: "I will pour out my Spirit upon all flesh; and your sons and your daughters shall prophesy, your old men shall dream dreams, your young men shall see visions." Even the servants will prophesy.

THE DAY OF THE LORD AND THE FUTURE GREATNESS OF YAHWEH, 2:28-3:21.

But the promise that the Spirit will come is a prelude to the announcement that the day of Yahweh is at hand: "The sun shall be turned into darkness, and the moon into blood, before the great and terrible day of the Lord come." Yahweh will gather the nations into the valley of Jehoshaphat where he will punish them for their cruelties to the Jews. Tyre and Sidon will be punished in kind for looting and for enslaving God's people. In a passage which reverses Isaiah and Micah (Isa. 2:4; Mic. 3:3), the nations are urged, "Beat your plowshares into swords, and your pruning hooks into spears . . ." Yahweh will judge the heathen, while "the sun and the moon shall be darkened, and the stars shall withdraw their shining" and "the heavens and the earth shall shake." But the Lord will protect His own people and give them great prosperity: "The mountains shall drop down new wine, and the hills shall flow with milk, and all the rivers of Judah shall flow with waters, and a fountain shall come forth of the house of the Lord and shall water the valley of Shittim."

Edom and Egypt, the enemies of Israel, will be destroyed, but Judah and Jerusalem will remain forever.

THE BOOK OF AMOS

INTRODUCTION

Amos was by his own account not a professional prophet[1] but a shepherd from the hills of Tekoa, a few miles south of Jerusalem. He also did seasonal work as a "dresser of sycamore trees" (R. S. V.), the fig-like fruits of which needed special treatment if they were to ripen properly. He evidently kept his eyes open on his travels, as his shrewd and penetrating comments show. He preached about the middle of the eighth century B. C., in the reign of Jeroboam II, at the great shrine of Bethel—that is, though a southerner from Judah, he preached in Israel, the northern kingdom. In Chapter 7, the priest Amaziah tells him substantially to go back where he came from.

Israel at this time was relatively properous. Assyria had temporarily withdrawn its attacks because of dissension at home. A flourishing international trade brought wealth to Israel. This wealth, however, became concentrated in relatively few hands, small holdings gave way to large estates, and the gulf between the very rich and the very poor widened. Social injustice was often accompanied by corruption in the courts. There was a great deal of religious activity at the numerous shrines, accompanied by complacency and optimism, but often not accompanied by high ethical standards. It is this false and superficial religion which Amos attacks. The book consists of oracles, visions, and short biographical passages. Note the vividness and imaginative power of his poetry and the penetrating exactness of his criticisms.

SUMMARY OF THE BOOK OF AMOS

TITLES AND MOTTO, 1:1-2.

The first verse is an editorial title to the whole book and tells us that Amos spoke in the time of King Uzziah of Judah and King Jeroboam of Israel. His opening motto declares that "the Lord will roar from Zion," i.e., that Yahweh is about to speak.

ORACLES AGAINST THE SURROUNDING NATIONS AND AGAINST ISRAEL, 1:3-2:16.

In the name of Yahweh, Amos attacks the enemies of Israel. Yahweh will punish Damascus for barbarously attacking Gilead, Gaza (i.e.,

Philistia) and Tyre for taking other nations into captivity, Edom for warring on his brother Israel, Ammon for greed and barbarity in war, and Moab for desecrating the remains of the king of Edom. (The attack on Judah for breaking God's laws was probably added later.) Each stanza is similarly constructed, beginning "For three transgressions of—and for four, I will not turn away the punishment . . ." Then the crime in each case is stated and the punishment announced in specific and vivid terms. This repetition has a powerful cumulative effect on the listeners, and they wait as each enemy is named to hear its crimes and fate proclaimed. Suddenly, when their emotions are thoroughly aroused against their enemies, Amos astonishes them by turning the attack on Israel. Israel, too, is guilty in Yahweh's eyes. She has sold the innocent for silver and the needy for a pair of sandals, she has committed moral and religious profanation. Yahweh's inescapable punishment awaits all classes of the nation.

ORACLES ON THE DOOM OF ISRAEL, 3:1-5:17.

Again Amos speaks for Yahweh, reminding Israel that she will be punished, as she has not acted as the chosen of Yahweh should act. Election involves responsibility: "You only have I known of all the families of the earth: therefore I will punish you for all your iniquities." In a series of analogies, the prophet shows that it is imperative that he prophesy. "Will a lion roar in the forest, when he hath no prey? . . . The Lord God hath spoken, who can but prophesy?" Because Israel has done wrong, her enemies will overcome her, and there will be no more of her left than the fragments a shepherd rescues from the mouth of a lion—two bones and a piece of ear.

The prophet addresses the rich women of Samaria (i.e., Israel) as cows of Bashan, who oppress the poor indirectly by urging their husbands to exploit the needy in order to have more money for luxuries. They will be dragged away with hooks and cast on the refuse heap. Ironically Amos bids the people gather at the sacred shrines: "Come to Bethel, —and transgress; at Galgal multiply transgressions." He implies that worship without justice is sacrilege. Yahweh has warned His people with many chastisements—famine, drought, blight, plague, and earthquake, but she has not returned to Him.

The prophet sings a formal lament for the fallen nation: "The virgin . . . Israel is fallen, she shall no more rise; she is forsaken upon her land; there is none to raise her up." He begs Israel "Seek the Lord, and ye shall live," but he knows that the people do not want to hear the word of Yahweh; they oppress the innocent, take bribes, and deny justice to the needy. Only if they seek good and not evil will even a remnant be saved.

THE DAY OF THE LORD, 5:18-6:14.

The prophet speaks next to those who look forward to a future day when Yahweh will enter into human history, overthrow Israel's enemies, and give her victory and power. The day of the Lord will be, he says, a day of darkness and destruction, not of light. Once again, in one of the most striking and famous passages in the Bible, he speaks in the person of Yahweh, reminding the people that ceremony and sacrifices mean nothing when they are divorced from justcie and righteousness: "I hate, I despise your feast days, and I will not smell (I.e., the sacrifices) in your solemn assemblies. . . . Take thou away from me the noise of thy songs. . . . But let judgment run down as waters and righteousness as a mighty stream." Amos goes on to paint a satirical pretense of the rich who do not care, who are at ease in Zion, "who lie on ivory couches" eating, drinking, and singing, and are not heart-sick over the state of the nation, "are not grieved for the affliction of Joseph." They shall be the first to go into captivity, for ruin and destruction are at hand.

THREE VISIONS OF JUDGMENT, 7:1-9.

Now Amos speaks in his own person of visions or perhaps actual events which seem to relate to Israel's relationship with Yahweh. First he sees Yahweh creating a great swarm of locusts—a symbol of destruction, for locusts are dangerous to the crops. He feels a moment of pity for Israel, and pleads, "O Lord God, forgive . . . by when shall Jacob (i.e., Israel) arise? for he is small." Yahweh seems to relent, but then comes a second vision, this time of a fire which devours the great deep (i.e., the primeval abyss of the creation story) and the land. Once again Amos pleads for Israel and once again Yahweh relents. But the third vision is stern and final. Yahweh stands with a plumbline in His hand, ready to test the nation. Israel does not meet the test, and Yahweh promises destruction to the sacred places and sanctuaries, destruction to the house of Jeroboam.

AMOS AND AMAZIAH, 7:10-17.

Now the visions are interrupted (for there are two others) by a narrative in the third person, apparently an extract from a longer account. Amaziah, the priest of Bethel, reports to the king (Jeroboam II) that the prophet has been conspiring against him and has even prophesied his death and the captivity of Israel. Amaziah tells Amos to go back to Judah, "there eat bread, and prophesy there," i.e., make your living by prophesying in your own country. In reply Amos denies that he is a regular prophet or a member of a prophetic order. He is a shepherd and dresser of sycamores. (The sycamore was a kind of fig tree, the "dressing" process either making strategic cuts to allow the best fruit to ripen or pricking the fruit to assist it in ripening.) Yahweh seized upon him one day and told him to prophesy to Israel.

THE BASKET OF SUMMER FRUIT AND THE INJUSTICE IN ISRAEL, 8:1-14.

The basket of summer fruit is the fourth vision. By a play on words—the word for fruit and the word for end sound alike in Hebrew—the prophet passes immediately to the thought that the end is about to come to Israel. Once again he lashes out at those who trample on the needy and long for the religious celebrations to be over so that they can sell their grain; who falsify their weights and measures, and sell the refuse of their wheat. Suffering and destruction will be the consequences.

THE FINAL DESTRUCTION OF ISRAEL, 9:1-8a.

In the fifth and final vision, Amos sees God standing on an altar and ordering the destruction of the sanctuary. (Perhaps Amos has Bethel itself in mind.) If any worshipers are left, they will die, slain by the sword. None shall escape.

EPILOGUE: THE RESTORATION OF ISRAEL, 9:8b-15.

This final passage seems to have been added by some later writer who perhaps felt that if Amos reconsidered, he might see hope for Israel. The optimism of this writer is striking contrast to the sternness and pessimism of Amos. The writer begins indeed pessimistically, saying that Yahweh will shake the house of Israel as one shakes a sieve, but he pronounces the promise of Yahweh to raise up the house of David, restore the fortunes of Israel, and replant His people on their own land. The restoration is unconditional; the favor of God is not, as elsewhere in the book, conditional on just and righteous conduct. For this reason and because of certain linguistic considerations, this part of the book is usually attributed to a post-exilic writer who believed that Yahweh as the Lord of history would secure the ultimate restoration of Israel.

THE BOOK OF OBADIAH

INTRODUCTION. The Edomites were supposed to be descended from Esau and therefore kinsmen of the house of Jacob. It was therefore resented deeply when the Edomites actually took part in the siege of Jerusalem and after its fall in 587 used the opportunity to occupy some of the lands of Judah. Obadiah expresses this resentment and desire for revenge. The vengeful spirit of the book, though understandable, can hardly be admired. Vengeance did, in fact, as Obadiah hoped, fall upon them, for the Edomites suffered from attacks of Arabs in the fifth century. The book is commonly dated in the latter part of the century.

SUMMARY OF THE BOOK OF OBADIAH

TITLE, 1:1a. The title gives the prophet's name and claims that his message concerning Edom is from God.

JUDGMENT AGAINST EDOM, 1: 1b-14. A messenger urges the nations to rise up against Edom. Yahweh addresses Edom, telling her He will make her small and despised and bring her down from her lofty and rocky fortresses. Esau's (i.e., Edom's) treasures have been looted and she has been conquered by her previous allies. Even the wise men will be destroyed and every man from the Mount of Esau will be slaughtered. This punishment will be just retribution for the fact that the Edomites actually took part in the attack on Jerusalem. "For thy violence against thy brother Jacob shame shall cover thee, and thou shalt be cut off for ever. In the day that thou stoodest on the other side, in the day that the strangers carried away captive his forces, and foreigners entered into his gates, and cast lots upon Jerusalem, even thou wast as one of them." This was a violation of the blood ties between Judah and Edom. Edom should not have gloated over his brother in his distress, or looted his possessions, or cut off his fugitives.

THE DAY OF THE LORD, 1:15-21. The day of the Lord is close for the heathen nations, of which Edom is one. Retribution is due. "As thou hast done it, it shall be done to thee." The heathen will be judged and must drink the cup of God's wrath and "shall be as though they had not been." But some of the house of Jacob will survive and will return to Mount Zion, the holy place, and will renew the attack on Edom. "And the house of Jacob shall be a fire, and the house of Joseph a flame, and the house of Esau for stubble, and they shall kindle in them, and devour them; and there shall not be any remaining of the house of Esau; for the Lord hath spoken it." Judah and Israel will reunite and will push back the Edomites to the south, the west, the north and the east. Delivers will go up "to Mount Zion to judge the Mount of Esau, and the kingdom shall be the Lord's."

THE BOOK OF JONAH

INTRODUCTION: This little book is one of the most delightful in the Bible, yet its message is a serious and lofty one. Its point is lost if it is treated as history. It is not history or an ordinary book of prophecy at all, but a story whose exaggerations, absurdities, and sudden turns of fate are part of the author's purpose. We might even call it a parable, since it is designed, like some of Jesus' parables, to make the hearer view a situation in a fresh light — ultimately, to look at himself.

The situation the author has in mind was a point in the post-exilic history when nationalistic feeling and particularism were stronger than the universalism preached by Second Isaiah (see above). Israel had suffered so many cruelties, disappointments, and disillusions that often her only feeling toward foreigners was hatred and a desire for revenge. These feelings are expressed in Obadiah and Esther and in part of Joel and Ezekiel. They are understandable, but the author of Jonah felt that such feelings were a violation of Israel's highest beliefs about God. In his story he tries to show that Jonah is actually repudiating his own image of God. He *knows* that God is "gracious-merciful, slow to anger and of great kindness," but this does not make it any easier for him to preach to the hateful Ninevites and he is furious when they repent and earn God's forgiveness. He cannot accept the fact that God cares for the ignorant heathen, too.

The pettiness and absurdity of his position is made clear when he is upset over the destruction of the plant which gave him shade, but becomes angry because God forgives thousands of helpless people who have shown every sign of repentance and sincerity.

Perhaps the author meant to go a step further, to show not only the absurdity and cruelty of bigotry, but the shortcomings of Israel in her role in history. The heathen among whom Jonah moves are not unreceptive to his religion. The sailors pray to his God and the Ninevites accept his prophetic message. The name Jonah means "dove," the symbol of Israel. Was the author trying to remind his countrymen that the chosen people were intended to be a light to the gentiles?

SUMMARY OF THE BOOK OF JONAH

THE DIVINE COMMAND, 1:1-2. The book begins, as any prophetic book might, by asserting that God spoke directly to Jonah. He has heard of the wickedness of Nineveh and orders Jonah to preach to the Ninevites.

JONAH'S FLIGHT FROM GOD, 1: 3-2:10. The author doubtless chose the Assyrians as the object of Jonah's mission just because they were the people most hated and feared by Israel, who had suffered so much from their cruel attacks. Jonah does not in the least want to preach to the Ninevites, so at Joppa he takes a ship to Tarshish (probably Tartessos, a Phoenician colony in Spain) in an effort to get as far as possible away, "away from the presence of the Lord" (R. S. V.). But the Lord sets in motion a mighty tempest, which so frightens the mariners that they pray, each to his own god, and toss some of the cargo overboard. Meanwhile Jonah is comfortably asleep in the ship's

hold. There the captain awakens him and bids him pray to his god, who might be the very one who could save them. (The captain's outlook is polytheistic; he assumes the storm is caused by the whim of some god who perhaps can be placated, if he can be identified.) When they cast lots to find whose presence is the reason for the storm, the lot falls on Jonah. He admits that he is the cause of the storm and declares his willingness to be cast into the sea. The good hearted soldiers make a valiant attempt to bring the ship in without having recourse to this desperate remedy, but eventually are obliged to carry it out. Jonah is cast into the sea, which immediately ceases from its raging. The sailors, who have prayed to Jonah's God, now offer Him vows and a sacrifice.

Meanwhile a great fish, which God has assigned to the task, swallows Jonah up and he remains in the fish's belly for three days and three nights. At this point a pious editor, evidently thinking that Jonah in these dire straights should pray, inserted a prayer which he thought appropriate, probably because of the words "the water compassed me about." It is not really appropriate, being a thanksgiving for deliverance, whereas Jonah is not really delivered until verse 10, when the fish vomits him out on dry land.

"THE RELUCTANT MISSIONARY," 3:1-4:11.

(The phrase is J. D. Smart's, see *IB,* VI, 888). Once again the word of the Lord comes to Jonah. He is to preach in Nineveh. Grudgingly he makes his way to the great city, so wide that it takes three days to cross it. His prophecy is a simple one: "Yet forty days and Nineveh shall be overthrown." Success is instantaneous. The people believe in God, proclaim a fast, and put on sackcloth. Even the king himself lays aside his royal robe, rules that all, even the animals, are to share the fast and the sackcloth. He urges prayer, hoping that the anger of God will be turned away, if the people change their evil ways. God is impressed with the transformation that has taken place and decides not to destroy the city.

This makes Jonah very angry. He seems bitterly disappointed that Nineveh is not going to be destroyed after all. He wishes he were dead. God asks him, "Doest thou well to be angry?" Jonah does not answer, but sulkily goes out to the east side of the city, where he makes a little booth and waits, perhaps still hoping for the city's destruction.

Next God orders a large plant (K. J. V. "gourd"), which suddenly grows up and shades Jonah's head. Jonah is delighted, but the next day God sends a worm which destroys the plant and a burning east wind which makes Jonah faint. Once more he wishes he were dead. Once again God asks him, "Doest thou well to be angry for the gourd?" Jonah replies that he is angry enough to die.

Gently God rebukes him and points the lesson: "Thou hast had pity on the gourd, for the which thou hast not laboured, neither madest it grow; which came up in a night, and perishes in a night: And should not I spare Nineveh, that great city, wherein are more than sixscore thousand persons that cannot discern between their right hand and their left hand; [i.e., ordinary, ignorant people] and also much cattle?" Jonah was deeply emotional about a plant which grew up and died in a day, yet he was enraged at God's pity for the helpless and repentant Ninevites.

THE BOOK OF MICAH

INTRODUCTION. Micah was a native of Moresheth, a little village in the Philistine Plain. He was a contemporary of Hosea and Isaiah, but seems to have been influenced most by Amos whose home, Tekoa, was only about twenty miles from Moresheth. Like Amos, he denounced the social injustice of the cities. He was also deeply dismayed by the ambitions of the Assyrians, who had already conquered Syria and Israel, leaving Judah an unprotected and helpless state between the Assyrian empire and Egypt. Micah seems to have felt that the corruption and social injustice in Judah would justify an Assyrian attack, and this is one argument he uses in trying to arrest the moral decay he saw all around him. However, the fall of Jerusalem, which he foretold, did not come in his time.

Although the superscription claims that he prophesied under three kings, it is usually thought that his ministry took place in the last years of the eighth century, perhaps 714-701. It is probable that he was active before the crisis of 711 and again before 701. His ministry apparently had some success, for the Book of Jeremiah (26:17-10) credits him with powerful influence for good over King Hezekiah, who destroyed the pagan images on the high places and kept the law of Moses.

The text of Micah has been carefully preserved, but editors have introduced much post-exilic material to balance Micah's rather gloomy outlook.

SUMMARY OF THE BOOK OF MICAH

SUPERSCRIPTION. The heading tells us that Micah was from Moresheth and that he focused his attention on Samaria and Jerusalem. It is thought that his ministry was confined to the reign of Hezekiah.

DANGER FROM ASSYRIA, 1:2-16. (A short eschatological psalm, verses 2-4, has been inserted as an introduction.) To call attention to his prophecy, Micah says he will walk about the city naked, crying out his indictment to fix attention on the big cities, Samaria and Jerusalem, as the sources of corruption. However, the cumulative list of towns suggests that he repeated his message in all the places he passed through. He warns the people that Jerusalem is in danger and a conqueror is coming who may take their children into exile.

THE EVILS OF JERUSALEM AND JUDAH, 2:1-3:12. Micah first directs his wrath against the wealthy men of Jerusalem who lie awake at night devising new plans for seizing their lands and homes of the poor. In the future their captors (i.e., the Assyrians) may take over and divide up their fields, but at present they do not want to listen to any criticism of their exploitation. Micah claims the right to criticize, for the Spirit of the Lord should not be restricted. (Another short passage describing the restoration of the remnant has been inserted here, verses 12-13).

Next Micah addresses the leaders, the "heads of Jacob" who "hate the good and love the evil," who tear the flesh of the people like butchers. He speaks to the prophets, who "cry Peace when they have something to eat, but declare war against him who puts nothing in their mouths" (R. S. V.). Such false prophets will dwell in darkness. He condemns the leaders who "build up Zion with blood," for "the heads thereof judge for reward, and the priests thereof teach for hire, and the prophets thereof divine for money. . . ." Because of their iniquity, Jerusalem will become a heap of ruins.

THE FUTURE OF ISRAEL, 4:1-5:15. There is wide agreement that these chapters are not by Micah, but belong to a later period. Two somewhat contradictory poems seem to have been combined. One written somewhat in the spirit of Second Isaiah looks forward to the "last days," after the reform from the Babylonian exile, when many nations will turn to Jerusalem and to the God of Jacob for law and for judgment. It contains the famous and beautiful passage "And he shall judge among many people, and rebuke strong nations afar off; and they shall beat their swords into plowshares, and their spears into pruning hooks: nation shall not lift up a sword against nation, neither shall they learn war any more." The other poem seems to be a hymn of hate, announcing that Zion will "beat in pieces many peoples" and annihilate their enemies. It closes with threats from Yaheweh that He will purge the remnant by destroying their armies, cities, fortresses, and heathen symbols.

TRUE RELIGION, 6:1-8. This famous passage is sometimes ascribed to an anonymous prophet in the reign of Manasseh, but the arguments against Micah's authorship seem less cogent than in the case of the previous section. In any case the poem is well worth studying carefully. It takes the form of a court trial, the case of Yahweh against Israel. The mountains are called as witnesses as the prophet in the name of the Lord summons Israel to present her case. He reminds Israel what God has done for her since He brought her out of Egypt and gave her Moses as her leader, implying that she has forgotten that the covenant relationship involves righteous acts on her side, too. Israel stands ashamed, with no case to plead: "Wherewith shall I come before the Lord, and bow myself before the high God? shall I come before him with burnt offerings, with calves of a year old? Will the Lord be pleased with thousands of rams, or with ten thousands of rivers of oil? shall I give my firstborn for my transgression, the fruit of my body for the sin of my soul? He hath showed thee, O man, what is good; and what doth the Lord require of thee, but to do justly, and to love mercy and to walk humbly with thy God?" It is often said that this summary of prophetic religion recalls Amos' dedication to justice, Hosea's affirmation of steadfast love, and Isaiah's insistence on tranquility in faith.

JERUSALEM'S SIN AND PUNISHMENT, 6:9-16. In the name of the Lord the prophet accuses the men of the city of dishonesty. Their measures, scales, and weights are designed to cheat the customers. For this Yahweh will punish them; they will sow, but not have time to reap. "You shall eat, but not be satisfied, and there shall be hunger in your inward parts" (R. S. V.). Because they have been as evil as the house of Omri, they will be scorned and despised by other nations.

THE PROPHET'S DESPAIR, 7:1-6. This poem may continue the thoughts of the last chapter. The prophet looks for a godly man, but it is like looking for fruit after it has all been gathered. All men are wicked: "they all lie in wait for blood, they hunt every man his brother with a net." Princes and judges take bribes and great men utter "mischievous desire." The best of them is like a briar or a thorn hedge. The passage concludes with a warning not to trust friends or neighbors, for even the members of a family can turn against each other.

A PSALM OF HOPE, 7:7-20. To conclude the book on a more cheerful note, some editor added a post-exilic psalm of hope which shows the influence both of Psalm 137 and of Second Isaiah. The speaker looks forward to the day when God will overthrow His enemies, trample them like mud, and restore the walls of Jerusalem, to which the dispersed Jews will return. God will be the shepherd of His people. The other nations will be ashamed of their power and will lick the dust and turn to God in fear. To the remnant of His chosen people, God will manifest His love and compassion as He promised in the days of old.

THE BOOK OF NAHUM

INTRODUCTION. For centuries the Near East had suffered from the Assyrians, whose cruelties were proverbial. Their power was extended even into Egypt, where Asshurabanapal conquered Thebes in 663 (the incident is referred to in Nah. 3:8-10). But in 612 B. C. Nineveh, the Assyrian capital, fell before a coalition of Babylonians, Medes, and Scythians. The prophet Nahum celebrates the fall of the city in this bloodthirsty hymn of revenge, notable for its intensity and its brilliant use of realistic detail. One can hardly call religious the spirit of hatred and vengeance which infuses the poem, but its literary power is of high quality and it must be remembered that Israel had suffered deeply at the hands of the Assyrians. It is not certain whether the book was written before or just after the siege.

SUMMARY OF THE BOOK OF NAHUM

TITLE, 1:1. The first verse contains the title of Nahum's poem and also the title of the acrostic poem which precedes it.

AN ACROSTIC ORACLE AGAINST NINEVEH, 1:2-10. This alphabetical acrostic, imperfectly recalled, was inserted by a much later editor to serve as an introduction. Some lines of it were woven into the passage which follows. For a reconstruction, see *IB,* VI, 995-6. The speaker reminds his hearers that Yahweh is a jealous God, whose power may be experienced in whirlwind and storm, in drought, in earthquake, and in volcanic disturbances. He will take vengeance on His enemies.

THE FALL OF NINEVEH, 1:11-2:12. Did not Nineveh plot evil against the Lord? Therefore she will be cut off, for "he that dasheth in pieces" (i.e., the coalition of Babylonians and Medes) has come up against her. The prophet pictures the preparation for the attack: "Man the ramparts; watch the road, gird your loins; collect all your strength" (R. S. V.). The war chariots rush back and forth. The officers stumble as they hurry to the walls. The iron gates are opened. Those who live in the palace are terrified. Nineveh is like a pool whose waters are draining away, her treasure is being looted. "She is empty, and void, and waste; and the heart melteth, and the knees smite together, and much pain is in all loins, and the faces of them all gather blackness." Yahweh vows that He will burn her chariots in smoke and devour her lions (a favorite Assyrian symbol).

THE RUIN OF NINEVEH, 3:1-19. "Woe to the bloody city!" cries the poet, "it is all full of lies and robbery." We hear "the noise of a whip, and the noise of the rattling of the wheels, and of the prancing horses, and of the jumping chariots." We see "the horseman lifteth up both the bright sword and the glittering spear: and there is a multitude slain. . . ." The shame of the harlot will be exposed. Ironically the prophet asks, "Are you better than Thebes?" (R. S. V.)—i.e., "Are you better than the city which one of your rulers captured?"—implying that Nineveh in her turn will be captured. The city will be dazed and drunken, as her fortifications fall like ripe figs and her gates lie open to the enemies. In mockery of Nineveh's helplessness, the speaker urges her, "Draw thee strongholds," make brick in vain, for, as he says, "There shall the fire devour thee, the sword shall cut thee off." The Assyrian leaders are useless: "Thy shepherds slumber, O king of Assyria: thy nobles shall dwell in the dust: thy people is scattered upon the mountains and no man gathereth them." The wound given to Nineveh is grievous (literally "festering") and all who hear rejoice, for all have suffered from the wickedness of Assyria.

THE BOOK OF HABAKKUK

INTRODUCTION. The reference to the Chaldeans in 1:6 would seem to date the work of Habakkuk in the end of the seventh century after the rise of Nabopolassar in 626 but before the fall of Jerusalem in 587. In the text, as we have it, the book's reply to the prophet's query about destruction and violence implies that the Chaldeans are an instrument of His chastisement, as much as the Assyrians were according to Isaiah 5:26-29. However, some editors think two separate poems have been interwoven here and would separate 1:5-11, 12b, 14-17, which deals with the Chaldeans, from the prophet's meditation on the problem of evil, 1:2-4, 12a, 13, 2:1-4. The psalm which rounds off the book was almost certainly added later. It is not in the Dead Sea manuscript of Habakkuk, which probably dates from the first century B.C.

The poet's struggle with the problem of evil should be compared to Job's.

SUMMARY OF THE BOOK OF HABAKKUK

TITLE, 1:1. The title gives the prophet's name (of Assyrian origin) and says his oracle came from God.

HABAKKUK'S QUESTION, 1:2-4. "O Lord, how long shall I cry, and Thou wilt not hear! even cry unto Thee of violence and Thou wilt not save!" The prophet addresses God directly. He sees destruction and violence in the world. Justice and the law are violated.

ORACLES ON THE BITTER AND HASTY NATION, 1:5-11. In the present text, this seems to be God's reply to the prophet's question. "For, lo, I raise up the Chaldeans, that bitter and hasty nation, which shall march through the breadth of the land, to possess the dwelling places that are not theirs." The Chaldeans, whose horses are swift and fierce, are dreadful, terrible, and violent; they take numberless captives, scoff at kings, laugh at fortresses.

HABAKKUK RENEWS HIS QUESTIONING, 1:12-17. "Art Thou not from everlasting; O Lord my God, my Holy One?. . . . Thou art of purer eyes than to behold evil, and canst not look on iniquity: wherefore lookest thou upon them that deal treacherously, and holdest thy tongue when the wicked devoureth the man that is more righteous than he?" How can God tolerate treachery and wickedness and look on in silence when evil men swallow up good? Men are like fish or crawling things, leaderless, ready to be caught by hook and net.

THE WATCHTOWER, 2:1-4. The

prophet decides to station himself on a watchtower to see what God will say in reply. God tells him to write down the answer plainly, so that anyone going by "on the run" can read it. The reply is as follows: the wicked who is not upright shall fail, but the righteous man shall live by his faithfulness.

THE WOES, 2:5-20. The prophet makes five pronouncements connected with tyranny. (All are given in the R. S. V. translation.) (1) "Woe to him who heaps up what is not his own," for rebellion will be the result. (2) "Woe to him who gets evil gain for his house," for it will not win him safety. (3) "Woe to him who builds a town with blood." (4) "Woe to him who makes his neighbors drink" and gazes on his shame. (5) "Woe to him who says to a wooden thing, Awake; to a dumb stone, Arise!"—i.e., to him who worships idols of wood and stone. At the end of the chapter, Habakkuk returns to the idea with which he started, that he will wait in silence before God: "But the Lord is in his holy temple: let all the earth keep silence before him."

HABAKKUK'S PRAYER, 3. The Book of Habakkuk concludes with a prayer of the prophet that resembles a psalm. It tells of a vision he has had of the Lord. In this vision the Lord appears as a figure of anger and wrath. He strides through the world and the entire creation trembles with fear. The Lord has come to smite the wicked and raise up his people. The prayer concludes on a note of joy: "The Lord God is my strength . . . he will make me walk upon mine high places."

THE BOOK OF ZEPHANIAH

INTRODUCTION. During the long reign of Manasseh (681-642) paganism had gained much ground in Judah. Manasseh imitated the Assyrians by worshiping the heavenly bodies as gods. He revived the worship of Canaanite Baals, believed in witchcraft and the cult of the dead, and possibly even practiced infant sacrifice. But after the death of Manasseh's son Amon (642-640) came the reforming king Josiah (640-609). It is thought that Zephaniah's work, which certainly attacks the syncretism favored by Manasseh, falls in the early years of Josiah's reign, perhaps about 626 B.C. Most of his warnings are not new, but he may have helped to prepare the ground for Josiah's reform of 621. His graphic picture of the day of Yahweh (1:14-16) lingered long in Judaeo-Christian memory and inspired the fine medieval Latin hymn "Dies Irae." The eschatological predictions of the last chapter, particularly verses 14-20, probably come from a later period.

SUMMARY OF THE BOOK OF ZEPHANIAH

TITLE, 1:1. The unusually long opening statement traces the prophet's ancestry back four generations to (apparently) King Hezekiah. If correct, this would make Zephaniah a cousin of King Josiah.

JUDGMENTS AGAINST JERUSALEM AND JUDAH, 1:2-18. Chapter 1 is disorganized and the opening verses, with their picture of total destruction, may have been added later. Then a genuine passage from

Zephaniah attacks the worship of Baal, those who worship heavenly bodies, the Ammonite cult of Malcham (a variant of Moloch), those who have adopted foreign clothes, and those who leap over the Temple threshold so as not to step on it (a pagan Philistine custom). Yahweh is represented as searching Jerusalem with lamps, ready to punish men who are complacent, "thick" like wine which has not been properly stirred up, who assume that God will do nothing, who say to themselves "The Lord will not do good, neither will He do evil." The day of the Lord, a day of wrath, suffering, desolation, and gloom is at hand, when even strong men will weep.

JUDGMENTS AGAINST THE NATIONS, 2:1-15.
The wrath of God is invoked against a "shameless nation" (R. S. V.)—Judah?—and again the Philistine cities. (Plea for humility in verse 3 may be editorial.) Oracles follow against Moab and the Ammonites, who will become as Sodom and Gomorrah, and against the Ethiopians, who will be slain by the sword. Assyria, too, is warned. Nineveh will become a desolation and a wilderness.

DENUNCIATIONS AND PROMISES, 3:1-20.
If any of this chapter is genuine, it is the opening attack, verses 1-7, on Jerusalem's rebelliousness and on the sins of the ruling classes. Her officials and judges prey on the people like animals, her prophets are untrustworthy, her priests blasphemous and lawless. Repeated warnings to the city have been disregarded. Yahweh will first assemble the nations to pour out His anger on them, but later will give them the gift of pure speech so that they may praise Him and serve Him with one accord. The proud will be removed and the humble remnant which is left will do no wrong, "for they shall feed and lie down and none shall make them afraid."

The book closes with a confident hope for a golden age. "Sing, O daughter of Zion, shout, O Israel," bids the prophet, "The Lord hath taken away thy judgments, he hath cast out thine enemy: the king of Israel, even the Lord, is in the midst of thee: thou shalt not see evil any more." God will "rejoice over thee with joy; he will rest in his love, he will joy over thee with singing. Sorrow will flee away, the lame and the outcast will be gathered in, the people will be gathered together, and will be "a name and a praise among all people of the earth."

THE BOOK OF HAGGAI

INTRODUCTION.
Both Haggai and Zechariah throw light on the year 520 and after, when the rebuilding of the Temple was commenced. Haggai was shocked to find that nearly twenty years after Cyrus had allowed the exiles to return, the Temple was still in a ruined state. His description of the poverty of the community (1:6) suggests that the people were too occupied in scraping a bare living to be concerned about it. They used the foundations for sacrifice anyway and were used to seeing them in their burned-out and damaged state. Haggai, however, felt that if they made the effort to rebuild the Temple, Yahweh would reward them with the fruits of the earth and with prosperity. He evidently convinced them, for the work of reconstruction was actually begun. Haggai is characteristic of post-exile Judaism both in seeing the Temple as the center of the community's life and in objecting to mingling with the Samaritans.

SUMMARY OF THE BOOK OF HAGGAI

SUPERSCRIPTION, 1:1. The opening sentence dates the first prophecy and declares that is came to Zerubbabel, governor of Judah, and to Joshua, the high priest.

CALL TO REBUILD, 1:2-15. The people are unwilling or unready to rebuild the Temple, for they live in great poverty, lacking sufficient food and clothes. Haggai tells them that the Lord wants them to rebuild it, so that He can appear there in glory. In his displeasure, He has withheld rain, grain, wine, and oil. Under the leadership of Zerubbabel and Joshua, the remnant of the people set to work. (Many editors consider 2:15-19 the second message and would place it here.)

THE OLD TEMPLE AND THE NEW, 2:1-9. People who remember Solomon's Temple in its former glory are urged to take courage. Yahweh's spirit is among them and He promises that the latter splendor of His house will be even greater than the former.

THE UNCLEAN, 2:10-14. The meaning of this passage is uncertain. Does Haggai mean that the people are unclean because they have not rebuilt the Temple? Or because they have sacrificed without a Temple? Or because they have mixed with the Samaritans? At any rate, for one of these reasons, Haggai considers that the offerings being made are unclean.

FRUITFULNESS, 2:15-19. Haggai here reverts to the theme that the fruitfulness of the earth is dependent on the restoration of the Temple. Many editors would move this passage to the end of Chapter 1.

ZERUBBABEL, THE CHOICE OF YAHWEH, 2:20-23. Yahweh says He is about to shake the heavens and the earth and overthrow kingdoms, apparently to remove obstacles to the rule of Zerubbabel, who is to be Yahweh's servant and His signet ring, to whom the heathen will surrender their powers.

THE BOOK OF ZECHARIAH

INTRODUCTION. Zechariah's oracles are dated in the year 520-18. His ministry overlaps slightly with Haggai's. Like Haggai, he is concerned with the rebuilding of the Temple, the leadership of Zerubbabel and the priest Joshua, and the coming of the Messianic age. Both writers are hostile to the Samaritans and anxious about ritual purity. Zechariah has touches of universalism which recall Second Isaiah.

The last six chapters of the book are not really the work of Zechariah, but a collection of oracles from various hands, probably from the Greek period.

SUMMARY OF THE BOOK OF ZECHARIAH

SUPERSCRIPTION, 1:1. The superscription gives Zechariah's ancestry and dates his first prophecy in 520 B.C., the "second year of Darius."

CALL TO REPENT, 1:2-6. Zechariah reports that Yahweh is angry with the ancestors of the people who did not turn away from their evil deeds.

He calls on the present generation to carry out his laws.

ZECHARIAH'S VISIONS, 1:7-6:8.
Zechariah sees a series of visions which are explained by an angelic interpreter. Four horsemen who have been riding about the earth report that all is peaceful. Four horses which represent enemies of Israel (Assyrians, Babylonians, Medes, Persians?) are frightened by four smiths who will cast them down. A man (angel?) with a measuring line is told that he need not be concerned about the walls of Jerusalem, for it will outgrow its walls and Yahweh will surround it with a wall of fire. The visions are now interrupted by an appeal to the Babylonian exiles to return home. Next Zechariah beholds Joshua confronted with "the Satan" (here means "the accuser"). However, Joshua's filthy garments, a symbol of (ritual?) impurity, are taken away, and he is clothed with fresh garments and a clean turban, and promised that he will have charge of the Lord's courts. A lampstand with seven lamps and near it two olive trees next appear, but the meaning of this vision is not very clear. Does it mean that the trees (Zerubbabel and Joshua) will supply oil (grace) for the lamp (Israel)? Or that the lamps signify Yahweh who enlightens the two anointed leaders? An enormous scroll about thirty by fifteen feet is inscribed with a curse on thieves and liars. A woman sitting in an ephah (a grain measure) represents wickedness. Finally, four chariots drawn by red, black, white and gray horses ride out from between two bronze mountains and go to the four points of the compass. Those who go to the north are to wreak Yahweh's anger on Babylon.

ZERUBBABEL CROWNED, 6:9-15.
The prophet is told to take gold and silver and make crowns for Joshua. This passage seems to have been altered. Originally it perhaps provided crowns for both Zerubbabel and Joshua, as the use of the plural indicates. If, as is sometimes supposed,

Zerubbabel led a rebellion which failed, the passage may have been altered after that event. At present it is obscure.

THE INQUIRY ABOUT THE FASTS, 7:1-8:23.
A deputation from Bethel asks whether the customary fasts should be continued. Zechariah replies that Yahweh prefers good moral standards to ritual. "Execute true judgment and show mercy and compassion every man to his brother: And oppress not the widow, nor the fatherless, the stranger, nor the poor; and let none of you imagine evil against his brother in your heart." A series of sayings relate to the coming happiness of Jerusalem. Yahweh is "jealous for Zion," and will return and dwell in her. Old men and women will sit happily in the street while children play. Yahweh does not seem to doubt Zerubbabel's success (though apparently some people did). The nation will be saved from Babylon and from Egypt and from internal strife. But when these happy days come, men must do right. "Speak ye every man the truth to his neighbor; execute the judgment of truth and peace in your gates: And let none of you imagine evil in your hearts against his neighbor; and love no false oath: for all these are things that I hate, saith the Lord." Then the fasts will be times of "joy and gladness and cheerful feasts," and people of all nations will turn to the Jews. They will say, "We will go with you: for we have heard that God is with you."

MISCELLANEOUS ORACLES, 9:1-14:21.
These oracles are anonymous and of uncertain date. The first (9:1-12) pictures the victory of a Messianic king. It may refer to the siege of Tyre by Alexander the Great in 322 B.C. The prophet thinks the siege presages the coming of the Messiah. The more belligerent end of the chapter (verses 13-17) may express Israel's disappointment when this expectation was not fulfilled. A brief petition from a time of drought (10:1-2) speaks scornfully of those who try

to make rain come by appealing to idols and diviners, and directs the people to "ask rain from the Lord," who alone can send it. The next three oracles probably date from the Ptolemaic period. A prophecy of war against tyrants (10:3-12) foretells the return of the Jews from the Diaspora. An ironic lament for the tyrants (11: 1-3) compares their destruction to the fall of great cedars and oaks. A puzzling allegory (11:4-14), in which the prophet says he is a shepherd of a flock doomed to perish, seems to lay the blame for Israel's troubles at home and abroad on their disloyalty to God. Details of the allegory are obscure and scholars do not agree on their interpretation. The last few verses of the chapter (15-17) speak of an evil governor, a "worthless shepherd," who "does not care for the perishing, or seek the wandering, or heal the maimed, or nourish the sound. . . ." (R. S. V.). The last chapters of the book (12-14) are apocalyptic and eschatological in character. The writer of the oracle in 12:1-13:9 expects that when the heathen nations rise to destroy God's people, God Himself will strike panic into their hearts, terrorizing horse and rider alike. Judah will be a blazing fire and Jerusalem, protected by God's shield, will stand secure. Its inhabitants will wash themselves in a cleansing fountain and the nation will be purged, only one-third surviving as a faithful remnant. In Chapter 14, another writer gives a different picture of the last days of Jerusalem. He says that after the city has been ravaged and half the population exiled, God in person will appear on the Mount of Olives, which will split in half, while the whole land becomes a plain. A terrible, rotting plague will afflict both people and beasts. If the nations who survive do not worship the Lord and keep the Feast of the Tabernacles (booths), they will be afflicted with terrible droughts. In that day Jerusalem will be so holy that pots to cook the sacrificial meals will have to be as large as ceremonial bowls, and, as a token of holiness, even the horses' bells will be inscribed "Holiness unto the Lord."

THE BOOK OF MALACHI

INTRODUCTION.
The book of Malachi belongs to the period just before the governorship of Nehemiah, who, in fact, corrected some of the abuses which are mentioned, such as mixed marriages and improperly carried out rituals. Malachi wrote at a time when both priests and people were depressed and discouraged by the realities which faced them after the return to Judah. They had come with high hopes but had had many disappointments. The land was poor and hardly offered a bare living. The nation was a powerless and unimportant little unit in the vast Persian Empire. Where were the glories of the return promised them by Second Isaiah? If they were really God's chosen, people asked, why was not their lot a happier one? Rewards and punishments seem to be very unevenly meted out. The people wanted to know why evil seemed to be rewarded and good not rewarded. They asked "Where is the God of justice?" The prophet attempts to give some answers to this question.

SUMMARY OF THE BOOK OF MALACHI

SUPERSCRIPTION, 1:1. This states that the oracle is addressed to Israel by Yahweh's messenger—for that, literally, is what Malachi means.

THE DOWNFALL OF EDOM, 1:2-5. The prophet explains that the downfall of Edom is one way in which Yahweh has demonstrated his love for Israel: "Yet I have loved Jacob but hated Esau" (R. S. V.). The Edomites will not be able to rebuild the ruins. They are "the people against whom the Lord hath indignation forever."

VARIOUS ABUSES, 1:6-2:17. Priests and people are guilty of sins before the Lord. This is one cause of their present suffering. The priests offer imperfect animals as sacrifices. They are not living up to their high calling because they have not kept the Lord's ways. Faithlessness in marriage and divorce are an offense to Yahweh.

THE FUTURE TIMES, 3:1-4:3. Yahweh will send his messenger who will purify the priests and people until they make the right offerings. Sorcery and adultery, perjury, and oppression of the helpless—the hireling, the widow, and the orphan—will be done away with. Now the people are robbing God by not paying proper tithes. But if they bring full tithes, He will send them blessings, so that the land and the vines shall bear fruit. The Lord keeps in His book of remembrance the names of those who fear Him, and they shall be His special possession. The day will come when the evildoers will be burned up like stubble and "the Sun of righteousness shall rise with healing in his wings," and the faithful shall tread down the wicked. This is the third point at which the prophet tries to answer the question, "Where is the God of Justice?"

EPILOGUE TO THE BOOK OF THE TWELVE, 4:4-5. "Remember ye the law of Moses my servant, which I commanded unto him in Horeb for all Israel, with the statutes and judgments. Behold, I will send you Elijah the prophet before the coming of the great and dreadful day of the Lord." He will turn the hearts of the fathers and the children toward each other, or the land will be cursed.

THE APOCRYPHA

The study of the Old Testament Apocrypha is attended with many problems, not the least of which is a satisfactory definition of the term. It is generally used to refer (in the King James Version) to the fourteen books* which, although written from about 200 B.C. to 100 A. D. (i.e., at about the same time as the last books of the Old Testament), are not part of the canon, or accepted text, of the Old Testament. The books were refused admittance to the canon for various reasons, the most important two of which were that they either were written too recently (e.g., I and II Maccabees) or that they were written in languages other than Hebrew, the "sacred tongue" (most of the Apocrypha were composed in Greek or Aramaic). The general name "apocrypha" comes from a Greek word meaning "hidden away"; that is, apocryphal books concern themselves with matters that were "hidden" from general view. [Those who favored such works believed they should be hidden because they dealt with doctrines too complicated or subtle for the population at large; their opponents also argued that such books ought to be hidden but they had different reasons for thinking so. They felt that they either made false claims as to authorship (e.g., some claimed to have been written by Abraham, Solomon, etc.) or else were heretical in content.] These books have led a curious existence during the last two thousand years; in some periods they have been widely read, in others practically ignored.

Unfortunately, this leads to a further complication in the definition. In the sixteenth century, the Roman Catholic Church stated officially that seven of the Apocrypha were divinely inspired and therefore just as authoritative as the rest of the Old Testament. Protestants do not share this position although they do believe the books should be read. (They also have another name for the book—*pseudepigrapha*, i.e., writing circulating under false titles.) This term is unsatisfactory, too, because it applies to some apocryphal works and not to others. Thus, there really is no generally agreed upon definition for the word. In this brief introductory survey, the term will have the meaning suggested at the beginning of this essay.

It is not to be thought that because the limits of the Apocrypha are ill defined, the books themselves are insignificant. The Apocrypha taken together are one-fourth as long as the entire Old Testament (and five-sixths as long as the New Testament). There are many different kinds of works within the Apocrypha: historical chronicles (I Esdras and I and II Maccabees), collections of wise sayings, "wisdom literature" (Wisdom of Solomon and Ecclesvasticus), short stories (Tobit, Bel and the Dragon, Susanna), and prophetic visions (II Esdras). The main interest of the Apocrypha lies not so much in their doctrines as in the insight they give into the attitudes and lives of their writers and compilers. The light they shed on these matters is especially valuable because we do not know too much about life in the period in which they were written. Because this literature is so extensive, and because there are so many problems relating to texts and dates of composition, all that can be attempted here are short summaries of and/or commentaries on each book. The interested student can easily pursue the matter further in the many books available on the subject.

* The books of the Apocrypha in the order in which they usually appear in the K. S. V. are: I and II Esdras, Tobit, Judith, The Additions to the Book of Esther, The Wisdom of Solomon, Ecclesiasticus, Baruch and the Letter of Jeremiah, The Prayer of Azariah and the Song of the Three Young Men, Susanna, Bel and the Dragon, The Prayer of Manasseh, and I and II Haccabees. In the R. S. V., Baruch and the Letter of Jeremiah are separated, thus making fifteen books.

FIRST ESDRAS

First Esdras is a chronicle that starts, abruptly, at II Chron. 35:1, with a description of the Passover held by King Josiah and then repeats the rest of II Chronicles, followed by the whole Book of Ezra and Neh. 7:73-8:12, finishing in the middle of a sentence. The main puzzle about I Esdras is its relation to Ezra-Nehemiah. It is clearly not a Greek translation of any Hebrew text we have today, and therefore it is reasonable to suppose that both the Biblical text and I Esdras derive from a common ancestor. I Esdras is noteworthy in that it rearranges the narrative of Ezra and Nehemiah by leaving out first seven chapters of Nehemiah and thus making Ezra run without a break into Nehemiah.

SECOND ESDRAS

Second Esdras is an example of *apocalyptic* writing which tries to foretell the future (other examples are the last chapters of the Book of Daniel, and the Book of Revelation of the New Testament). Apocalytic writing is usually difficult to understand because it imparts its meaning through elaborate and difficult symbols, and II Esdras is no exception. The heart of this book, chapters 3 to 14, is a record of seven revelations seen by Ezra of Babylon. In the first vision Ezra is downcast over the sad fate of the Jewish people, and he meditates about the problem of evil. In the second vision there is a discussion of those who will die before the present age is concluded. The main subject of the third vision is the small number who will be saved. The fourth is a vision of the sad plight of the Jewish people; the fifth and sixth are complicated allegories of the coming of the Messiah. The seventh shows Ezra told by God that he is soon to be taken to Heaven.

TOBIT

Tobit is a well-told short story that points a moral. Its chief lesson is that although God allows evil to befall the righteous, He watches over them and saves them when they are threatened with disaster. It is the story of Tobit, a Palestinian Jew who, along with his family, is taken as a prisoner to Babylon (see II Kings 18:9-11). There he becomes famous for his charity and good works. He loses his fortune, goes blind, and quarrels with his wife; however, although he is alone and destitute, he never loses his faith in God. Meanwhile, his relative Sarah, who lives in far-off Media, is also desperately unhappy. She has been married seven times, and each of her husbands has been killed before the marriage can be consummated. Like Tobit, she is pious and prays to God for death to lift her misery from her shoulders. Tobit believes himself about to die, and he gives his last instructions to his son Tobias, who must make a journey to Media at this time. Tobias travels with a young man who is really the angel Raphael in disguise, and after several miraculous occurrences the story ends happily, with Tobias marrying Sarah and Tobit's sight and wife restored.

JUDITH

Judith is another effective tale that enforces a moral. In this case, the events have a military setting (it is thought that the author was a Palestinian Jew who wrote during the troubled times following the Maccabean uprising). The lesson the book teaches is that religion and patriotic self-defense are inextricably bound up with each other. If the Jews observe the law of Moses exactly, then the Lord will surely protect them; if not, then He will give them into the hands of the enemy. The heroine, Judith, combines bravery and piety to outwit her adversaries. It should be said that although the story has an appearance of historical accuracy, it is in fact wholly fictional.

The narrative begins with a quarrel between the Assyrians and the Medes in which the Medes are totally defeated. The Assyrian king Nebuchadrezzar decides to conquer the many nations that had sided with the Medes and therefore fits out a great army under the command of Holofernes. Holofernes demolishes the power of all the nations on the Mediterranean coast and finally comes to the Israelites in Palestine, who decide to oppose him. Holofernes is told that the Jews cannot be beaten unless they sin against their God, but he is infuriated by their opposition and surrounds Jerusalem and cuts off its water supply. Soon the Jews become desperate, and the beautiful and pious widow Judith tries to think of a plan to save them. She succeeds, and after suitable prayer, she goes over to the Assyrians and tells Holofernes that she has left Jerusalem because the Jews, in their desperation, are preparing to eat forbidden foods. Holofernes is delighted with her beauty and holds a banquet for her. When he is reeling drunk, she cuts off his head and returns to Jerusalem. The Jews then rush upon the Assyrians, who flee in panic when they discover that their general is dead.

THE ADDITIONS TO THE BOOK OF ESTHER

This puzzling material can best be understood if one has some knowledge of the text. Early in the Christian era the man who translated the Book of Esther into Greek added a large selection (107 verses) to the book. When Esther came to be rendered into Latin, the translator translated these additional sections but placed them at the back of the book as notes. These notes were often omitted by careless scribes, and the confusion was made even worse when the chapters of Esther were numbered consecutively to make it appear as if the additions were a kind of continuation of the narrative of the book. Thus what we now have printed as one Apocryphal book was once scattered through the Book of Esther.

WISDOM OF SOLOMON AND ECCLESIASTICUS

Both these books are collections of sage reflections on life made by a wise man; in this they resemble the "wisdom" books of the Old Testament: Job, Ecclesiastes, and Proverbs. Although these two works belong to the "wisdom" tradition, they do not resemble one another. Ecclesiasticus mainly treats of wisdom in its practical aspect; it is concerned with ethics and social conduct and, like the Book of Proverbs, offers its wisdom in the form of brief sayings. The Wisdom of Solomon, on the other hand, is a much more ambitious work. It aspires to be a contribution to religious philosophy, and therefore presents a prose narrative argument. While both works stem from traditional Old Testament Judaism, the influence of Greek thought is clearly to be seen in the Wisdom of Solomon; its author attempts to show that Jewish and Greek philosophies are compatible.

BARUCH AND THE LETTER OF JEREMIAH

The Book of Baruch was supposed to have been written by the Baruch who was the secretary of Jeremiah (Jer. 32:12), and it is the only one of the Apocrypha that is written in imitation of the prophetical books of the Old Testament. It begins in Babylon, with Baruch telling the captives that they should confess the sins that led to their conquest by the Babylonians. Then comes a plea for Divine forgiveness and mercy. In the middle of chapter 4 the style and tone changes.

The language becomes more poetical (it is thought that a second author's contribution begins here), and the book becomes somewhat more optimistic. It ends on a note of hope for the restoration of the people to Palestine. The Letter of Jeremiah is usually printed as the sixth and last chapter of Baruch, but it really has no connection to either Baruch or Jeremiah. Instead it is a little tract against idolatry.

THE PRAYER OF AZARIAH AND THE SONG OF THE THREE YOUNG MEN

The Prayer of Azariah is an addition to the canonical Book of Daniel. It will be remembered that Azariah, who is better known by his Babylonian name of Abednego, was put into the fiery furnace along with his two fellow Jews Shadrach and Meshach. This was done to him because he persisted in his belief in Yahweh and refused to worship the golden image (Dan. 3:23-24). It is at this time that he offers up his prayer. Contrary to

what one might expect, Azariah does not ask God to extinguish the flames, but rather he praises the Lord and begs that his people be delivered from oppression. In response, an angel causes a cooling wind to blow on the three martyrs. The Song of the Three Young Men is the long hymn of praise to the Lord offered up by Azariah and his two friends in the furnace.

SUSANNA

Like the Prayer of Azariah, Susanna is an addition to the Book of Daniel; it is an excellent, suspenseful short story and is inserted either as chapter 1 or chapter 13. It involves the beautiful and pious Susanna, the wife of an eminent Babylonian Jew, Joakim. It is the custom for lawsuits to be heard at Joakim's estate in the morning. Two elderly judges who regularly come to Joakim's house are overcome

with lust for Susanna. One hot day Susanna decides to bathe in her pool, and she sends her maids to shut the doors. The two judges have hidden themselves by the pool and rush out as soon as the maids have gone. They tell her that if she will not submit to them, they will say that they caught her in adultery with a young man. She refuses, and they bring the charge. She is tried for the offense, and she denies it, praying to God to prove her innocence. She is convicted and sentenced to death. As she is being led away, a young man named Daniel (the prophet) intervenes and demands to question the witnesses. He catches them in a lie, and Susanna is set free and the judges are executed. The moral is clear: purity and trust in God will sustain and protect one in difficulty.

BEL AND THE DRAGON

Bel and the Dragon is still another addition to the Book of Daniel. This book consists of two short episodes that purport to be scenes from the life of the prophet. The king of Persia asks Daniel why he does not worship the idol called Bel. Daniel replies that he worships only the one true God and not any manmade thing. The king thinks that Daniel is wrong. If Bel is not living, he asks him, how is it that the idol consumes the enormous amount of food that is sacrificed to it daily. The king asks the priests of Bel's temple whether they are eating the food, and they deny it. They are not worried when the king proposes, as a test, that the sanctuary be sealed up, because they have a trapdoor under the idol through which they can enter. Daniel, however, spreads ashes over the floor, and when the sanctuary is opened the next day he is able to show the king the footprints of the priests in the ashes. The king is furious, and orders the priests killed. The story of the Dragon concerns another god worshiped by the Babylonians—this one a huge dragon or serpent. Daniel agrees that this god is alive, but he denies the king's claim that the beast is immortal. Daniel manages to poison it, whereupon many people are furious with him and demand that he be killed. The king orders Daniel placed in the lions' den (this is a different occasion from that narrated in chapter 6 of the biblical text, in which Daniel is also placed in a lions' den). After seven days with the lions Daniel emerges unharmed, and the king throws the men who have clamored for Daniel's death into the den.

THE PRAYER OF MANASSEH

It will be recalled that Manasseh is the wicked son of King Hezekiah (II Kings 21 and II Chron. 33). As a punishment for the evil that he does, he is captured and taken into exile in Assyria. There he experiences a change of heart. He prays to the Lord, and his prayer is received. This prayer, the Book of Chronicles says, is recorded in a narrative that has not survived. Therefore the Apocryphal Prayer of Manasseh was composed in later times to supply this lack. This short work begins with praise for the Lord. This is followed by a confession of sins, and then a humble request for pardon. The prayer ends on a note of petition for grace and with more praise for the Almighty.

FIRST AND SECOND MACCABEES

First and Second Maccabees are two accounts, by different authors, of the struggle for religious liberty carried on by the Jewish patriot Judah Maccabee (also called Judas Maccabeus) in the second century B.C. Although the two books recount largely the same events, there are great differences between them in terms of style and intention. First Maccabees is straightforward, simple chronicle; Second Maccabees is much more complicated and rhetorical, and its author uses the historical narrative to point a moral.

When the action opens, Antiochus Epiphanes has just come to the throne (175 B.C.); when it ends Simon Maccabee has just died (134 B.C.). A very short introduction gives the minimum of historical background necessary to understand the book, and is followed by a description of the terrible situation of the Jews under King Antiochus. Antiochus has decided to force the Jews to worship Greek gods, and he therefore forbids, under severe penalties, the observance of the Jewish religion. Mattathias and his sons refuse to obey this law, and flee to the mountains. From the mountains they and the group that collects about them wage guerrilla war on the Greeks; the main part of the book deals with the actions of three of Mattathias' sons: Judah, Jonathan, and Simon. The narrative is one of battles won and lost against the numerically superior Greeks, climaxing in the gaining of political independence under Simon Maccabee in 142 B.C. However, Simon and two of his sons are murdered in 134 B.C., and another of Simon's sons, John, seizes power and continues the Maccabean tradition of Jewish independence. When one thinks of the exciting and inspiring story told in Maccabees, it is somewhat strange that the books were not made part of the Old Testament. Despite this omission, the history of the Maccabees has been popular through the centuries and is commemorated yearly in the Jewish holiday of Hanukkah.

ESSAY QUESTIONS AND ANSWERS ON THE OLD TESTAMENT

1. What is meant by the Lower and Higher Criticism of the Bible?
Lower Criticism of the Bible (often known as Textual Criticism) involves studying the available texts of the Bible in order to determine the original wording as far as is possible from a comparative analysis of existent manuscript copies. Higher Criticism (often known as Historical Criticism) is more comprehensive in scope: authorship, dates, sources, etc., are the focuses of study in Historical Criticism. With the advance in science and the development of archeology the progress in this field of criticism has been stupendous. Obviously the commentary in this book follows the current best Historical Criticism.

2. Does the Bible have any overall unity?
It does. It is the continuous tale of the growth in religious spirit of the Hebrew and early Christian peoples. It contains the history and literature of both Judaism and Christianity. Its 66 books unfold a moral and spiritual truth that provides great comfort and satisfaction to distressed human

beings. Its message? Good is at the heart of the universe, that time and the stars are on the side of Right and Justice, that all men are brothers and God their Father.

3. Is there a discernable progress in the conception of God if the Bible is read chronologically? Discuss.

There is. If one thinks of the growth of the God conception as a long-term one with reflections and retrogressions in an overall upward line: there is reflected a *polytheism* in Genesis in the use of plural names for the Deity and the anthropomorphic God who walks and talks like a human being; he is jealous and often angry, requiring the murder of thousands of women and children. Tribal worship of this fearful and angry deity was by animal sacrifice as atonement for sin. The God of Moses was a *tribal deity*, the saviour and protector of the Hebrews, but in Canaan, Baal-worship (agricultural polytheism) was mingled with tribal monotheism. Elijah the prophet established the supremacy of monotheism over Baal, while the prophet Amos (eighth century B.C.) made of the Deity a God of justice and righteousness, as did Hosea who added to Him a God of mercy and compassion; and to climax the process Second Isaiah adds universalism to high ethical monotheism. It is important to remember that the standard order of the O. T. is not chronological but topical.

4. Where is the gold mine of Biblical archaeology?

It is located in the cradle of civilization, the fertile valley of the Tigris and Euphrates rivers. Mesopotamia (modern Iraq) contains the earliest remains of civilized life. Within eight hundred miles of Jerusalem as the center of a circle will be found the gold mines of modern biblical archaeology.

5. Name some heroes of modern archaeology and philosophy and briefly cite their individual contributions.

1. Champollion in the early nineteenth century deciphered the hieroglyphs of the Rosetta Stone to unlock the mysteries of ancient Egypt.

2. Henry C. Rawlinson was the first to decipher the perplexing and baffling Persian and Babylonian cuneiform (1846); his daring and courage are records of a great man at work.

3. Botta, Layard, Rich, Place, Oppert, and Sarzec are only a few of the names of renown in archaeological studies. George A. Barton's *Archaeology and the Bible*, C. W. Ceram's *Gods, Graves, and Scholars*, and Jack Finegan's *Light From the Ancient Past* are all good books in this field (see Bibliography).

6. In what way does the Gilgamesh epic of the Flood story tally with the account in Genesis?

They tally in so many ways that scholars are certain that either the Hebrew account is dependent upon the Babylonian or both are versions of an earlier original. In both versions the hero is told by a deity that a Deluge will occur; both are similar in the description of the building of the ark, the embarkation, the ceasing of the rain, the final rest on a mountain peak, the three birds, the disembarkations, and the sacrifice.

7. What is the significance of the Code of Hammurabi biblically?

There is considerable dependence in the Old Testament on the laws of the Code of Hammurabi, and in fact there are some fifty articles in the so-called Mosaic laws in which the similarity is practically verbatim.

8. What is the significance of the Poem of the Righteous Sufferer?

The Poem (about 2000 B.C.) deals with a righteous man who suffers unjustly at the hands of the gods, one who questions their goodness and sense of justice. A good man suffers terribly, one who has not sinned.

He questions the conception that irreligiousness brings suffering and righteousness in man brings prosperity. God's justice is inscrutable, and is so stated in a stormy and violent demonstration. This Poem of the Righteous Sufferer (Babylonian) is quite similar to that of Job as demonstrated above.

9. What is the significance of the Ras Shamra texts biblically?

Clay tablets dug up in 1929 reveal an alphabet earlier than that of the fabled Phoenicians. They date from the fifteenth century B.C. and were found in Ras Shamra (then called Ugarit) in northwest Syria; their significance is that they reveal the Canaanite myths, beliefs, and religious practices, many of which were absorbed by the invading Hebrews. Hebrew religion was definitely syncretistic in its origins.

10. What was the first form of Hebrew prophecy?

That of the dervishes or ecstatics, politico-religious leaders of the Hebrews in the eleventh century B.C. They roamed about like minstrels and worked themselves into mad frenzy through music. They lived a parasitic life, and had no real moral or religious message. The great eighth century reformers knew them as "false prophets."

11. Who was the first literary prophet?

Amos (750 B.C.), often known as the Prophet of Righteousness; in chronological terms his book is the first written book of the Old Testament, or Tanak. He spoke of a Yahweh of righteousness and higher ethics, above that of mere ritual.

12. What was the prophet Isaiah's contribution?

The doctrine of Messianism begins with him (Yahweh would deliver Israel by means of a divinely appointed Messiah). He also insisted that political Israel be subordinated to its priests. Faith in God is superior to military alliances; some think this is the key to the survival of the Jewish community in spite of political downfalls.

13. Discuss the authorship of the Ten Commandments according to the Higher Criticism.

Moses cannot have been the author of the Ten Commandments in their present form (Exod. 20; Deut. 5). Laws grow naturally from social and civil situations: they are not revealed *before* the history of a people. As conditions change, laws are modified and some are added. Thus the Decalogue implies an agricultural (and not a tribal) setting that can only refer to the Hebrews settled in Canaan and not to the prior days in Egypt. In addition, the Decalogue has an advanced ethical tone reflecting much later times than the harsh and primitive times of the Mosaic wanderings.

14. What forms of writing does the historical narrative take?

Such forms as early war songs, ballads, tales of the patriarchs, legends around the conquest of Canaan, the histories of kings, temple records, the annals of royalty, and even post-Exilic redactions.

15. Discuss two examples of the "Literature of Revolt."

1. The Book of Ruth (about 400 B.C.) is a kind of short story rebelling against the Hebrew prohibition of intermarriage with foreigners.
2. The Book of Jonah (400-300 B.C.) is a parable satire dealing a blow against religious exclusiveness and sectarianism. God even loves the foreign and miserable Ninevites!

16. What is the most pronounced expression of apocalyptic in the Old Testament? Discuss its outstanding features.

The Book of Daniel (168 B.C.) was written to give courage to the Jews in their resistance to the Greeks, and also to assure the Jews of final victory over the heathen. There will be a New Kingdom ruled over by "the Son of Man" which shall not pass away. The righteous shall be rewarded in the hereafter and the enemy crushed!

17. What is the final canon of the Old Testament? List in order by title.

The Law: Genesis, Exodus, Leviticus, Numbers, Deuteronomy.
The Former Prophets: Joshua, Judges, I and II Samuel, I and II Kings.
The Latter Prophets:
Major: Isaiah, Jeremiah, Ezekiel.
Minor: The Book of the Twelve: Hosea, Joel, Amos, Obadiah, Jonah, Micah, Nahum, Habakkuk, Zephaniah, Haggai, Zechariah, Malachi.
The Writings:
Poetic Books: Psalms, Proverbs, Job.
The Five Rolls: Canticles, Ruth, Lamentations, Ecclesiastes, Esther.
The Remainder: Daniel, Ezra, Nehemiah, I and II Chronicles. There are 39 books in all, grouped into a larger category of 24 books in the official Hebrew list.

18. What is the Septuagint? Discuss its main features.

Jews scattered about the Mediterranean world (the Diaspora) had forgotten Hebrew and knew only Greek (about 300 B.C.), especially those in and around Alexandria in Egypt. In 250 B.C. arrangements were made for the translation of the Hebrew Bible into Greek for the benefit of the Diaspora. This translation is called the **Septuagint** from the Latin for 70 (**septuaginta**), and according to a tradition 70 scholars worked for 70 years on the translation. This version is typically more liberal than the Hebrew in that it includes 14 more books than the official 39 of the Hebrew canon. Those 14 books outside the canon are known as the Apocrypha ("hidden" or "spurious" in Greek).

19. How does the official Catholic Bible (the Vulgate) handle the so-called Apocrypha in contrast to the Protestants?

In 404 B.C. the Vulgate was finished by Jerome; it became the Bible of western Christendom for a thousand years and still is the official Catholic Bible. Jerome called the Septuagint's extra 14 books "Apocrypha" but still included them in his translation. Later the Catholic Church was to call the 14 books officially canonical. The Protestants (led by Luther) reject the 14 books as non-canonical.

20. List the Septuagintal Apocrypha.

First and Second Esdras; Tobit; Judith; The Remainder of Esther; The Wisdom of Solomon; Ecclesiasticus; Baruch; Susanna; Song of the Three Children, Bel and the Dragon, Prayer of Manasseh, I and II Maccabees.

A NOTE ON ENGLISH TRANSLATIONS OF THE BIBLE

1320-84: John Wyclife was the first to translate the complete Bible into English. He was a pre-Reformation Protestant who translated the Bible from the Latin Vulgate (340-420 A.D.). The Old Testament appeared in 1382 and the New Testament in 1380. He knew neither Greek nor Hebrew. An extremely popular translation in its time.

1484-1536: William Tyndale is the greatest name in the history of the English Bible: his was the first English translation directly from the Greek and Hebrew—the Old Testament was left incomplete at his death (by burning at the stake). His influence is tremendous: 80% of the K.J.V. retains his phraseology; his prose style "unparalleled in grace, felicity of expression, and vigor" (see F. G. Bratton's *A History of the Bible*, 1959, p. 251; his book is the best so far on biblical history for the non-scholar).

1610: Roman Catholic scholars fleeing persecution published this English translation in 1610. The preface, however, warns against reading the Bible by the profane laity. The translation is directly from the Vulgate. The vocabulary is stilted and Latinized. Greek and Hebrew sources were additionally utilized in the Bishop Challoner version in 1741. Known earlier as the Douay-Reims version.

1611: The King James Bible of 1611 was begun in 1607 with 47 scholars participating; they used existing translations (Bishops' Bible mainly, then the Geneva, Douay-Reims, Luther's German Bible, etc.). Actually the KJV is virtually the Tyndale Bible by a series of transmissions thus: Tyndale — Matthew's — Great — Bishops'—KJV.

It is often known as "The Authorized Version," and many revised editions have been published. Their sources were inferior to those of later translations, their knowledge of Greek and Hebrew was not profound, their archaisms, solecisms, errors (many, indeed!) abounded. It became for 270 years *the* Protestant Bible. Its influence on English speech and writing is vast (e.g., from 1900 to 1950 some 1,100 titles of books were taken from the KJV). Its bond on the people has survived better, more accurate, and more readable translations. To this day the parishoner feels "un-Biblical" should he hear the pastor read from some modern translation.

1881-85: The Revised Version broke the monopoly of the KJV. The accumulated scholarship of two centuries produced an accurate, scholarly, and literal translation in current English. There was much opposition to the unseating of the KJV. The American Standard Version (1901) is an Americanized Revised Version. The Revised Standard Version (1946-52) was a gigantic scholarly effort, outstripping all previous translations for accuracy and fluency and modernity. In America it has already supplanted the ASV of 1901. The best private, modern (almost colloquial) translations are those by James Moffatt (1913) and J. M. P. Smith (OT only) in 1927.

SELECTED BIBLIOGRAPHY

BASIC REFERENCE WORKS: ENCYCLOPEDIAS, COMMENTARIES, ETC.

Dictionary of the Bible, ed. James Hastings (New York: Charles Scribner's Sons; 1903-4). Conservative and slightly out of date.

Encyclopedia Biblica, ed. T. K. Cheyne and J. S. Black (New York: The Macmillan Co.; 1899-1903). More liberal and thoroughly professional. Not for the layman.

Harper's Bible Dictionary, ed. M. S. and J. L. Miller (New York: Harper & Brothers; 1952). A good, liberal one-volume encyclopedia for the layman.

Interpreter's Bible Dictionary, ed. G. A. Buttrick and others, in 12 volumes (New York; Nashville: Abingdon Press; 1956). Gives the scriptural text in both the King James and Revised Standard Versions in parallel columns. There is scholarly historical commentary and beneath that, on each page, is theological apparatus for preachers. A great and superlative achievement. These volumes formed the basis of much of the higher criticism in this book.

Interpreter's Bible Dictionary (1962) by the same press as above; it is the best encyclopedia of the Bible existing. Its roster of scholars of all shades of opinion is appallingly impressive.

A Catholic Commentary on Holy Scripture (Nelson). For the official Catholic interpretation.

The International Critical Commentary, ed. S. R. Driver and others, (New York: Charles Scribner's Sons); also Allensen (publishers), all volumes (40). The standard and the most exhaustively learned. Come armed with Hebrew and Greek.

The best one-volume commentaries are those by J. R. Dummelow (*Commentary on the Holy Bible,* New York: The Macmillan Co.; 1909); Frederick C. Eiselen and others, *Abingdon Bible Commentary,* New York: Abingdon Press; 1911).

The best atlases are those by G. E. Wright and Floyd V. Filson, *The Westminster Historical Atlas to the Bible* (Philadelphia: Westminster Press; 1956); and Herbert G. May, *The Oxford Bible Atlas* (New York: Oxford University Press; 1962).

INTRODUCTIONS AND DISCUSSION OF THE OLD TESTAMENT

Bewer, Julius A., *The Literature of the Old Testament* (New York: Columbia University Press; 1933), third edition.

Driver, Samuel R., *An Introduction to the Literature of the Old Testament* (New York: Charles Scribner's Sons; 1891). For the advanced student.

Pfeiffer, Robert H., *Introduction to the Old Testament* (New York: Harper & Brothers; 1948). Scholarly, and standard.

Anderson, Bernhard, *The Old Testament* (Prentice-Hall, Inc., Englewood Cliffs, N. J.).

——, *Understanding the Old Testament* (Prentice-Hall; 1957). Both books clear and readable for the layman and student.

RELIGIOUS HISTORY OF ISRAEL

Gottwald, Norman K., *A Light to the Nations* (New York: Harper; 1959).

Meek, Theophile J., and M. Miller, *Hebrew Origins* (New York: Harper Torchbooks; 1960).

Wawtor, Bruce, *The Conscience of Israel* (New York: Sheed and Ward; 1952).

Muilenberg, James A., "The History of the Religion of Israel," *Interpreter's Bible,* I, pp. 292-348; the best single essay.

Oesterley, W. O. E., *The Hebrew Religion* (New York: The Macmillan Co.; 1937).

Wright, G. Ernest, "The Faith of Israel," *Interpreter's Bible,* I, pp. 349-89; a fine essay also.

TEXT, CANON, AND TRANSLATIONS

Roberts, Bleddyn J., *The Old Testament Text and Versions* (Cardiff: University of Wales Press; 1951); advanced but the best.

Margolis, Max L., *The Hebrew Scriptures in the Making* (Philadelphia: Jewish Publication Society of America; 1922); useful for the layman.

THE PRESENT-DAY SCIENTIFIC APPROACH

Robinson, Wheeler H. (ed.) *Record and Revelation* (Oxford: Oxford University Press; 1952). Standard and best.

Rowley, H. H., *The Old Testament and Modern Study* (Oxford: Oxford University Press; 1952); a thrilling if difficult book. Now in paperback.

Hahn, Herbert F., *Old Testament in Modern Research* (Philadelphia: Muhlenberg Press; 1954); better for beginners.

ARCHAEOLOGY AND HISTORY OF ISRAEL

Pritchard, James B., *The Ancient Near East in Pictures* (Princeton: Princeton University Press: 1955). Fascinating!

——, *The Ancient Near East: An Anthology of Text and Pictures* (Princeton: Princeton University Press; 1958). Combines his picture and textbook in one neat volume.

Scott, R. B. Y., *The Relevance of*

the Prophets (New York: Macmillan; 1953).

Bright, John, *A History of Israel* (Philadelphia: Westminster Press; 1958). Conservative.

Thomas, Winton D., *Documents from Old Testament Times* (New York: Harper Torchbooks; 1961).

Robinson, Theodore H. and Oesterley, W. O. E., *A History of Israel* (2 vols.; Oxford: Oxford University Press; 1932); standard and thorough.

Finegan, Jack, *Light from the Ancient Past* (Princeton: Princeton University Press; 1959).

Burrows, Millar, *What Mean These Stones?* (New Haven: American Schools of Oriental Research; 1941).

Albright, William Foxwell, *The Archaeology of Palestine* (London: Penguin Books Inc.) standard.

Glueck, Nelson, *The River Jordan* (Philadelphia: Westminster Press; 1946). Standard.

*   *   *

Note. The clearest, most accurate, and vivid account without any jargon whatsoever is Samuel Sandmel's *The Hebrew Scriptures: An Introduction to Their Literature and Religious Ideas* (New York: Alfred A. Knopf; 1963). This is a delightful introduction to the Old Testament for the layman, done with humor and verve. Dr. Sandmel's learning is carried with grace and style. The Bibliography carries useful criticisms on each book cited. In similar terms, Fred G. Bratton's *A History of the Bible* (Boston: Beacon Press; 1959) does the same excellent job in the story of the development of the Bible.

NOTES

NOTES

NOTES

NOTES

NOTES

NOTES

NOTES